THE LIGHTNER LIBRARY
Keuka College
Keuka Park, New York 14478

The Negotiation and Administration of Hotel and Restaurant Management Contracts

The Negotiation and Administration of Hotel and Restaurant Management Contracts

Third revised and expanded edition

James J. Eyster

School of Hotel Administration
Cornell University
Ithaca, NY

© 1988 James J. Eyster

First edition published 1977
Revised edition published 1980
Third edition, revised and expanded, 1988

ALL RIGHTS RESERVED. No part of this work may be reproduced, copied, or transmitted in any form or by any means without written permission of the publisher.

Printed in the United States of America

ISBN 0-937056-04-9

School of Hotel Administration
Statler Hall, Cornell University
Ithaca, NY 14853

KF
2042
.H6
E97
1988

Table of Contents

List of Exhibits

Preface to the Third Edition

SINCE the publication of the second edition in 1980, the use of management contracts in the hospitality industry has been affected by many factors. The most significant of these are the following:

— Chain and independent operating companies are continuing to expand almost exclusively through the use of management contracts, both domestically and internationally.

— Competition among chain operating companies is intensifying due to the emergence of new domestic chain operators, the mergers of smaller regional and national operators, and the entry into the U.S. market of foreign-based hotel chain operators.

— The shake-out among independent operating companies continues. The more competent operators are increasing in size and are expanding their services. As weak operators disappear, small, new operators appear, trying to take advantage of the opportunities afforded by the explosive growth of small, market-specific budget, economy, and suite-type properties.

— Hotel developers and owners are becoming more sophisticated in their knowledge of the hospitality industry and of contract management and are demanding more of operators. Sometimes these demands are reasonable, and sometimes they are not.

— Lenders are taking a more active role in the negotiating process to protect their interests in the project.

— With bargaining power shifting more toward owners, negotiated management contracts more frequently contain provisions specifying operator equity or loan contributions, management fees tiered to ownership returns, shorter initial and renewal terms, operator performance criteria, and greater ownership involvement in budgeting and expenditure decisions.

— As operators more often enter into joint-venture agreements with developers to construct and own properties, their dual role as operator and joint venture partner is creating conflicts of interest with the developer.

— Contracts are more frequently terminated before the originally agreed-upon termination date, because owners and operators are unable to settle contract disputes successfully. Mechanisms are therefore needed to deal more efficiently with contract disputes and to settle claims of each party in a unilateral termination.

The purpose of this revised edition is:
— To update and expand the 1980 edition's database and analysis regarding the provisions of concern and the negotiation outcomes of these provisions, in light of the significant changes noted above;
— To suggest to owners, operators, and lenders a rigorous approach, including self- and cross-evaluations, to employ when preparing for and entering into negotiations;
— To provide guidelines, based upon a project's discounted cash flow potential, for evaluating a project's return to serve as a basis for negotiating a management-fee structure that will provide an adequate equity return to the owner and an adequate incentive-base return to the operator;
— To provide data on negotiated management contracts for specific types of lodging facilities (full-service, budget, economy, suite, domestic, international) and for commercial restaurant operations that were not a part of the previous edition.

The above revisions and additions are the product of extensive data collection and analysis made possible through the cooperation of hospitality industry operators, owners, leaders, and consultants who provided data, opinions, and insight, and through the funding of a research grant provided by Cornell University's School of Hotel Administration. Since much of the individual management-contract data collected was of a confidential nature, the author grouped the data by operator and owner type so as not to identify the original sources. It is my hope that the study will prove useful to everyone interested in the management-contract concept and its practice.

—**J.J.E.,** *Ithaca, New York*

Acknowledgments

THE AUTHOR gratefully acknowledges the support of the several hundred hotel owners, operators, lenders, and consultants who willingly and candidly shared their management-contract experiences and concerns with me.

I am especially grateful to Robert A. Beck, John J. Clark, William H. Kaven, Joe P. Bail, and William J. Wasmuth for their support during the project and to the research committee of the School of Hotel Administration for funding to complete the research.

I wish to acknowledge additional thanks: to A. Neal Geller for his assistance with the development of the owner and operator assessment procedures in Chapter V; to Jochen Schaeffer-Suren for his computer-model program development to assess owner and operator financial returns in Chapter V and in Appendix D; to Michael Smaldone for his assistance with the text's data presentation and word processing; and to Glenn Withiam and *The Cornell Quarterly* staff for their editing and production efforts.

Most of all, the author expresses his deepests appreciation to his wife, Susan, and to his children, Jennifer and James, without whose patience and understanding this study could not have been produced.

I

Introduction

The management-contract form of operating agreement was introduced in the American lodging industry in the late 1960s by hotel and motor-inn operating companies as a means of expanding their earnings bases—the number of rooms managed—more rapidly. Developer-owners with no experience or expertise in the operation of lodging facilities also found the contract form attractive, for it enabled them to take advantage of the potential high returns from hotel and motor-inn ownership.

The industry readily adopted the use of management contracts. In 1970, the ten major U.S. chain operating companies had just 22 management contracts. By 1975, these ten companies were employing 182 contracts, and by the end of 1979, they were managing 299 properties under management contracts. By 1979, other newly formed independent operating companies accounted for almost 500 more management contracts. During the 1980s, the management contract continued to be the operating agreement used for most new properties larger than 100 rooms. By early 1987, 20 chain operating companies operated close to 700 properties under management contracts, and more than 60 independent operating companies managed approximately 950 hotel and motor-inn projects.

Despite widespread press coverage of the advantages and disadvantages of management contracts, many owners and operators who have entered into management contracts have expressed reservations about their contracts and about the owner-operator relationship the contract establishes. Their concerns, heightened by the unexpected economic recessions of the mid-1970s and overbuilding of the mid-1980s, have resulted in a wide range of opinions among owners, operators, and hospitality consultants as to the fairness of the owner-operator arrangement under the standard provisions of the management contract.

A. Purpose and Scope of the Study

This study will analyze the management-contract provisions causing these concerns. The analysis includes: **(1)** the identification of owners' and operators' concerns during contract negotiations; **(2)** an investigation of how an owner's and operator's relative bargaining strengths affect the outcome of their negotiations; **(3)** the identification of owners' and operators' concerns during the term of the contract; and **(4)** an examination of the underlying factors contributing to those concerns. Finally, the study suggests negotiating strategies that should lead to an equitable contract for both parties.

For the original 1977 database, the researcher obtained data through extensive field interviews with major chain operating companies, independent operating companies, and owners of hotels and motor inns. These data were revised in 1979 and again in 1986 and 1987. The 1986-87 data collection and analysis, presented herein, were expanded to include budget and economy lodging properties, suite-type lodging properties, restaurants located within lodging properties, and freestanding commercial restaurants.

From this analysis, three models were developed to aid owners and operators in assessing at any time their contractual arrangement and their individual positions. The first model, the continuum of relative bargaining strength, reflects the factors that determine the bargaining strengths of an owner and an operator during contract negotiations and the specific effects their relative positions have on the outcome of the negotiations. Four "zones" are set up along the continuum to illustrate the effects on the negotiations of shifts in owner and operator bargaining strengths.

The second model, the hierarchy of concerns, illustrates the tendency of concerns not resolved during negotiations to escalate during the term of the contract and shows that these concerns can diminish when certain operating results or owner-operator compromises are reached. The model examines the underlying factors causing these concerns.

The third model, depicting the working relationship of the owner, the operator's corporate staff, and the property's general manager, illustrates the intricacies of the triangular relationship established in the contract, the division of operational and legal responsibilities, and the effects upon the relationship when the owner attempts to influence operating policies and procedures.

To assist the reader in understanding the negotiating process, two preparatory steps are discussed and illustrated. The first consists of an evaluation procedure whereby owners and operators test their prospective counterparts and establish their own expectations of the project's promise. The second illustrates a discounted-cash-flow evaluation of the project, a technique employed to ensure a realistic assessment of the project's probable financial performance. The study ends with a summary of findings, conclusions based on those findings, and implications for the future use of management contracts.

This chapter provides the background for the study presentation and analysis and includes: operational definitions, a summary of contract provisions and owner and operator risks, the factors influencing the rapid adoption of management contracts, and the other major operating-agreement forms from which owners and operators can choose.

Chapter II identifies the major components of bargaining power that determine the relative bargaining strength of the owner and the operator. Chapter III identifies and analyzes the major provisions of concern in hotel contracts during contract negotiations and presents the negotiated settlements of each provision in relation to owner-operator relative bargaining strength. Chapter IV identifies owner and operator concerns that arise during the term of the contract and strategies used by each party to ameliorate these concerns. Chapter V presents the process of evaluating prospective owners and operators and a financial-performance decision model for project analysis. Chapter VI identifies and analyzes the provisions of concern in commercial restaurant operations. The conclusions and implications of the research are summarized in Chapter VII.

Four appendices are included in the study. Appendix A is an annotated list of hotel contract provisions, and describes variations observed in contracts provided by owners and operators participating in the study. Appendix B discusses the major market, economic, and business-policy factors influencing the rapid adoption of management contracts. Appendix C contains present-value tables to be used in making capital budgeting decisions. Appendix D describes the components necessary for a reliable quantitative model to analyze project and management-fee returns.

B. The Study's Limitations

The study is subject to the following biases and limitations. First, it represents a business approach to the use of management contracts, and focuses on the business and economic objectives of owners and operators; it does not discuss the legal status of individual contract provisions.

Second, the sample selection of operators and owners was limited to those willing to cooperate in the research. In addition, some operators may have attempted to restrict the author's access to owners critical of their performance. However, due to the large number of owners and operators cooperating in the study and to the researcher's independent search for owners, the possible bias attributable to the sample's composition appears to be minimal.

Third, the study focused upon the concerns and problem areas of management contracts and not upon the potential benefits derived from the contracts. The reader should not assume, therefore, that all contractual relationships are plagued by problems resulting from unresolved concerns. Where possible, the degree to which concerns have been resolved by owners and operators is documented throughout the study.

C. Definitions

The following definitions are used throughout the study and are supplemented by additional definitions where appropriate.

- Management Contract: a written agreement between the owner and the operator of a hotel or motor inn by which the owner employs the operator as an agent (employee) to assume full responsibility for operating and managing the property. As an agent, the operator pays, in the name of the owner, all operating expenses from the cash flow generated from the property, retains management fees, and remits the remaining cash flow, if any, to the owner. The owner supplies the lodging property, including any land, building, furniture, fixtures, equipment, and working capital, and assumes full legal and financial responsibility for the project.
- Operator: a chain operating company or an independent operating company, whose function is the professional management of a hotel property.
- Chain Operating Company: a hotel company providing management and operating expertise to lodging properties it owns, leases, or manages, and using its national trademark and reservations system as an integral part of the management of the property.
- Independent Operating Company: a hotel company providing management and operating expertise to lodging properties it owns, leases, or manages, without the use of a national trademark or reservations system of its own. It may operate a franchised property carrying a national lodging chain's trademark, however, and may therefore have access to a national chain's reservations system. The operating company may be a separate and distinct entity from the owner, in which case the contract is considered to be an arms'-length contract. If, on the other hand, the operating company is a subsidiary of the owner, or the owner and the operating entities have common ownership, the negotiated contract is not considered to be at arms' length. A distinction will be made in the text between these two categories when the negotiated provisions differ.
- Owner: a developer-owner or an owner-in-foreclosure that holds title to the property.
- Developer-Owner: a business entity (usually a proprietor, partnership, corporation, or joint venture) that owns the hotel or motor inn and has not defaulted on the property's outstanding loan commitments.
- Owner-in-Foreclosure: a business entity (usually a commercial bank, savings-and-loan association, real-estate investment trust, or savings bank) originally acting as a lender to a developer-owner but later assuming ownership of the

property as a result of the developer-owner's inability to honor outstanding loan commitments.

• Provision of Concern: a provision in a management contract creating anxiety or dissatisfaction on the part of either the owner or the operator during the negotiation of the contract or during the term of the contract.

• Bargaining: the act of negotiating a provision of concern between an owner and an operator. In such negotiations the participants are (theoretically, at least) working toward a balanced position—one to their mutual benefit—rather than assuming adversary positions, as is the case in labor-management collective bargaining.

• Term: the length of time a contract is to remain in effect.

• Basic Management Fee: the remuneration the owner agrees to pay the operator for performing the duties specified in the contract. The fee is usually an agreed-upon percentage of gross revenues, but is sometimes a fixed-dollar amount independent of the volume of revenue realized.

• Incentive Fee: the remuneration the owner agrees to pay the operator for generating a predetermined profit, income, or cash-flow level from the operation. The fee is usually an agreed-upon percentage of gross operating profit, or cash flow after debt service and other ownership obligations, and may be paid in addition to or in lieu of the basic fee, depending upon the contract provisions.

• Operator System-Reimbursable Expenses: expenses paid by the owner to the operator for centralized services provided by the operator as part of the operator's system-wide efforts in support of the owner's property. They include expenditures for system-wide advertising, national and regional sales offices, centralized reservation systems, centralized accounting and management information systems, centralized procurement services, and centralized educational and training programs.

• Gross Revenue: all revenues and incomes of any kind derived directly or indirectly from the property, including store and building rentals or other payments from sublessees and concessionaires.

• Income Before Fixed Charges (Gross Operating Profit): profit after deducting from gross revenue all operational expenses, including the basic management fee, but excluding the following: depreciation, interest, property taxes, and insurance; amortization of pre-opening expenses; capital expenditures, including replacement of furniture, fixtures, and equipment; and the incentive management fee.

• Working Capital: funds provided from the operation's cash flow and from the owner as required to make timely payments of all operating expenses.

• Lodging Property: used to describe in the broadest sense any commercial lodging accommodations available for transient guests, including hotels, motor inns, motor hotels, and resorts. This expanded definition also applies to the word "hotel" as used in this text.

- Property: a hotel, motor-inn, or restaurant building; its furniture, fixtures, and equipment; and the land it occupies.

D. The Background

Since management contracts are a relatively recent phenomenon in the domestic lodging industry, this section of the text will explain the basic concept of the management contract. It summarizes the major owner-operator agreements in a typical contract, the risks involved for both owners and operators, and the factors that have influenced the adoption of management contracts and shaped the goals and expectations of owners and operators.

1. Summary of Contract Provisions

The basic contract concept consists of three underlying components: **(a)** the operator has sole and exclusive right to manage the property without ownership interference; **(b)** the owner pays all operating and financing expenses and assumes ownership risks; and **(c)** the operator is indemnified from his actions except for gross negligence or fraud. Thus, the concept assigns all operating responsibilities to the operating company and all financial responsibilities to the owner. As a result, owners often feel they are at a disadvantage because they turn over to the operator complete operating control of their properties without having adequate leverage to affect the operator's behavior or actions. On the other hand, operators claim that they are being hired to perform a service for which they have expertise, that ownership interference would diminish their ability to perform effectively, and that it is they, and not the owners, who are creating the economic value of the project from which the owners will ultimately benefit.

Exhibit I-1 summarizes the duties agreed to by the operator and the owner in a typical contract. The length of the contract term varies, depending upon the owner's and the operator's bargaining strengths. Chain operators usually require a 15- to 20-year term; the term for independent operators ranges from one to ten years. Both the owner and the operator have the right to terminate the contract if the other party fails to fulfill any material covenant. The operator can terminate the contract if the owner is unable to meet financial obligations, files for bankruptcy, or sells the property; the owner can exercise the right to terminate if the operator files for bankruptcy, is found guilty of gross negligence or fraud, or fails to meet operator performance levels that may be provided for in the contract. The parties may, of course, terminate the contract at any time by mutual consent.

Management fees paid by the owner to the operator may consist of a basic fee, a basic fee plus an incentive fee, or the greater of a basic fee or an incentive fee. Basic fees are usually a specified percentage of gross revenues; incentive fees are usually a specified percentage of gross operating profit or a percentage of cash

EXHIBIT I-1

Major Operator and Owner Agreements in a Typical Contract

Operator agrees:

1. To select, employ, terminate, supervise, direct, train, and assign all employees of the owner engaged in the operation of the property;

2. To establish all price and rate schedules and to collect all receipts for all services or income of any nature from the operation;

3. To install a suitable accounting system, to maintain bookkeeping records, and to pay, in the owner's name, all expenses incurred in the operation of the property;

4. To negotiate and arrange leases for store, office, or lobby space within the property and to obtain and grant concessions, subject to owner's approval;

5. To apply for, obtain, and maintain, in the name and at the expense of the owner, all necessary licenses and permits;

6. To negotiate all service contracts, subject to owner's approval;

7. To purchase on behalf of the owner inventories, provisions, supplies, and equipment reasonably necessary to maintain and operate the property;

8. To plan, prepare, and conduct advertising and promotional programs for the property;

9. To prepare annual budgets (operating, replacement, and capital additions) for operating the property and to obtain owner's approval of the budget;

10. To make or cause to be made all necessary repairs, replacements, and improvements;

11. To conduct business in a lawful manner and in full compliance with all governmental laws and regulations; and

12. To provide (in the case of chain operator) the hotel or motor-inn chain's name and access to its national reservations system.

Owner agrees:

1. To provide lodging property, equipment, furniture, fixtures, inventories, working capital, reserve for replacement funds, and, if applicable, a referral or franchise agreement;

2. To resupply working capital if the working-capital balance falls below a stipulated amount;

3. To grant the operator sole and exclusive right to supervise, direct, and control the management and operation of the property for and on behalf of the owner, in the name of the owner, and for the owner's account;

4. Not to interfere with the operator's supervision, direction, and control of the management and operation of the property, nor to give orders or instructions to any personnel employed on the property;

5. To assume that all personnel, including the general manager, are in the sole employ of the owner and that all salaries, wages, and other compensation will be determined by the operator but be paid by the owner; if the operator pays an employee (such as the general manager) from the operator's payroll, the operator will be reimbursed by the owner;

6. To carry minimum fire, general liability, workers' compensation, employer's liability, and bonding insurance and to hold the operator harmless for any loss sustained, irrespective and regardless of any negligence on the part of the operator;

7. To compensate the operator through the basic management fee (a stipulated percentage of gross revenues) and the incentive fee (a stipulated percentage of gross operating profit or cash flow after ownership obligations);

8. To assume a *pro-rata* share of charges made by the operator's central office for advertising, accounting, and computerized management-information services, and to assume travel and maintenance costs of operator's central-office personnel assigned to projects on the owner's property; and

9. To give the operator the right of first refusal or the right of first offer to purchase the property if the owner sells the property during the term of the contract.

flow after debt service and other ownership obligations. In addition to the management fee, the owner pays operating and financial obligations including the salaries of the property's general manager and staff and a *pro-rata* share of the operator's system expenses attributable to the operation of the property.

A complete description of provisions contained in contracts, the frequency with which each provision occurs in the contracts studied, and variations on the standard provisions are contained in Appendix A.

2. Summary of Owner and Operator Risks

The distribution of risks between owner and operator depends upon two factors. First, the high risk and commensurate return of hotel investment are assumed by the owner, not by the operator, under a management contract. Unlike the traditional lease, in which the owner is guaranteed a fixed lease payment that covers debt service, insurance, and taxes, leaving the operator to benefit or suffer from fluctuations in cash flow, the management contract guarantees the operator a management fee and passes the remaining cash flow on to the owner for meeting debt service, insurance, and taxes. If operating cash flow is high, the owner enjoys a high return; if operating cash flow is low, the owner suffers a loss.

Second, the owner assigns all operating responsibility to the operator and is restricted from interfering with or influencing the operation of the property. As a result, the owner must rely completely upon the operator's ability to promote the property effectively, operate it efficiently, and generate adequate profits to cover the owner's debt service and other costs.

Operator and owner risks in a typical management-contract agreement are summarized in Exhibit I-2. It should be noted that risks are shared according to the relative bargaining strengths of the two parties and each party's ability to negotiate effectively; they can therefore be redistributed to some degree during contract negotiations.

3. Factors Influencing the Rapid Adoption of Management Contracts

Although U.S. hotel companies operating internationally had employed management contracts since the 1950s to expand operations in foreign countries while minimizing their risks, U.S. lodging firms did not employ contracts in domestic properties until the early 1970s. Following Hyatt's lead, most major chain operators soon began using management contracts to supplement traditional ownership, joint-venture, lease, and franchise arrangements. Exhibit I-3 illustrates the rapid growth of management contracts among franchised, company-owned, and company-leased properties since 1970 for major chain operators.

In addition to the chain operators, at least 60 independent operating companies manage approximately 950 properties under management contracts. They

EXHIBIT I-2

Operator and Owner Risks in a Typical Management Contract

Operator risks:

1. Financial risk is low compared to operator-leased or operator-owned properties. Assuming that the managed property is operating *above* its break-even volume, a lower return on sales is realized compared to an operator-leased or operator-owned property. If the property is operating *below* its break-even volume, cash deficits must be made up by the owner, not the operator. The operator gives up a certain amount of profit in return for a smaller investment and reduced risk.

2. Dependence on owner's continued financial strength. Since the owner is required to supply additional funds when cash flow is inadequate to meet operating and debt-retirement needs, the operator is dependent upon the owner's ability to provide, if needed, long-term cash infusions.

3. Little influence on ownership decision-making. Unless the operator has made an equity contribution to the project, he has minimal influence on ownership decisions regarding the sale or disposition of the property.

4. Risk of contract termination. Termination of contract by the owner prior to or at the end of the agreed-upon term can result in the operator's loss of a competitive location and loss of prestige.

Owner risks:

1. Loss of control. By turning over all responsibility for the day-to-day operations to the operator, the owner has no control over the hiring and firing of personnel, the setting of prices, the determination of costs, and the use of cash generated before all expenses, including the management fees, have been paid. He must rely completely upon the operator's discretion. His input is generally limited to the approval of the annual budget; even here, his approval cannot be unduly withheld.

2. Fee. The management fee is paid over and above the normal operating expenses of the operation, thereby lowering the profit the owner would receive if he operated the property himself. Consequently, the owner must be convinced that the operator is generating adequate additional income to more than cover the management fees.

3. Financial risk. Since no fixed rental income is required from the operator, as in a lease, the owner bears the full risk of the operation's inability to meet operating expenses and debt payments. Conversely, however, the owner's return will be greater under a management contract than under a lease if the property experiences above-average volume and is efficiently operated.

4. Difficulty of contract termination. The owner can generally terminate the contract only if he can prove gross negligence on the part of the operator, or in the event of bankruptcy, insolvency, merger, or corporate reorganization of the operator. Gross negligence is extremely difficult to prove.

5. Possibility that operator favors operator-owned to operator-managed properties. Many owners express the belief that operators place their best managerial talent in their owned properties and favor them with group business bookings at the expense of their managed properties, since the return from an operator-owned property is greater than from an operator-managed property.

EXHIBIT 1-3

Operating Agreement Forms of Properties Affiliated with Chain Operating Companies (Number of Properties and Percentage of Each Type of Form to Total Properties Within Chain: 1970–1986)

	Franchises				Management Contracts				Company —owned/leased				Total Properties			
	1970	1975	1979	1986	1970	1975	1979	1986	1970	1975	1979	1986	1970	1975	1979	1986
Holiday Inn	987 77%	1450 81%	1493 86%	1484 88%	4 0%	14 1%	27 2%	65 4%	284 22%	318 18%	217 12%	139 8%	1275	1782	1737	1688
Quality International	285 93%	270 15%	301 17%	721 43%	0	0	5 0%	18 1%	22 7%	40 13%	26 8%	13 2%	307	310	332	752
Ramada	232 78%	515 78%	532 80%	514 90%	0	12 2%	7 1%	14 2%	65 22%	130 20%	125 19%	43 8%	297	657	664	571
Sheraton	104 59%	263 74%	315 79%	349 72%	0	32 9%	49 12%	112 23%	71 41%	59 17%	36 9%	27 6%	175	354	400	488
Howard Johnson	368 88%	402 76%	392 75%	325 72%	0	0	0	0	52 12%	124 24%	130 25%	125 28%	420	526	522	450
Travelodge	99 22%	154 33%	237 44%	182 41%	0	24 5%	43 8%	0 0%	343 78%	290 62%	263 48%	261 59%	442	468	543	443
Days Inn	0	0	14 5%	379 86%	0	0	0	37 8%	0	244 100%	294 95%	25 6%	0	244	308	441
Hilton Domestic	42 49%	105 70%	141 75%	218 82%	0	26 17%	31 16%	23 9%	44 51%	19 13%	17 9%	25 9%	86	150	189	266
Marriott	5 36%	12 27%	18 27%	34 23%	0	18 18%	25 38%	97 65%	9 64%	24 55%	23 35%	18 12%	14	44	66	149

Inter-Continental	NA	NA	NA	17 17%	NA	NA	NA	41 41%	NA	NA	NA	41 41%	NA	NA	NA	99
Radisson	0	0	0	59 61%	0	2 17%	10 45%	33 34%	6 100%	10 83%	12 55%	4 4%	6	12	22	96
Hilton International	0	0	0	0	16 30%	18 29%	32 42%	41 46%	37 70%	45 71%	44 58%	49 54%	53	63	76	90
Hyatt	0	0	0	0	23 100%	54 100%	66 85%	61 72%	0	0	12 15%	24 28%	23	54	78	85
Westin	0	0	0	0	6 11%	10 22%	29 66%	19 37%	49 89%	35 78%	15 34%	33 63%	55	45	44	52
Omni (Dunfey)	NA	NA	NA	0	NA	NA	NA	34 74%	NA	NA	NA	12 26%	NA	NA	NA	46
Clarion (AIRCOA)	0	NA	NA	NA	0	NA	NA	21 81%	0	NA	NA	5 19%	0	NA	NA	26
Four Seasons	0	0	0	0	0	0	1 8%	4 20%	5 100%	5 100%	11 92%	16 80%	5	5	12	20
Doubletree	0	0	0	0	4 100%	5 100%	6 100%	14 82%	0	0	0	3 18%	4	5	6	17
Royce	0	0	0	0	0	0	0	15 100%	0	0	0	0	0	0	0	15
Totals	2122 67%	3171 67%	3443 69%	4282 74%	53 2%	205 4%	331 7%	649 11%	987 31%	1343 28%	1225 25%	863 15%	3162	4719	4999	5794

manage both independent (non-affiliated) properties and properties affiliated with national referral associations or franchises. Most of these independent operators were established since 1971, are regional, and manage properties smaller than those managed by chain operators. AIRCOA, Horizon, Hospitality Management Corporation, MHM Corporation, and Mariner Corporation are examples of independent operating companies.

The major market, economic, and business-policy factors leading to the adoption of management contracts are summarized in Exhibit I-4; those with the earliest influence on contract use are listed first, followed by those having an impact more recently. These factors stemmed from the compressed real-estate boom-and-bust cycle affecting the U.S. economy in the late 1960s and early 1970s and the rapid growth of new properties through the late 1970s and early 1980s. Each factor contributed to shaping the objectives and expectations of owners and operators. A discussion of each factor appears in Appendix B.

Both chain and independent operating companies appear eager to continue their expansion programs through the use of management contracts. An executive with a major chain operating company made the following comments in a recent interview:

> Public corporations have been experimenting in the last 15 years with a number of operating arrangements—leases, franchises, joint ventures, and now management contracts—and will continue to evaluate each of these in light of changing economic conditions, tax regulations, and Wall Street evaluations. However, it looks as if management contracts will be the way to go, at least into the foreseeable future and probably into the long-term future—especially in the hotel business, where ownership is highly dependent upon specialized services.

Whether the use of management contracts will continue to expand, however, depends on the ability of owners and operators to remedy the financial, operational, and legal concerns identified in Chapters II and III.

E. Other Major Operating Agreement Forms

The management contract is only one of several major forms of operating agreements and, depending on the circumstances, may not be the most favorable form for either the owner or the operator.

1. Choices of Operating Alternatives

An owner can choose from five basic operating arrangements; each has its advantages and disadvantages. The choices are: **(a)** *self-operation*—owner operates independently of any second-party assistance or management; **(b)** *self-operation with membership in a referral system;* **(c)** *self-operation under a franchise agreement;* **(d)** *leasing to an operator;* and **(e)** *signing a management contract with a chain or independent operating company.* These operating arrangements may be

EXHIBIT I-4

Factors Influencing the Adoption of Management Contracts

Factor #1: Market concentration and increasing competitiveness on the part of chain operating companies attempting to expand earnings bases. **Influence:** Construction of new properties, and intensified competition both between chain-affiliated properties and independent properties and among chain operating companies.

Factor #2: Increased availability of money for real-estate ventures in the late 1960s, early 1970s and early 1980s. **Influence:** Increase in the number of owners with little or no lodging experience; overbuilding in most lodging markets; and development of marginal projects whose survival depended upon high volumes of business.

Factor #3: Increased size of new lodging properties, new design and location trends, and larger investment required. **Influence:** Increased risk for owners due to high fixed operating costs and high debt-service commitments.

Factor #4: Policy decisions by chain operating companies to change from being real-estate companies to operating companies. **Influence:** Gave operating companies more control over properties they managed; shifted investment risk from operator to owner; and improved operating companies' ability to raise funds for rapid growth by improving earnings per share and balance-sheet ratios.

Factor #5: Lenders' insistence on professional hotel or motor-inn management. **Influence:** Increased opportunity for chain and independent operating companies to obtain management contracts.

Factor #6: Inadequate supply of professional management personnel to operate expanded number of properties. **Influence:** Spurred the formation of independent operating companies and increased opportunity for both chain and independent operating companies to obtain management contracts. Ease of entry resulted in establishment of both chain and independent operating companies offering inadequate management expertise, in addition to companies offering experienced, talented personnel.

Factor #7: The recession of the mid-1970s. **Influence:** Strained operator-owner relations under existing contracts; increased the number of contracts between owners-in-foreclosure and operators; and led ultimately to greater flexibility in contract provisions.

Factor #8: The Economic Recovery Tax Act of 1981. **Influence:** Major tax incentive for real-estate developers to construct hotels; many projects developed for tax-shelter benefits rather than for economic reasons; developer has no hotel-operating experience and relied on hotel operator for management.

Factor #9: Market segmentation of the mid-1980s. **Influence:** Chain operating companies expanded their lodging product lines to target a range of specific market segments in an effort to gain market share; most of these properties developed by nonoperators, thus increasing use of contracts.

combined, as in the case of an owner's signing a management contract with an independent operating company and utilizing a franchise or referral agreement, or an owner's entering into a joint venture with a chain operating company. In this case, the joint venture might negotiate a management contract with the operating company.

Owners should be aware of the primary advantages and disadvantages of each of the five basic choices as they evaluate which choice is most appropriate to their property. Outlined below are the advantages and disadvantages to the owner and to the second party (referral association, franchisor, or management company) of each choice. Exhibit I-5 provides a brief summary of this analysis. Exhibit I-6 summarizes the fees and costs charged to the owner by the second party for each operating agreement form.

a. Self-Operation. An owner operating independently of any second party enjoys the maximum freedom to operate and can receive maximum returns if he markets his property effectively and manages efficiently since there are no fees to be paid to a second party. To benefit, owners must have expertise and a strong operational record, because they lack the advantages of national affiliation, referral, reservation, and operational systems provided under other forms of operating agreements. Also, financing is often difficult to obtain without having the benefits of a referral, franchise, or recognized hotel operating company. However, for an owner with a unique property, strong operational experience, and a market consisting of significant repeat business, this choice is preferable.

b. Self-Operation with Membership in a Referral System. Joining a referral association such as Best Western or Preferred Hotels provides the owner with membership in an association that provides national affiliation and referral, access to a reservation system, ability to take advantage of lower cost supplies, equipment, and insurance, and a network organization of other owner-operators. At the same time, the owner can maintain his property's distinct identity and individuality and most of the operational flexibility possible if he were operating independently of a second party. These advantages must be weighed against the costs associated with membership, which range between two and three percent of room sales (refer to Exhibit I-6), and the owner's assessment as to whether membership in the referral system will generate the additional volume of business to cover the referral fees and costs.

The referral association's strength is in its ability to offer advantages to its members that they cannot achieve on their own. The success of an association depends upon its ability to choose member properties that have the operational and financial capability to maintain the required standards, to monitor and enforce standards consistently, and to provide effective system-wide services.

c. Self-Operation under a Franchise Agreement. An owner signing a franchise agreement benefits from the services provided by a referral association, plus the following: **(a)** during development: assistance with site selection, feasibility analysis, architectural design prototypes, restaurant plans and speci-

EXHIBIT I-5

Comparison of Major Operating Agreement Forms

	Owner		Second Party	
	Advantages	**Disadvantages**	**Advantages**	**Disadvantages**
Owner operation (independent)	• Complete freedom to operate • Maximum return (no fees to an operator)	• No national affiliation, referral, or reservations system • Maximum downside risk, but no fee commitment	(No second party)	
Owner operation with referral	• National affiliation and referral; access to reservations system • Virtually complete freedom to operate • Maximum return, less referral fees and charges of 2% to 3% of room sales	• Maximum downside risk plus referral fees	(Referral association) • Increase size of chain network with minimal investment • Increase in referral-fee revenue with minimal costs	• Minimal control of property standards and quality of service • Revenues limited to referral fees
Owner operation under franchise	• National affiliation, referral, and guidance • Assistance during development, preopening, and operating phases • Freedom to operate, within bounds • Maximum return, less franchise fees and charges (5% to 7% of room sales)	• Maximum downside risk plus franchise fees and charges • Possible negative image if franchisor is weak	(Franchisor) • Increase size of chain network with minimal investment • Increase in franchise-fee revenue with minimal costs	• Minimal control of properties and quality of service • Revenues limited to franchise fees
Owner lease to operator	• Hotel investment with no hotel management expertise • Known financial return, either as fixed rental or fixed plus percentage-of-sales rental (adequate to cover carrying costs) • Minimal downside risk • Financing easier with reputable operator	• Loss of operating control • Minimal return, since limited to rental agreement	(Lessee) • Increase size of chain network with minimal or moderate investment • Increase in revenues once operating expenses are met • No depreciation and carrying costs (therefore maximum earnings per share) • Sole control of operation	• Increased downside financial risk, including rental payment • Loss of property on lease termination
Management contract (no operator equity)	• Hotel investment with no hotel management expertise • Financing easier with reputable operator • Maximum return, less management fees and charges (5% to 9% of gross revenues)	• Loss of operating control • Maximum downside risk, plus management fees • Difficult to remove operator	• Increase size of chain network • Increase in management-fee revenues with minimal costs • No minimum payments to owner • No depreciation and carrying costs (therefore maximum earnings per share)	• Revenues limited to management fees • Minimal input in ownership decisions • Dependence on owner's financial strength • Loss of property on termination of contract

EXHIBIT I-6

Comparison of Fees and Charges for Major Operating-Agreement Forms

	Minimum Initial Fee	Royalty Fee[2] (% Room Sales)	Management Fee (Basic and Incentive)	System Expenses[1,2] (% Room Sales)
Referral agreements:				
Best Western	$12,000	1.7%	—	0.7%
Friendship Inns	$ 9,000	1.5%	—	0.5%
Preferred Hotels	$14,000	0.5%	—	2.3%
Franchise agreements:				
Days Inns	$30,000	5.0%	—	2.0%
Econo Lodges	$11,000	2.5%	—	2.5%
Hilton	$62,000	5.0%	—	1.0%
Holiday Inns	$30,000–$100,000	4.0%	—	2.5%–3.5%
Marriott	$80,000	6.0%	—	1.8%
Quality	$32,000	3.0%	—	2.2%
Ramada	$25,000	3.0%	—	3.5%
Sheraton	$35,000	5.0%	—	1.6%
Super 8	$16,000	4.0%	—	1.0%
Management contract:				
Representative independent operating companies	—	—	2½–3½% gross revenue plus 5–8% gross operating profit	0.0–1.5% gross revenues
Representative chain operating companies	—	—	3–4½% gross revenue plus 10% gross operating profit	1.5–3.3% gross revenues

[1]System expenses include marketing and advertising fees, reservation expenses, and accounting, purchasing, and training fees and are calculated based upon representative size properties.
[2]For referral and franchise agreements, system expenses percentages are percentages of room sales; for management contract agreements, system expenses are percentages of gross revenues.

fications, and leads for mortgage and equipment financing; **(b)** during pre-opening: extensive operating and systems manuals and franchisor visitation to assist key property personnel; and **(c)** during operation: extensive consultation and technical services (at additional cost) and stronger on-going training programs. As a franchised operation, the owner is subject to greater uniformity and standardization of his physical plant and operational controls. For an owner with little or no operational expertise, this may be beneficial; for a strong owner, this standardization may be considered an impediment.

The benefits associated with a franchise must be weighed against the fees and charges, the strength and ability of the franchise system to generate additional business, and the requirement, if any, by the lender of a national affiliation as a prerequisite for obtaining financing. Annual franchise charges, including royalty fees and advertising, marketing, and reservation costs, range from three to seven percent of room sales. (Refer to Exhibit I-6 for representative franchise fees and charges.)

For the franchisor, as with the referral association, long-term success depends upon the ability to select experienced developers and operators as franchisees, to monitor and enforce standards consistently, and to provide efficient system-wide services. Franchisors have adopted different strategies for expansion. Some have elected to expand their market shares and franchise-fee revenue as quickly as possible. Consequently, less consistent operating standards exist among their franchised properties, since prospective franchisees were not screened as carefully as with other franchisors who chose a more deliberate, controlled-growth strategy. Conversely, franchisors who expanded slowly and maintained exceedingly high standards in selecting franchisees tend to have a more reliable and valuable franchise and also find themselves in a stronger bargaining position when negotiating management contracts because of their reputation in the marketplace for providing a higher quality product and service.

d. Owner Leasing a Property to an Operator. Hotel operating companies will usually not consider leasing a property because they prefer management contracts, which do not contain the downside risks associated with leases. If an operating company wants to benefit beyond its management fee from the upside returns of a strong property, it will usually attempt to negotiate a joint-venture position with the owner. If the developer is unwilling to share an ownership position, the operator may sign a lease in order to benefit from the upside return and to secure its position at the property.

When an owner is able to negotiate a hotel lease, he trades the potential gains or losses inherent in the other four choices for the relative safety of a definite but limited upside return. His rental basis can be a fixed rental amount geared to an agreed-upon index, a percentage of gross revenue, or a combination of a fixed amount and percentage of gross revenue.

e. Owner Signs a Management Contract with a Chain or Independent Management Company. An owner lacking hotel operating expertise can achieve the benefits of hotel ownership by contracting with an operator who provides the operating know-how and charges a management fee plus a *pro-rata* share of his system-reimbursable expenses. After paying these fees and reimbursable expenses, the owner keeps for himself all additional cash flow. With both a management contract and a lease the owner has professional management operating his property. The difference between the two is that with a lease, the operator enjoys the upside return in a profitable property and takes the downside risk, whereas the owner is in that position with a management contract.

Management fees and system-reimbursable expenses charged under a management contract are significantly higher than those charged under a referral or a franchise agreement. The combined fees and expenses range from four to seven percent of gross revenues for independent management companies and from five to ten percent of gross revenues for chain management companies. (Refer to Exhibit I-6).

The three major questions an owner must address concerning the contract option are: **(a)** is he capable of managing the property himself either as an independent, as a referral-system member, or as a franchisee? **(b)** can the benefits of an operating company exceed the disadvantages and costs of employing one? and **(c)** does the lender require a professional management company to operate the property as a condition of granting a mortgage? If the owner chooses the management-contract option, he must identify operators whose strengths match the needs of the property and negotiate a contract that meets his needs.

For the operator, the advantages of a management contract are: an increase in the number of properties managed with little or no financial investment or depreciation and carrying charges, an increase in management-fee revenues, little or no downside financial risk, and a more consistent product compared with properties operated under franchise agreements. The disadvantages are: limitation of financial returns to the management fees earned, minimal input in ownership decisions, dependence on the owner's financial strength, and loss of the property on termination of the contract. Negotiating a joint-venture agreement with the owner, however, negates to a great extent these disadvantages.

2. Implications for Owners, Operators, and Lenders

Since a number of operating alternatives exist, each of which provides certain advantages and disadvantages not present in the other choices, owners, operators, and lenders must carefully analyze which alternative will best meet the needs of the project concept, its market position, and the level of management expertise necessary for effective promotion and efficient management of the property.

The owner must determine whether he possesses the time commitment and expertise to manage his property as an independent or with the assistance of a referral or franchise company, or whether he would be better off turning over management of the property to an operator through a management contract or a lease. If he chooses to operate the property himself, he must evaluate the benefits and costs of managing the property as an independent or as a nationally affiliated property. He should analyze the specific referral and franchise companies in light of his specific project to determine which arrangement would reinforce and strengthen his project. Selecting a referral system or franchise that does not assist in targeting the project to the appropriate market may detrimentally affect the positioning and operating results.

If the owner hires a management company, he must choose between an independent operator (possibly in combination with a referral or franchise agreement) and a chain operator. Here he must select an operator who has the expertise and ability to effectively promote and manage that type of property in that type of market. Often a smaller operating company is more effective than a larger independent or chain operator in promoting and managing small- to medium-size or specific-type properties. The owner's ability to match the appropriate operating company with the specific needs of his property is probably the most critical decision he will make.

The operator's choice depends on whether the operator is a chain or independent operating company. Most chain operators evaluate projects with three alternatives: as a management-contract property (with or without an operator-equity position), as a franchise property, and, as a last resort, as a leased property. The operator evaluates the property's size, its potential to expand market share or enhance market presence, the property's projected operating returns, the owner's development and financial strength, and other potential operating and ownership opportunities in the area. If the project entails fewer than 250 rooms, has less than above-average earnings potential, or is in an area in which the operator is restricted by another management contract from operating, the operator will consider negotiating a franchise. If the project can add significantly to the operator's market share and market presence and if the property is large enough to generate adequate management fees, the operator is usually willing to negotiate a management contract. If the project's upside potential is significant or if the owner's bargaining power is strong, the operator may be willing to assume an ownership position in the project, thus increasing his upside return beyond the management fees earned and securing a voice in ownership decisions. Several chain operators, however, are expanding solely with management contracts and do not offer franchise agreements.

The independent operator evaluates a project either as a management contract or as a leased property. He evaluates the property's management-fee potential, his ability to service the project, and the owner's strength and intent to maintain ownership in the property. Independents are often called in to manage a property for an owner-in-foreclosure while that owner is attempting to improve the property's cash flow prior to its sale.

The lender is the important third party in the choice of an operating agreement, because of his financial exposure in the project. To protect this exposure, the lender wants to ensure that the property can generate its projected volume of business, profitability, and coverage ratios to meet debt service and adequate maintenance standards. As a result, the lender will usually insist upon national affiliation and professional management either in the form of a referral or franchise arrangement with an independent operating company or in the form of a chain operating company. In addition to determining which forms or combinations of agreements are acceptable and, in many cases, which specific affiliations and operating companies are acceptable, lenders are often active players in determining the outcome of the negotiated provisions in a management contract.

Owners and operators come to the bargaining table with different strengths and weaknesses. Their relative bargaining positions play an important role in determining the outcome of the negotiated provisions of concern. Chapter II identifies the factors that influence this bargaining power.

II

Components of Owner and Operator Bargaining Power

The bargaining power each party brings to the negotiating table influences his ability to alter the contract agreement form originally presented as the basis for negotiations. Bargaining strength involves fifteen factors—eight of them affecting the operator's strength, and seven influencing that of the owner. The combined interplay of these factors determines in part the contract provisions each party will ultimately accept. This chapter describes the factors that determine owners' and operators' relative bargaining strength.

A. Determinants of the Operator's Bargaining Power

The eight factors affecting the operator's bargaining power are listed in Exhibit II-1, along with an indication of the relative importance accorded to each factor by the two categories of owners (developer-owners and owners-in-foreclosure) and the two categories of operators (chain operators and independent operators).

1. The Operator's Market Position and Consistency of Product (as perceived by the public, other owners, and lenders)

The perception held by the public, other owners, and lenders of an operator's market position and ability to deliver a product consistent with that market position and image is considered to be a major factor in determining the operator's bargaining power. This factor is much more apparent with chain operators than with independent operators, but the factor is significantly important for each.

In recent years, many chain operators have attempted to expand their market share by entering new markets with multi-level, market-segmented product

EXHIBIT II-1

Factors Influencing the Bargaining Power of Operators

Factor	Degree of Importance as Perceived by: Developer-Owner	Owner-In-Foreclosure	Chain Operator	Independent Operator
• Operator's market position and consistency of product	3	2	3	2
• Number of properties operated	2	1	3	2
• Operator's stability and continuity	3	3	3	3
• Services offered by operator:				
—Marketing, sales, reservations	3	3	3	3
—Operational controls	3	3	3	2
—Development, Technical, and pre-opening	3	1	3	2
• Quality of operator supervision	2	2	3	3
• Operator's willingness to contribute equity and/or debt financing	3	2	2	2
• Operator's flexibility in negotiating contract provisions	3	3	2	2
• Operator's responsiveness to owner's goals	3	2	1	2

3 = extremely important
2 = moderately important
1 = somewhat important
0 = not important

lines, while other operators have continued to rely upon a single focused product. Chain operators who have chosen to develop multiple product lines (e.g., budget/economy, moderate-priced, first-class luxury), have been successful only by developing, marketing, and managing clear-cut product choices. Several of these operators have reorganized their corporate structure into separate divisions to reflect these individual product lines and to develop expertise and delivery systems tailored to each line.

The stronger independent operators tend to focus their talents and delivery systems on particular types of properties (e.g., limited service, highway, suburban, conference-oriented, suburban), or on one or two specific franchise lines. Operators who fail to differentiate successfully and who attempt to be "all things to all people" usually do not offer as effective a marketing or management organization.

Owners unfamiliar with the hospitality industry bring with them images of chain and independent operators that have been formed over time and from many informal sources. This background can be focused and supplemented with additional input from hospitality consultants, owners of other company-managed properties, and hotel lenders. Input from these sources can assist the owner in assessing an operator's marketing effectiveness, management depth and effectiveness, and ability to achieve expected profitability for the specific types of property the owner wishes to develop.

2. Number of Properties Operated

The number of properties managed by a particular operator is viewed as an important factor in bargaining power. An owner looks to a chain operator to provide an established system of properties that will promote the image of the owner's property and provide referral business without creating direct competition with his property. The owner also evaluates how rapidly the operator is expanding in order to assess the degree of assistance and support his property will receive as well as the possibility of future competition from the operator's new properties in either the same or in different product lines. Therefore, it is important to evaluate not only the existing network of properties but also the number of the operator's properties coming on line during the next three to five years.

Both chain and independent operators must manage at least six to eight properties to support a central staff that can provide specialized assistance in marketing, food and beverage, accounting, training, and procurement. As the number of properties increases, however, owners express concern about the operator's ability to supervise their individual properties effectively, and they place greater importance on the operator's regional staff resources.

3. The Operator's Stability and Continuity

The owner's perception of the operator's stability and continuity is a factor exerting a significant impact on an operator's bargaining power. Operators who have either grown too rapidly or experienced losses in the number of properties managed are viewed with some suspicion and generally have less bargaining power. An operator with a record of steady growth, on the other hand, is perceived by the owner as prudent in his evaluation and selection of properties. The operator's care in assimilating properties before expanding further is interpreted by the owner as a characteristic to the benefit of both owner and operator.

Savvy owners view internal policy shifts and key personnel changes in an operator's organization with concern because these changes indicate internal problems that could eventually affect the owner's property. An owner usually does not become aware of an operator's organizational problems until after the contract is negotiated. With more owners now involved in management contracts, however, an operator's ability to manage his organization effectively is more visible, and internal stability is becoming a greater factor in the operator's bargaining effectiveness.

4. Services Offered by the Operator

Owners and operators identified four major categories of services influencing an operator's bargaining power: **(1)** marketing, sales, and reservations; **(2)** operational controls; **(3)** financial reporting systems; and **(4)** development, technical assistance, and pre-opening management services. Owners assess an operator's ability to perform these functions on the basis of the operator's experience, the quality and experience of the operator's staff, and the mechanical systems developed to implement each service.

The category of marketing, sales, and reservations was considered the most important by both developer-owners and owners-in-foreclosure. Owners have become especially sensitive in the past few years to operators' promotional abilities due to overbuilding in many markets. Developer-owners with large properties rely on the operator's ability to attract group and conference business. Hence, these owners favor chain operators large enough to offer total marketing packages that include brand names, national reservations systems, and strong national and regional sales offices.

Owners of medium-size (250-300 rooms) and smaller properties with franchise licenses and access to national-chain reservations systems tend to favor independent operators, thinking them better qualified than chain operators to analyze regional and local characteristics and to promote a property to a particular market or clientele. Many owners consider chain operators less flexible than independent operators in developing custom approaches for local markets because a chain's strength lies largely in its established uniform procedures.

An operator's ability to provide effective operational controls increases the strength of his position in bargaining with owners who have experience in lodging operations. The operator's record in this area has less effect upon owners with little or no experience, however, unless they have researched the operator's reputation among other owners, lenders, and consultants. The quality of an operator's financial and managerial accounting system—in providing accurate payroll, accounts receivable, accounts payable, cash-management functions, and current managerial-reporting data—is considered extremely important by both operators and sophisticated owners since an effective system is necessary for the operator to identify and correct operating deficiencies, to manage cash effectively, and to determine realistic budget projections. Sophisticated owners often independently track an operator's performance in keeping expenses in line with revenues and in adjusting operating procedures to maximize profits. An operator who combines effective promotion with efficient cost management greatly enhances his bargaining power with the owner in any subsequent negotiations for other owner-developed properties.

An operator's ability to offer extensive development, technical assistance, and pre-opening services, coupled with a reputation for performing these services well, increases his bargaining power. Some operators offer extensive development and technical-assistance services. These include chain operators who have chosen to develop and construct hotels as part of their expansion program and independent operators who are operating subsidiaries of development companies. These operators can offer their development and construction experience and expertise and can even serve as project managers. All operators offer (and most require the owner to purchase) technical-assistance services for to-be-built projects, since operator input at this stage has a significant effect on the operational efficiency of the project. Technical-assistance services include consultation in architectural design, interior design, energy systems, security systems, procurement, and food-facilities planning. For an owner with no experience in developing hotels or motor inns, the extent and quality of these services is critical.

For to-be-built projects, all operators require the owner to purchase their pre-opening services, since effective management of the pre-opening phase has a significant impact on the property's market penetration and operating performance for the first several years of operation. Owners who have had no significant hotel experience tend to underestimate the importance, impact, and cost of the pre-opening phase. Pre-opening services include the developing a market plan and pre-opening budget; managing marketing and pre-selling; selecting, hiring and training personnel; purchasing inventories and supplies; negotiating leases and service contracts; and ensuring that the property is ready to receive guests on the opening date. Operators assuming the management of existing properties usually require the owner to accept a transition plan that permits the operator to gain access to the property prior to the takeover date to assess the level and quality of the existing operations, the status of advanced reservations and group business bookings, the effectiveness of existing property personnel, and the condition of the physical plant.

An operator with in-house development expertise or with a reputation for effective administration of technical and pre-opening management services has significant bargaining power. Owners and lenders of existing properties managed by an operator are reliable sources for assessing that operator's capabilities.

5. Quality of Operator Supervision

Although all operators emphasize the quality of their staff's management abilities during negotiations and rely heavily on this salesmanship to strengthen their bargaining power, only owners who have researched the operator's quality of supervision with other owners, lenders, and consultants can realistically assess operator claims. Experienced owners suggest that the quality of supervision an operator offers depends on several factors: the expertise of the operator's corporate and regional support staff and the linkage between these staff levels; the number of properties each staff group supervises; the support staff's distance from the property; and, prior to the property's opening, the linkage among the operator's development, technical-assistance, and pre-opening teams. These owners look for an experienced staff with minimal turnover that supervises fewer than eight properties and is so located that a staff member can reach the property within half a day. When evaluating independent operators, experienced owners tend to scrutinize the achievement record of the operator's chief executive officer since that person is central to the organization and embodies the operating company's performance capability.

6. The Operator's Willingness to Contribute Equity or Debt Financing

The extent to which an operator is willing to make an equity or loan contribution and the terms of that contribution have a considerable effect on his bargaining power. Owners view the operator's contribution as a sign of faith in the property's financial viability. Until recently, owners were at a disadvantage in asking operators to contribute equity or to make a loan to the ownership entity. In only a few cases did chain or independent operators agree to make equity contributions; in these cases, operators took the initiative for making an equity contribution because they wanted to share as a joint-venture partner in the profits of a lucrative project or to protect their management interest by gaining a voice in ownership decision-making.

Today, although most operators are still reluctant to make significant equity or debt contributions, many will do so to meet the competition in bidding for prime projects and locations or to meet lender requirements. Owners-in-foreclosure usually prefer to award a contract to an operator with a strong equity base in the hope that the operator will eventually purchase the property.

An owner's acceptance of an operator contribution can have disadvantages as well as benefits. This topic will be discussed in greater detail in Chapter III.

7. The Operator's Flexibility in Negotiating Contract Provisions

Owners and operators identified the following areas in which an operator's ability to remain flexible during negotiations increases the operator's bargaining power: **(1)** operator equity or loan contributions; **(2)** length of contract term and number of renewal terms; **(3)** management-fee structure; **(4)** conditions for contract termination, including operator performance standards; **(5)** personnel;

and **(6)** operator budgeting and spending restrictions. Each of these areas will be analyzed in detail in Chapter III.

8. The Operator's Responsiveness to the Owner's Goals

Owners cite special attention from a particular person on the operator's staff as an important factor in the operator's bargaining strength. A person's expressing genuine concern about the success of the owner's investment, or having ownership experience himself creates such a sense of individual attention. If an owner perceives an operator or his representative as honest, capable, agreeable, and able to see the enterprise from both the operator's and the owner's perspective, the owner's willingness to trust the operator increases significantly.

Most owners interviewed believed a small independent operator with ownership experience had distinct advantages over a larger independent or chain operator. In instances where an owner could establish a positive working relationship with an individual (e.g., a regional supervisor in an operator's organization), the owner usually favored the operator over other operators. Owners considered "the person with whom I will be working" a major factor in choosing an operator and noted that a good relationship reduced their concern about contract provisions in which they had to rely on the operator's discretion.

B. Determinants of the Owner's Bargaining Power

While provisions of management contracts seemed to favor the operator in the early years of their use, ownership entities were not without their bargaining strengths. Moreover, as the discussion of the seven factors presented below (and summarized in Exhibit II-2) indicates, owners have enjoyed increasing power at the bargaining table as the management-contract concept has continued to mature and as competition among operators has increased.

1. The Owner's Intent to Maintain Ownership

The owner's intent to maintain ownership is a pivotal factor influencing his bargaining power. If the owner intends to hold the property for an extended period, the operator enjoys the following benefits: a long-term presence in that market, a relatively secure and predictable management-fee revenue stream, and a commitment by the owner to maintain the property adequately to protect his capital investment. The operator therefore feels more disposed to accommodate the owner's concerns if he wants to obtain the contract. If the owner plans to use the operator only as a "caretaker" until he can sell the property, the project will not contribute to the stability of of the operator's organization, and the operator is seldom willing to concede points of contention during negotiations.

Some operators, however, do seek out properties that an owner plans to hold for only a short time. These operators include smaller independent operators

EXHIBIT II-2

Factors Influencing the Bargaining Power of Owners

Factor	Developer-Owner	Owner-In-Foreclosure	Chain Operator	Independent Operator
	Degree of Importance as Perceived by:			
• Operator's intent to maintain ownership	2	1	3	2
• Owner's experience and management capability:				
—Experience and reputation as developer	3	1	3	2
—Ownership of other lodging properties	3	2	2	2
• Owner's financial commitment and stability:				
—Equity investment in property	2	1	3	3
—Ability to fund losses	2	1	3	3
• Type of owner: institutional or individual entrepreneur	1	1	2	1
• Property's ability to meet operator's financial goals	3	2	3	3
• Property's ability to enhance operator's position:				
—Location	3	1	3	3
—Quality of design	3	2	3	3
• Competition among operators	3	3	3	3

3 = extremely important
2 = moderately important
1 = somewhat important
0 = not important

making their livelihood from the management of foreclosed properties that they eventually may purchase or for which they will assume the mortgage; independent operators whose main objective in managing is to earn the brokerage fee for setting up the sale of the property to a third party; and chain operators who have reluctantly agreed to manage a property on a short-term basis as a favor to an owner-in-foreclosure who is a potential source of future business or financing.

2. The Owner's Experience and Management Capability

In a position paper written by members of one of the operating companies studied, the developer-owner was described as "the crucial coagulant to a successful real-estate project, bringing the diverse elements of any development together." Most operators held this view. The bargaining power of an owner is enhanced by a record of success in commercial real-estate development, especially in other hotel projects. The developer's ability to interact well with local governments, zoning boards, and major lending institutions and to manage the development process expedites the completion of construction. If the developer-owner has experience with other hotel projects, he is more likely to understand the peculiarities of hotel development and operation: substantial pre-opening expenditures, significant negative cash flows during the start-up years, the constant need to refurbish public spaces, and the management-intensive nature of hotel operation. Operators view owners with previous hotel experience as generally more predictable and cooperative but also as more demanding concerning operator performance standards.

3. The Owner's Financial Commitment and Stability

All operators interviewed preferred that owners hold substantial equity in the property and maintain adequate cash reserves to fund potential cost overruns, negative cash flows during the project's start-up period, capital improvements, and replacement of furniture, fixtures, and equipment. A number of operators insist on reviewing and approving the owner's equity funding and structure, debt-financing package, and loan guarantees prior to making a management-contract commitment. When an owner possesses the financial resources to fund the project adequately on a long-term basis, his bargaining power increases significantly.

4. The Institutional Owner versus the Individual Entrepreneur

Most of the operators interviewed generally prefer to deal with institutional owners rather than individual entrepreneurs. Operators consider institutional owners more consistent in their decision-making, believe they measure operator performance in financial rather than in operational or personal terms, and feel they are more likely to refrain from interfering in the operation of the property. Operators often perceive business relationships with individual owners as being unpredictable, because the personalities and idiosyncrasies of individual owners play a greater role in the owner-operator relationship. Individual entrepreneurs are also more likely to interfere with the operator's management of the property, since they typically live near the property, frequently partake of its services, and bear the brunt of any criticism directed at the operation by local clientele.

However, operators also cited several advantages to dealing with an individual entrepreneur: he can be extremely influential in generating local support and business for the operation, since he is generally a well-known, successful businessperson in the community, and he can usually make decisions more promptly than institutional owners who are often hindered by multi-level decision-making mechanisms.

5. The Property's Ability to Meet the Operator's Financial Goals

Owners and operators agree that a property's potential for achieving the operator's financial goals is a primary component of the owner's bargaining power, and that the owner's bargaining power improves as the potential of the operator's achieving a relatively high return increases. The operator may be willing to accept a lower return, however, in an effort to enhance his market posture, to gain presence in a new market, or to meet the competitive bidding of other operators.

6. The Property's Ability to Enhance the Operator's Position

The ability of the property to enhance the operator's market posture, visibility, and competitive position in the industry is considered especially important by chain operators who are competing for larger shares of the national market. Most operators who consider specific areas or locations important to their overall growth objectives are willing to make concessions during negotiations and to accept a lower potential return than they might receive from a less desirable location. At this writing, center-city and suburban locations in major regional markets and resort properties in exclusive resort areas are considered prime locations.

An operator also considers the quality of a property's architectural and interior design when assessing whether a project would enhance or detract from the operating company's market posture, visibility, and competitive position. A developer-owner who can offer unique architecture and tasteful interior design, thereby contributing to a customer's favorable impression, enjoys bargaining power superior to that of owners whose properties are unremarkable. One operator commented, "It is important to establish facilities that provide perceived value to customers. The impressions of quality and uniqueness are important in attracting customers and improving our image, and they enable a property to earn the premium rates required for profitable operation."

7. Competition Among Operators

Increased competition among operators has contributed significantly to the increased bargaining power of owners. This increased competition results from several factors: **(1)** the need for operators to increase market share continually as a necessity for continued growth in a market that is not expanding; **(2)** the slowdown in construction of first-class, full-service properties in prime locations; **(3)** the entry of additional foreign-based chain operators in the U.S. market; **(4)** the formation of recently-formed chain operators that developed originally as operating subsidiaries of owners and now offer their own chain-affiliated services; **(5)** the continued ease of entry into the market of newly-formed independent management companies; and **(6)** increased knowledge and sophistication of owners and lending institutions about the hospitality industry and about management contracts. The result of the increased competition is forcing operators intent on obtaining contracts to make greater concessions during negotiations.

C. The Relative Bargaining Strength Continuum

The continuum of relative bargaining strength appearing in Exhibit II-3 illustrates the interaction of operator and owner bargaining power factors. The continuum is divided into four zones, reflecting varying degrees of relative strength. Zone I represents a relationship in which the operator has far more bargaining clout than the owner, while Zone IV, at the opposite end of the range, represents a relationship in which the owner is at a significant advantage.

Placing any particular owner-operator relationship in its appropriate position on the continuum requires a careful assessment of the factors peculiar to that situation and the time of the negotiations. Below are some representative examples of owner-operator relationships classified into zones according to the parties' relative bargaining strength.

- Zone I (heavily favors operator):

— Most operators and developer-owners (1970-1973).

— Most operators and owners-in-foreclosure (1970-1982).

— Strong chain and independent operators and developer-owners (usually entrepreneurial) with single properties in poor or average locations (1974-present).

— Strong chain and independent operators managing single properties for owners-in-foreclosure who ask the operator to assist (1983-present).

- Zone II (slightly favors operator):

— Chain and independent operators and developer-owners (entrepreneurial) with multiple properties or with single properties in good locations (1974-1976).

— Strong chain and independent operators and developer-owners (entrepreneurial and institutional) with one or several properties in average locations (1972-1985).

— Strong independent operators and owners-in-foreclosure with single properties (1974-1975).

- Zone III (slightly favors owner):

— Chain and independent operators and developer-owners (institutional) with several properties (1975-1981).

— Chain and independent operators and developer-owners (entrepreneurial) with several properties in good locations (1974-1981).

— Independent operators and owners-in-foreclosure with several properties (1975-1981).

EXHIBIT II-3

The Continuum of Relative Bargaining Strength

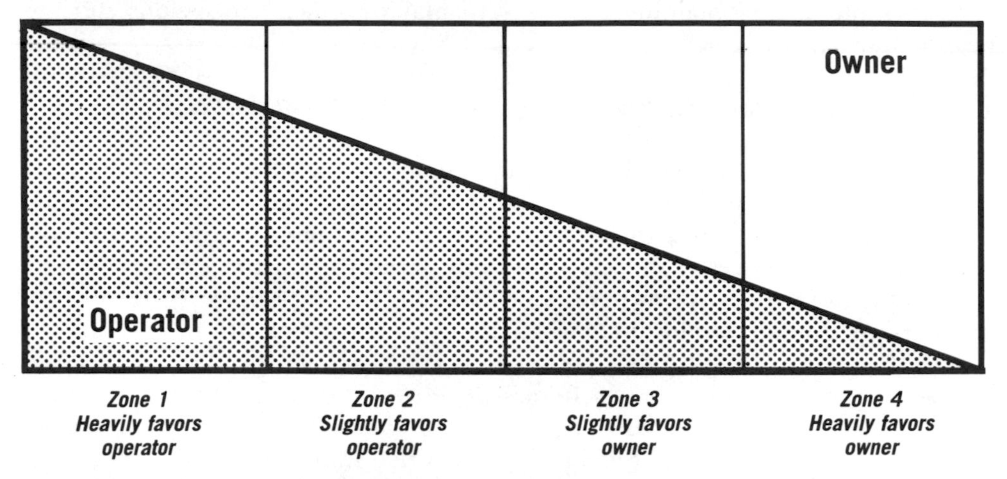

Factors enhancing operator's bargaining position

- Excellent opinion of operator held by public, other owners, and lending institutions.
- Adequate number of properties managed to support centralized staff and to indicate experience.
- Stable and continuous history of operator growth.
- Complete and competent services in: marketing, sales, reservations; operational controls; financial reporting; and pre-opening management and technical services.
- Maximum operator equity contribution.
- Experienced and thorough national and regional staff supervision.
- Maximum operator flexibility in contract negotiations.
- Owner's perception that the operator is responsive to the owner's goals.

Factors enhancing owner's bargaining position

- Intent to maintain ownership for extended period of time.
- Sound experience and management capability of owner.
- Adequate financial commitment by owner to the project and stable financial background of owner.
- Institutional ownership, rather than entrepreneurial ownership.
- High potential to achieve operator's financial-return goals.
- Excellent opportunity for operator to enhance market posture, visibility, and competitive position in the industry.
- Substantial competition among operators for the property.

- Zone IV (heavily favors owner):

— Chain and independent operators and developer-owners (institutional) with many properties (1981-present).

— Chain and independent operators and developer-owners (entrepreneurial) with exceptional locations (1978-present).

— Independent operators and owners-in-foreclosure with many properties (1976-1978).

As the above classifications indicate, a general shift has occurred along the continuum away from the operator-dominated end toward the owner-dominated end. This shift is attributable to two factors: increased competition among an increasing number of operators and a growing knowledge and sophistication of owners about management contracts and the hotel industry.

III

Provisions of Concern during Negotiations

The contract form that serves as the basis for negotiations is usually provided by the operator, and its provisions accordingly favor the operator's position. The operator hopes to maximize his control over the property's operation for an extended and uninterrupted period. The owner, on the other hand, wants the freedom to monitor the operator's performance, the authority to change or influence the operator's behavior during the term of the contract, and the power to terminate the contract if he becomes justifiably dissatisfied with the operator's performance. As a result, certain provisions of a typical operator's contract proposal cause owner concerns. During negotiations the owner attempts to reduce or eliminate these concerns, while the operator tries to resist revisions that would weaken his position or create problems for him during the contract term.

It is extremely important during management-contract negotiations that the concerns of both the owner and the operator are recognized and dealt with, or these concerns can undermine the contractual relationship later. This chapter analyzes the provisions of concern to owners and to operators during negotiations (see Appendix A). How the relative bargaining strengths of owner and operator affect the contract provisions negotitated is summarized at the end of the chapter.

A. Eleven Provisions of Concern

The provisions of concern to owners and operators during negotiations usually center on the following eleven areas: **(1)** the nature of the contractual arrangement; **(2)** operator loan and equity contributions; **(3)** the length of the contract term and the option to extend the term; **(4)** management fees, to include technical assistance fees, pre-opening and post-opening management fees; **(5)** operator system-reimbursable expenses; **(6)** conditions for contract termination, to include operator performance provisions; **(7)** personnel; **(8)** budgeting and spending limitations; **(9)** banking, accounting, and financial reporting; **(10)** dispute-settlement procedures: and **(11)** restrictive covenants. The eleven areas are listed in the order in which they usually arise during negotiations. The first six are considered of major importance, so they receive the greatest emphasis during negotiations. The remaining five areas are usually dealt with after the first six are tentatively resolved.

As mentioned earlier, because the contract form is usually provided by the operator and tends to favor the operator's position, negotiations usually proceed first with the owner's response to standard provisions, and then the operator's reaction to that response, followed by possible compromises that may be made.

1. The Nature of the Contractual Arrangement

Owner concerns regarding the nature of the contractual arrangement are central to all negotiations. These involve the following provisions of the owner-operator relationship: the operator as agent; the indemnification of the operator; and the operator's sole and exclusive right to manage the property free from owner interference. Provisions relating to these issues are listed below. (The numerals and letters in parentheses indicate the location of that provision in Appendix A.)

a. The Concept of Agency

• Operator shall act solely in behalf of and as agent for owner and not in his own behalf (I:F.1).

• All debts, obligations, and other liabilities incurred by the operator in performance of his duties shall be incurred in behalf of the owner, and the operator shall not be liable for the payment of any such debts, obligations, and other liabilities (I:F.2).

• No partnership or joint venture. Nothing contained in this agreement shall constitute or be construed to be or create a partnership or joint venture between the owner, his successors or assigns, on the one part, and operator, his successors or assigns, on the other part (X:A).

• Operating expenses. Owner shall be solely liable for the costs and expenses of maintaining and operating the property and shall pay all debts and expenses of maintaining, operating, and supervising the operation of the property, including, without limitation, the salaries of all its personnel (IV:C).

b. Indemnification of Operator

• Operator shall not be liable to owner or to any other person for any act or omission, negligent, tortious or otherwise, or any agent or employee of owner or operator in the performance of this agreement, except only the fraud or gross negligence of operator (IV:G.1).

• Owner hereby agrees to indemnify and hold harmless operator from and against any liability, loss, damage, cost, or expense (including attorney's fees) by reason of such act or omission (IV:G.2).

- Operator makes no guarantee, warranty, or representation that there will be profits or that there will not be losses from the operation of the property (X:C.2).

c. Operator's Sole and Exclusive Right (to manage the property free from owner interference)

- Sole and exclusive right. Owner grants sole and exclusive right to supervise and direct the management and operation of the property [without interference from owner] (I:E).
- Personnel. Owner shall not interfere or give orders or instructions to personnel employed at the property (IV:D.9).

Taken collectively, the provisions detailed above place the operator in full control of managing the operation, while all legal and financial liability rests with the owner. The concept of agency establishes an employer-employee relationship between the owner and the operator and protects the operator from any liability of debt, including all costs and expenses incurred resulting from the ownership or operation of the property. The provision stating that no partnership or joint venture has been established reiterates this strict employer-employee relationship. Provisions indemnifying the operator extend his nonliability to include all actions he undertakes—short of fraud or gross negligence—in performance of the agreement. Owners are aware that gross negligence is extremely difficult to prove and that litigation involving allegations of either fraud or gross negligence would extend over a long period, during which the operation would suffer from an unresolved adversary relationship between owner and operator.

Owners are usually reluctant to relinquish control of the operation completely, especially if they have been actively engaged in planning and constructing the property or if the property is their first lodging venture. If, during the construction and pre-opening, the operator has relied upon the owner to facilitate the operator's takeover of the property (and, as a result, a working relationship has been established in which each party views the other as an equal), the no-interference clause may prove difficult for the owner to accept. Even as they sign the contract, many owners fail to realize the significance of the operating restrictions placed upon them; their misconceptions about their role in a property's operation often lead to conflicts between owners and operators almost immediately after the contract comes into force.

Owners often attempt to replace the agency relationship with a relationship that establishes the operator as an independent contractor. There are several advantages for the owner in an independent-contractor relationship, including: **(1)** the ability of each party to indemnify the other party for negligence or fraud; **(2)** the establishment of property employees as employees of the operator, placing the liability of employee witholding taxes, worker's compensation, and public-liability insurance on the operator, even though the cost of the above will be reimbursed from the owner's account as property operating expenses; and **(3)** a potential limitation on the operator's authority to commit the owner in the areas of the negotiation of leases, service contracts, and labor contracts, and the signing of checks in the name of the owner.

Prior to establishing a negotiating position on the agency-independent contractor issue, an owner should seek legal advice on the advantages and disadvantages of each position and weigh these on the basis of: **(a)** restrictions placed upon him by law on his ability to operate non-related businesses; **(b)** his liability exposure to lawsuits that may be initiated by guests, employees, suppliers, or other parties; and **(c)** his tax position. Some ownership entities—namely, insurance companies, pension funds, and real-estate investment trusts—may not legally be able to manage or supervise a hotel operation. When this restriction applies, the operator must be an independent contractor who is responsible for the management of the property.

The potential exposure to lawsuits is of significant concern because a lawsuit brought by a guest, employee, supplier, or other party usually names both the owner and the operator as parties to the action. The court then weighs not only what the owner and the operator intended in the contractual relationship as stated in the contract but also how each acted in supervising and controlling the day-to-day operations of the property and how they portrayed that supervision and control to the public. The extent to which the owner exercises or influences supervision or control on operations may have an impact on whether he is considered to share responsibility for actions that precipitated a lawsuit. The owner should ensure that he carries adequate liability insurance or that the operator's insurance includes coverage for the owner.

The Tax Reform Act of 1986, which states that losses from limited partnerships or other businesses in which the taxpayer does not materially participate cannot be used to offset income from other sources, has provided an impetus for the principals in limited partnerships to achieve greater influence in operating decisions. To establish material participation, these owners are more willing to accept the agency concept and negotiate hard for the right to participate in determining major operating policies and to obtain approval rights in budgeting and staffing decisions.

In recent years, owners have often been able to negotiate an indemnification-of-owner provision in both agency and independent-contractor agreements. A typical provision is presented below:

> To the extent that Owner shall not be fully covered by insurance, Operator will indemnify Owner and hold it harmless from and damages, liability, cost, claim, or expense, including attorneys' fees, arising out of or in connection with the operation

of the Hotel or Operator's operations other than at the Hotel. The costs of such indemnity shall be borne as follows:

1. if the damage, liability, cost, claim, or expense is attributed to Operator's negligence, willful misconduct, willful violation of any legal requirements of breach of this agreement (other than Operator's covenant to comply with the legal requirements), the cost of such indemnification shall be borne solely by Operator and shall not be charged against Profit; and
2. if the damage, liability, cost, claim or expense is attributable to any other reason or cause, the cost of such indemnification shall be paid by Operator out of the operating accounts and may be charged against the Profit, unless such losses, expenses, or damages arise from any matters relating to the structural integrity of the Hotel or other matters relating to defects in design, materials, or workmanship in the construction of the improvements (other than alterations or additions made by Operator and agreed upon by Owner and Operator).

Owners believe that the above provision provides a better indemnification balance than exists in most contracts provided by operators.

The operator's sole and exclusive right to manage without interference from the owner may be influenced by the owner's ability to negotiate the other ten major provisions of concern. The owner's objective in this matter is to ensure that the operator has adequate latitude to exercise its best judgment and adequate incentives to meet the owner's objectives, while the owner maintains some influence through various incentives, options, and approval rights on the overall direction of the hotel's operation.

2. Operator Loan and Equity Contributions

Most owners attempt to negotiate into the contract an operator loan or equity contribution because the contribution increases the operator's risk and incentive in the project. The incidence of operator loan and equity contributions by both chain and independent operators has increased significantly in the past several years. This shift has been due primarily to the increased competition among operators for contract properties and to a more aggressive position taken by some operators, who as joint-venture partners or as general partners of a limited partnership desire to initiate and control the expansion of their hotel real-estate and operations networks.

Most operators still prefer not to lend or contribute equity but may do so if they want the property badly enough or if they find the owner willing to concede on other major provisions if an operator contribution is forthcoming. Both owners and operators report that the most conclusive factors in contract negotiations often are the willingness of the operator to make a contribution and the type and amount of that contribution. "We primarily want to manage," stated one operator who summarized a common operator viewpoint, "but often we have to buy a contract by putting up equity or a loan." "We prefer," stated another, "to evidence our intent by way of concessions on our fees in the form of deferrals or waivers. This concession indicates our willingness to take risk." This second viewpoint is viewed by most owners as a second-best settlement since it does not produce upfront cash toward the development, furnishing, pre-opening, or operational funding for a new property.

Operator reluctance to contribute equity or loans is due to a number of factors. In many cases, operators do not have access to funding. They have developed and positioned themselves as operating and service firms, not as real-estate firms. For those that are publicly held, equity interest would have an adverse impact on their operating statement, because of allocations of start-up losses and on-going interest, depreciation, and liability charges. "In order to take ownership risks inherent in making a contribution," one operator stated, "we need to be pretty darn sure the property will contribute significantly to expansion of our own market share and provide a healthy and steady management-fee stream."

Exhibit III-1 summarizes negotiated operator loan contributions made by domestic and international chain operators and by independent operators in terms of the principal loan amounts, the length of the loan, the length of the amortization period, the interest-rate base, and the specified funding objectives. The loan amount is usually specified to cover an identifiable project component such as working capital; inventories; furniture, fixtures, and equipment; operating deficits; or a specific combination of these. The loans are often funded only after the equity cash and mortgage funding has occurred. Terms of the loan usually range from eight to ten years with the provision that the loan becomes immediately due if the contract is terminated. The length of the amortization is usually greater than the length of the loan's term with approximately one-quarter of the loans being non-amortizing (interest only). The repayment structure is heavily influenced by the property's projected operating cash flows. Interest rates are based upon either a fixed or floating rate and are negotiated at an amount to represent the operator's cost of borrowing plus from one to two percentage points.

Operator equity contributions have also increased significantly in the past several years, because of increased competition among operators and the desire by some operators to obtain the decision-making rights of ownership in properties with strong potential. The form of the contribution differs significantly depending upon whether the operator is the developer-owner or a minority-interest owner. When the operator takes the lead as a developer-owner, he usually does so either as a 50-percent owner in a joint venture with a money partner or as a general partner in a limited partnership. The establishment of the percentage of ownership among joint-venture partners depends upon the relative values of the assets, services, and benefits each party brings to the

EXHIBIT III-1
Operator Loan Contributions

	Chain Operator		Independent Operator with Developer-Owner
	Domestic	International	
Percentage of properties managed in which operator loan contributions were made:			
Prior to 1982	17%	4%	10%
Since 1982	25%	13%	21%
Principal amounts of loans:			
Minimum	$ 150,000	$ 100,000	$ 40,000
Median	$ 450,000	$ 500,000	$ 110,000
Maximum	$5,000,000	$2,000,000	$2,000,000
Term of loan:			
Minimum	3	5	3
Median	10	8	6
Maximum	15	10	10
Amortization period:[1]			
Minimum	6	5	5
Median	10	8	8
Maximum	20	20	10
Interest rate:			
Fixed	8–14½%	10–13%	8–12%
Floating	prime	prime to prime +2	prime to prime +2; prime ÷ .85
Amount specified for:			
Working capital and/or inventories	53%	46%	48%
Furniture/equipment	14%	—	3%
Operating deficits	21%	23%	17%
Non-specified	38%	30%	41%

[1]Approximately 24% of loans are non-amortizing (interest-only) loans due at the end of their stated terms.

project. As a developer-owner, the operator's basis is determined by the value of the assets he may contribute (e.g., land, cash, other assets), the value of the services he may contribute (e.g., development, technical assistance, pre-opening, below-market management fees), and the value of other benefits (image, marketing services, etc.) The money partner's basis is determined by the value of assets he may contribute (e.g., the amount, terms, and interest rates of construction and permanent mortgage financing and secondary loan financing), the values of services he may contribute (e.g., loan-placement fees), and the value of

EXHIBIT III-2

Joint-Venture Agreement Example with Developer, Money Partner, and Operator as Partners

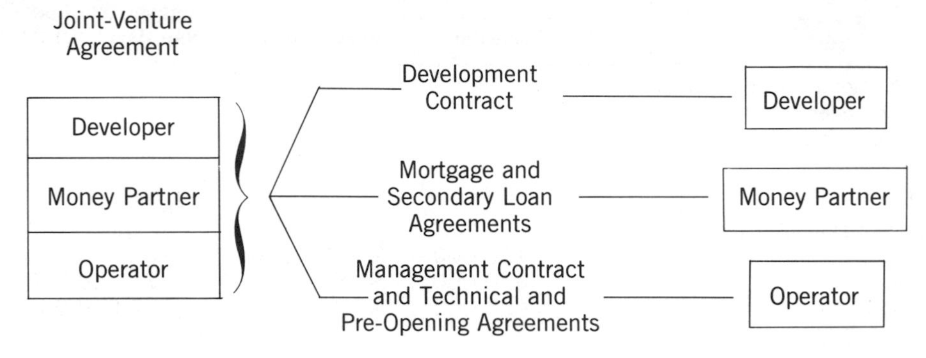

Key provisions to be negotiated in the joint-venture agreement:

1. Establishment of the joint-venture percentage of ownership for each joint-venture partner and what contributions constitute the basis for the percentages: cash, land, other assets, services provided, other value brought to the project.
2. Specific roles and voting rights of each partner during each of the three major phases of ownership: development and acquisition; operation; disposition.
3. Funding requirements: amounts, method and terms of funding, release schedule, additional funding for unexpected circumstances (project-cost overruns, greater-than-anticipated negative cash flow from operation), adjustments in joint-venture ownership percentages if any partner fails to meet its funding obligations.
4. Provisions for termination of any contract or agreement between the joint venture and any partner and for termination of the joint-venture agreement.

other benefits. When the operator is not developing the property, his equity ownership is based upon his contribution of the above relative to two other partners—the developer and the money partner.

Exhibit III-2 illustrates the structure of a three-partner joint venture in which the operator is not in the developer role. The joint-venture arrangement comprises four agreements: the joint-venture agreement itself; the development contract; the mortgage and secondary-loan agreements; and the management contract and technical and pre-opening agreements. Although each of the agreements is separate and distinct from the other three, negotiation of the four takes place simultaneously because concessions by any one of the three partners in one agreement is usually reflected in an adjustment in one of the other agreements. For instance, an operator may receive a greater proportion of the joint-venture equity by agreeing to any one or a combination of the following: a

EXHIBIT III-3
Operator Equity Contributions

	Chain Operator		
	Domestic	**International**	**Independent Operator with Developer-Owner**
Percentage of properties managed in which operator equity contributions were made:			
Prior to 1982	17%	10%	6%
1982 and after	28%	13%	17%
Type of equity contribution:[1]			
Cash	40%	30%	25%
Technical service/pre-opening management fees	60%	75%	80%
Conversion of incentive-management fees	5%	—	5%
Other	15%	10%	10%
Percentage of equity structure:[2]			
Minimum	5%	5%	5%
Medium	12%	10%	10%
Maximum	50%	20%	50%

[1]Types are often in combination with each other.
[2]For contracts in which operator has 50% or less equity interest in project.

lower base for his technical service or pre-opening fees or contributing these services to the venture; negotiating a lower basic or incentive management fee; contributing cash to the venture; or providing a loan to cover a portion of expected operating deficits. Conversely, increased assets or benefits provided to the joint venture by other partners may offset or decrease the operator's equity percentage. These contributions may include, for example, an increase in mortgage-principal amounts or a decrease in interest rates on the part of the money partner, or an increase in cash or a decrease in development fees by the developer.

When an operator is the developer-owner in a limited partnership, he is the general partner and must structure his equity base upon the value of the assets and services he contributes and the value of the benefits he provides to the limited partners (tax-shelter benefits, preferred returns, and capital apprecia-tion).

Exhibit III-3, which illustrates operator equity contributions negotiated by domestic and international chain operators and by independent operators, reflects the trend in increased operator equity contributions. The most prevalent type of contribution in each category is the contribution of technical services and

EXHIBIT III-4

Typical Initial and Renewal Terms

	Chain Operator			Independent Operator		
	Domestic			With Developer-Owner		With Owner-in-Foreclosure
	No Equity	Equity Interest	International	No Equity	Equity Interest	
Length of initial term (years):[1]						
Minimum	5	10	10	1	5	½
Median	15	20	20	3	8	1
Maximum	30	30	30	20	20	3
Number of renewal terms:[2]						
Minimum	0	1	1	0	0	0
Median	2	2	3	1	2	1
Maximum	5	5	5	3	2	2
Length of each renewal term (years):						
Minimum	5	5	5	2	3	½
Median	10	10	10	3	5	1
Maximum	10	10	10	5	5	2

[1]Frequently, initial contract terms between independent operators and owners-in-foreclosure state that the contract continues indefinitely until notice of cancellation is given with or without cause by either owner or operator.
[2]Option to renew is most always the option of the operator. Occasionally, operator performance standards must have been met for renewal term to take effect; if performance level is not met, owner has the option not to renew contract.

pre-opening management fees, although this type of contribution is often made in combination with cash or other forms of contributions. In several cases, owners have the option to convert earned incentive fees into equity.

3. Term of the Contract

The length of the contract's intial term, the number of renewal terms, the length of each renewal term, and who holds renewal options are major concerns to the owner, the operator, and the lender.

A long contract term provides stability for all three parties but decreases the owner's and lender's flexibility and can be a significant disadvantage to an owner if he unilaterally removes the operator, since the remaining term and renewal periods serve as a basis for a negotiated owner-operator settlement. A shorter contract term increases the flexibility of each party but is considered to be a major drawback for the operator who wants to manage the property over an extended period of time so he can realize his return for the significant up-front costs and effort involved. The lender is often the party that determines the initial term length because he wants to ensure that the contract's term coincides with the term of the permanent financing.

Exhibit III-4 illustrates the lengths of initial terms, number of renewal terms, and lengths of each renewal term stipulated in the contracts of owners and operators interviewed. Chain operators can negotiate longer initial and renewal terms than can independent operators because they bring with them an established brand recognition that contributes significantly to the identity of the property. Chain operators estimate that they need, on average, a term of at least eight to ten years to recover their start-up costs and to make their time and effort in the project worthwhile. Independent operators state that they need a minimum of five years for start-up properties and two to three years for existing properties to make the contract worth their while. Due to increased competition and decreased terms of permanent financing vehicles within the United States, chain operators and lenders are often willing to accept initial terms of ten to 15 years instead of the 20-year contract that was the industry standard for many years. Independent operators, who do not benefit from a chain name, can usually negotiate a maximum initial term of only ten years. When either a chain or independent operator contracts with an owner-in-foreclosure, contract terms usually range from six months to one year with a minimum of one year's management fee to be paid in the event the contract is terminated within the year.

In addition to the length of the initial term and subsequent renewal terms, two other issues are of significant importance. The first involves which party can exercise the option to renew. The second involves what becomes of the contract if the owner sells the property during the initial or subsequent terms of the contract.

Historically, negotiated contracts gave the operator and not the owner the option to renew, and this position is still the most prevalent. In cases where the owner possesses significant relative bargaining strength, however, an owner sometimes achieves the option to renew or negotiates conditions on the operator's option to renew—usually, the achievement of specified performance levels.

What becomes of the contract when the owner wishes to sell or sells the property prior to the expiration of the contract's full term is a significant negotiating issue. The major negotiating points center on the following: whether the operator has a preferential right to purchase the property; whether the operator has the right to approve the purchaser; whether the management contract survives the sale; and, if the contract is terminated on sale, what the basis is for operator compensation. These issues will be discussed in the section dealing with termination, later in this chapter.

Both chain and independent operators state that although the length of the contract term provides a feeling of stability or flexibility, the parties can agree to terminate the contract at any time if the owner-operator working relationship becomes untenable or if termination is mutually beneficial for other reasons.

4. Management Fees

Payments by the owner to the operator for services rendered fall into four categories: technical-assistance fees, pre-opening management fees and services, post-opening management fees, and system-reimbursable expenses.

a. Technical-Assistance Fees. Technical-assistance fees are charged by operators who take an active consultation role in the design and planning of lodging facilities. The major areas in which operators offer consultation services include architecture, interior design and lighting, mechanical installations, food-facilities layout and equipment, and such other areas as energy, entertainment, security, and financing. The degree to which operators are competent consultants in these areas varies widely. The owner can obtain information concerning a particular operator's competence in a given area from other owners who have used the operator's services. Some operators are considerably more demanding than others in their insistence that specific operating specifications be met in the design and planning of facilities. Most chain operators offer a wide range of consultation services, but the availability of these services among independent management companies varies from operator to operator.

All of the major chain operators surveyed offer technical assistance services (consultation) in architecture, interior design and lighting, and food-facilities layout and equipment. Nine operators offer consultation for mechanical installations, and six operators offer consultation for energy analysis. Less frequently, operators offer consultations in entertainment, security, and financing. Participation in technical assistance ranges widely. Two operators offer their services as project managers, while others will only be consultants. Four operators require that they participate in all phases of technical development.

Most independent operators offer some consultation services in architecture and food-facilities layout and equipment, but, in most cases, these services are less extensive than those offered by chain operators. Because their staffs are small, few independent operators can offer expertise in interior design and lighting or in mechanical systems.

The amount of the technical-assistance fee is based upon the specific services required by the operator or chosen by the owner, the amount of time spent by operator personnel on the project, the project stage at which operator involvement begins, and the complexity of the project. Chain-operator technical-assistance fees range from $100,000 to $250,000 depending upon their degree of involvement. Independent operator fees ranged from $40,000 to $150,000.

Chain operators base their fees for these services upon direct payroll costs, often multiplied by a set amount, for all regional and corporate personnel performing services. Of the chain operators studied, three use a multiple of 2.5, three use a 2x multiple, four charge the direct payroll cost (with no multiple), and two operators quote a flat fee for the entire technical-assistance package without reference to time spent. Four operators expressed willingness to negotiate technical-assistance fees or to include them as a component of their equity participation. Out-of-pocket expenses incurred in the performance of technical services are charged in addition to technical-assistance fees in all cases. Most independent operators charge a flat fee for their technical assistance, but several base their fees on direct payroll cost, to which they apply a multiple of two.

Technical services are usually negotiated in a technical-service agreement which is either separate and distinct from the management contract or is included as an addendum to the management contract. The technical-services agreement must delineate what each party—owner and operator—is expected to accomplish through each step of the development process. Confusion usually arises from general contract wording, and disagreements occur when wording does not specifically define whether the operator performs given services or advises and consults on those services.

b. Pre-Opening Management Fees. Pre-opening management fees are paid to operators for developing the pre-opening plan and budget and for supervising pre-opening activities, including staffing the operation, training personnel, installing operating systems, marketing the property, procuring all supplies and inventories, and negotiating in the name of the owner leases and service contracts. Since the hotel's performance during the first several years of operation is extremely important, the operator's ability to provide highly professional pre-opening services is critical. Owners with no previous hotel experience usually grossly underestimate the amount of effort and cost involved in planning and carrying through the pre-opening phase.

Pre-opening budget amounts, which include the pre-opening management fees, range from $1,200 to $2,500 per room, or 1.5 percent to 1.9 percent of total project cost, depending upon the size of the project and type of service and facilities offered. Pre-opening management fees range from $80,000 to $120,000 depending upon the size of the project, the type of service and facilities offered, and the length of the period over which the pre-opening phase occurs. Most operators require the owner to pay ten percent of the pre-opening fee when the contract is signed and then make equal payments of the remainder of the fee over the pre-opening period. If delays in the opening date occur, additional fee payments are required during the delay period.

All 12 major chain operators surveyed offer pre-opening management services, including development and supervision of the pre-opening plan. For these services, two operators charge no fee, three operators charge a fee covering only the payroll of personnel not at the property, three operators charge two times payroll costs, two operators charge 2.5 times payroll expense, and two operators charge a flat fee. Four operators reported that their pre-opening management fees are negotiable, and three said they would be willing to include the fees as part of their equity contribution. Out-of-pocket expenses incurred in the performance of pre-opening services are charged in addition to the pre-opening management fees in all cases.

System-wide marketing charges during the pre-opening period are handled in the following manner. Six operators charge at cost, pro-rated by the number of rooms in their system; and two charge at cost, pro-rated by the number of properties in their system. Four operators assess no charge. Of those operators who do charge, five begin the charge on the date the contract is signed, and the remainder begin the charge a predetermined number of months prior to the expected opening date. Purchasing and procurement services are offered by eight operators. Seven charge fees based on a percentage (ranging from four to eight percent) over invoice. One operator charges only for the time involved in rendering the service.

Most independent operators offer pre-opening management services that include all the services offered by the chain operators except system-wide marketing. The quality of these services varies widely among independent operators. Some offer extensive and effective services, while others offer few services. Although without the nationally recognized name of a chain operator, a number of independent operators offer very effective local and regional pre-opening marketing programs.

The owner should key in on the following critical areas that the operator is responsible for providing during the pre-opening phase: **(1)** the development of a detailed market plan tailored to the specific local, regional, and national target markets; **(2)** the installation of an adequate internal control and management information system that is fully operational before the property's opening; **(3)** the placement of a property management team early enough to train employees sufficiently; and **(4)** the deployment of a corporate pre-opening team to assist the property's management staff during the opening.

c. Post-Opening Management Fees. The management fee paid by the owner to the operator is the operator's compensation for managing and supervising the property and, in the case of a chain operator, for providing the benefit of using the chain's name and reservations system. An owner who employs an independent operator and desires the use of a national chain name and reservations system must obtain a franchise or referral license in addition to his management contract with the independent operator.

The owner additionally bears the full operating costs associated with the permanent, on-property management and supervisory staff, but is usually not charged for supervisory or trouble-shooting services rendered by the operator's regional and national staffs, either for work performed at the property or for work at the regional or corporate offices. These services are usually covered by the management fee. However, the owner must bear the travel and maintenance expenses incurred by regional and national staff members in the performance of supervisory services directly relating to the property.

Operators structure their management fees in the following ways: **(1)** *a basic fee only;* **(2)** *a basic fee plus an incentive fee;* **(3)** *a basic fee or an incentive fee, whichever is greater;* and **(4)** *incentive fee only.* The basic-fee-only arrangement gives the operator no incentive to increase profits if the fee is a fixed dollar amount and only minimal incentive if the fee is based upon a percentage of revenues. This arrangement is most common when the owner has minimal bargaining power (e.g., an owner-in-foreclosure of a severely depressed property) or in a less-than-arm's-length contract between an owner and an operating-entity subsidiary of the owner.

The second fee type—basic fee plus incentive fee—provides the operator with greater incentive to produce profits because the incentive fee (usually based upon a percentage of income before fixed charges or cash flow after debt service) is earned in addition to the basic fee. The vast majority of contracts between chain or independent operators and developer-owners are of this type. Negotiations on the basic fee plus incentive fee structure center primarily on the incentive-fee component, which comprises: **(a)** what performance line will be used as a basis of the fee; **(b)** whether the calculation of the incentive fee will begin in the first year or in subsequent years of operation; **(c)** whether the incentive fee or a portion of the incentive fee is subordinated or tiered to debt service and to a return on equity or is waived if debt service or a specified return on equity is not achieved; and **(d)** whether deferred incentive fees bear interest and, if so, at what rate. Usually the project lender has significant influence in the negotiation of the incentive portion of the management fee, since he wants to ensure that the incentive management fee is subordinated to debt service. Each of the above will be discussed in the latter part of this section.

The third type of fee structure—payment of a basic fee or an incentive fee, whichever is greater—can increase the operator's incentive to generate profits only if there is a realistic possibility that the proceeds from the incentive fee will be greater than the proceeds from the basic fee. The basic-fee portion can be either a fixed dollar amount or a percentage of revenues. Operators negotiating for the management of properties with highly uncertain futures or with accounting records that do not accurately reflect past operating results prefer a fixed-dollar basic fee and want to maintain an incentive component for improving the property's operating results.

The fourth fee structure type—incentive fee only—is the least-used fee structure since it can create volatile fluctuations in fee revenue for the operator. However, emerging chain and independent operators will sometimes offer this fee structure to obtain a competitive negotiating advantage.

d. Owner Concerns. The three major areas of owner concern relating to management fees are: **(1)** what specific operator services are received for the fees; **(2)** what proportion of the basic fee represents operator-cost recovery and what proportion represents operator profit; and **(3)** what fee-structure combination(s) establish adequate incentives for the operator to cover debt service and achieve the owner's required return on equity.

Owners should require operators to specify clearly in the contract what services are performed for the management fee, what specific services will entail additional fees or charges, and the specific basis (cost or cost-plus) of the fee or charge. Usually, non-recurring technical services or extensive operational analyses to determine the need for major capital expenditures are considered to be services above and beyond on-going management services and will incur additional fees. Services like these should be clearly defined in the contract.

Chain operators maintain that they generally need to earn between two and two and one-half percent of gross revenues (or an equivalent amount in dollars from another fee-structure type) to cover their corporate overhead expenses that are not directly reimbursed by their system-reimbursable expenses. The relatively small income of properties with fewer than 300 rooms generally precludes chain operators from bidding on them, because smaller properties cannot realistically afford the chains' management fees (except for smaller properties projecting exceptionally high room rates, occupancy, or restaurant volume). Independent operators, with their lower overhead, need to earn from $36,000 to $80,000 per year per property to cover their overhead expenses. Within this range, the amount required depends upon the size of the operator's corporate staff, the depth of the operator's group services, and the number and sizes of the properties managed. When a chain operator and an independent operator bid against each other, the independent operator's fee structure must be low enough so that his fees, when combined with the property's franchise or referral fees, are favorable compared to the chain operator's management fees.

The negotiation of a fee structure that the property can afford and that provides an effective management incentive calls for flexibility on the part of both the operator, the owner, and the lender. Since each property has different market, operating, and financing factors affecting it, the management-fee structure must be tailored to the unique characteristics of that property. The wider range of management-fee structures and of the negotiated conditions for incentive-fee payments within the past several years indicates the increased sophistication of the negotiating process and a rejection of a presumed "industry-standard" fee structure.

Exhibit III-5 illustrates variations within each of the four fee classifications found in international and domestic chain-operator management contracts. Exhibit III-6 illustrates variations within each of the four fee classifications in independent-operator management contracts for contracts with developer-owners.

Summarized below are the recent major trends in negotiated management-fee structures:

— The *basic fee* as a percentage of gross revenues has stabilized around three percent. In order to match the fee structure with the ability of the property to pay the fees, a sliding-scale base fee is negotiated during the first several years of operation or a portion of the fixed basic-fee percentage is deferred.

— The basis for *incentive fees* is shifting from being a function of income

EXHIBIT III-5

Chain Operator Management-Fee Structures

Fee Structure	Domestic		International
	No Equity	Equity Interest	
Basic fee only:			
1. Percentage of gross revenues[1]	4–6%	3–8%	4–7%
2. Percentage of gross revenues, with portion of fee subordinated to cash flow after debt service	4–5% with 1% subordinated	—	—
3. Fixed fee (annual)[2]	$1,000,000–$1,400,000	—	$800,000–$1,000,000
Basic fee plus incentive fee (no subordination of incentive fee)[3,4]			
1. Percentage of gross revenues, plus percentage of income before fixed charges (IBFC)	3–4% + 10% IBFC; 3% + 15% IBFC	2–4% + 10% IBFC	2½–3½% + 8–12% IBFC; 3% + 10% IBFC
2. Percentage of gross revenues, plus percentage of cash flow after property taxes, insurance, reserve for replacement, and debt service (NCF)	3–5% + 18–25% NCF	3–4% + 10–20% NCF	—
3. Percentage of gross revenues, plus percentage of cash flow after property taxes, insurance, reserve for replacement, debt service and return on equity (NCFAROE)	3–5% + 18–30% NCFAROE (8–12% ROE)	—	5% + 18–30% NCFAROE (8–10% ROE)
4. Fixed fee plus percentage of income before fixed charges (IBFC)	$500,000–$600,000 + 10% IBFC	—	$500,000–$700,000 + 10% IBFC
Basic fee plus incentive fee (with subordination of incentive fee):[3,5]			
1. Percentage of gross revenues, plus percentage of income before fixed charges (IBFC): incentive fee (or portion) subordinated to property taxes, insurance, reserve for replacement, and debt service	3–5% + 10–12% IBFC subordinated; 3–4% + 5% IBFC + 5% IBFC subordinated	3–4% + 10% IBFC subordinated	2½–4% + 12–16% IBFC subordinated
2. Percentage of gross revenues, plus percentage of income before fixed charges (IBFC); incentive fee (or portion) subordinated to property taxes, insurance, reserve for replacement, debt service, and return on equity	3–4% + 10–15% IBFC subordinated; 3–4% + 5% IBFC subordinated to debt service + 5–10% IBFC subordinated to return on equity (8–10% ROE)	—	4–5% + 10% IBFC subordinated

EXHIBIT III-5, Chain Operator Management-Fee Structures (continued)

Fee Structure	Domestic		International
	No Equity	**Equity Interest**	
3. Percentage of gross revenues, plus percentage of income before fixed charges less property taxes and insurance and reserve for replacement (CFBDS); incentive fee (or portion) subordinated to debt service	3% + 15–20% CFBDS subordinated; 3% + 10% CFBDS + 10% CFBDS subordinated	3% + 15–20% CFBDS subordinated; 3% + 10% CFBDS + 10% CFBDS subordinated	—
4. Percentage of gross revenues, plus dollar amount by which income before fixed charges percentage amount exceeds gross revenues	3–5% + incentive fee of amount by which 20% IBFC exceeds basic fee	3–5% + incentive fee of amount by which 20% IBFC exceeds basic fee	—
Basic fee or incentive fee, whichever is greater:			
1. Percentage of gross revenues or percentage of income before fixed charges	3½–4% or 12–18% IBFC	4% or 15–20% IBFC	4% or 20% IBFC
Incentive fee only:			
1. Percentage of income before fixed charges	18–30% IBFC	18–30% IBFC	20–30% IBFC
2. Percentage of income before fixed charges, plus percentage of cash flow after property taxes, insurance, reserve for replacement and debt service (NCF)	10–12% IBFC + 20–25% NCF	—	—
3. Percentage of income before fixed charges, plus percentage of cash flow after property taxes, insurance, reserve for replacement, debt service, and return on equity (NCFAROE)	10–15% IBFC + 20–40% NCFAROE (8–10% ROE)	—	—

[1]Occasionally the percentage of gross revenues begins at a lower rate and increases to a higher rate over the start-up period. (Example: 4% first two years, 5% next two years, 6% each year thereafter).
[2]Stated in 1986 dollars.
[3]Sometimes the basic-fee percentage and/or the incentive-fee percentages begin at a lower rate and increase to the full rate when the operation's stabilized year is achieved. (Example: basic fee—3% first two years, 3½% next two years; 4% each year thereafter; incentive fee—5% first two years; 8% next three years, 10% each year thereafter).
[4]Occasionally only the basic fee is earned during the start-up period, and the incentive fee begins and may be increased as the operation reaches its stabilized year or as specific profit levels are achieved. (Example: basic fee—3% each year; incentive fee—none first two years; 5% next two years; 10% each year thereafter.)
[5]Subordination provisions vary significantly. Usually when inadequate cash flow is available to pay incentive fees, fees are deferred until such time as cash flow is available; when deferred, fees are usually but not always subject to interest (fixed or floating rate). Occasionally, incentive fees are waived in the early years of a project's life if cash flow is not available.

EXHIBIT III-6

Independent Operator Management-Fee Structures

Fee Structure	With Developer-Owner: No Equity	With Developer-Owner: Equity Interest	With Owner-in-Foreclosure
Basic fee only:			
1. Percentage of gross revenues[1]	4–6%	4–5%	3–4%
2. Percentage of gross revenues with portion of fee subordinated to cash flow after debt service	4–5% with 1–1½% subordinated	4–6% with 2% subordinated	—
3. Percentage of room revenues and of food and beverage revenues	3–5% rooms and 5% food and beverage	—	4–5% rooms and 3–5% food and beverage
4. Fixed fee (annual)[2]	—	$80,000–$300,000	$45,000–$120,000
Basic fee plus incentive fee (no subordination of incentive fee):[3,4]			
1. Percentage of gross revenues, plus percentage of income before fixed charges (IBFC)	2½–3½% + 5–10% IBFC	2½–3% + 5–10% IBFC	3% + 5–8% IBFC
2. Percentages of gross revenues, plus percentage of cash flow after property taxes, insurance, reserve for replacement, and debt service (NCF)	3½–4½% + 10–18% NCF	2½–3½% + 10–15% NCF	—
3. Percentage of gross revenues, plus percentage of cash flow after property taxes, insurance, reserve for replacement, debt service, and specified return on equity (NCFAROE)	3–3½% + 10–20% NCFAROE (8–10% ROE)	3–3½ + 10–20% NCFAROE (8–10% ROE)	—
4. Percentage of room revenues and percentage of food and beverage revenues, plus percentage of income before fixed charges	3% rooms and 5% food and beverage + 5–8% IBFC	3% rooms and 5% food and beverage + 5% IBFC	3% rooms and 4–5% food and beverage + 5% IBFC
5. Fixed fee, plus percentage of income before fixed charges[2]	—	—	$40,000–$72,000 + 4–10% IBFC
6. Fixed fee, plus percentage of increase in income before fixed charges[2]	—	—	$48,000–$60,000 + 8–20% increase in IBFC
Basic fee, plus incentive fee (with subordination of incentive fee):[3,5]			
1. Percentage of gross revenues, plus percentage of income before fixed charges (IBFC); incentive fee (or portion) subordinated to property taxes, insurance, reserve for replacement, and debt service	2½–4% + 6–10% IBFC; 3% + 3–5% IBFC + 3–5% IBFC subordinated	—	—

EXHIBIT III-6, Independent Operator Management-Fee Structures (continued)

Fee Structure	With Developer-Owner: No Equity	With Developer-Owner: Equity Interest	With Owner-in-Foreclosure
2. Percentage of gross revenues, plus percentage of income before fixed charges (IBFC); incentive fee (or portion) subordinated to property taxes, insurance, reserve for replacement, debt service, and return on equity	2½–3½% + 8–10% IBFC; 3% + 5% IBFC subordinated to debt service + 5% subordinated to return on equity	—	—
3. Percentage of gross revenues, plus percentage of income before fixed charges less property taxes, insurance, and reserve for replacement (CFBDS); incentive fee (or portion) subordinated to debt service	3% + 8–10% CFBDS subordinated; 3% + 5% CFBDS + 5% CFBDS subordinated	3% + 8–10% CFBDS subordinated; 3–3½% + 4% CFBDS + 4% CFBDS subordinated	—
Basic fee or incentive fee, whichever is greater:			
1. Percentage of gross revenues or percentage of income before fixed charges	3–4% or 10–12% IBFC	3–4% or 10–12% IBFC	3% or 10% IBFC
2. Fixed fee or percentage of gross revenues and percentage of income before fixed charges[2]	$36,000–$60,000 or 3% + 8% IBFC	—	—
3. Fixed fee or percentage of gross revenues or percentage of income before fixed charges[2]	—	—	$35,000–$75,000 or 3% or 10–15% GOP
Incentive fee only:			
1. Percentage of income before fixed charges	7½–20% IBFC	10–18% IBFC	—
2. Percentage of income before fixed charges, plus percentage of cash flow after property taxes, insurance, reserve for replacement, and debt service (NCF)	6–10% IBFC + 15–25% NCF	6–10% IBFC 10–20% NCF	—
3. Percentage of income before fixed charges, plus percentage of cash flow after property taxes, insurance, reserve for replacement, debt service, and return on equity (NCFAROE)	8–12% IBFC + 20–25% NCFAROE (7–10% ROE)	—	—

[1]Occasionally, the percentage of gross revenues begins at a lower rate and increases to a higher rate over the start-up period. (Example: 2½% first year; 3% second year; 3½% third year; 4% fourth year; 5% each year thereafter.)

[2]Stated in 1986 dollars.

[3]Occasionally, the basic-fee percentages and/or the incentive-fee percentages begin at a lower rate and increase to the full rate when the operation's stabilized year is achieved. (Example: basic fee—2½% first two years, 3% next two years, 3½% each year thereafter; incentive fee—none for first two years, 4% next two years, 4% each year thereafter.)

[4]Sometimes only the basic fee is earned during the start-up period, and the incentive fee begins and may be increased as the operation reaches its stabilized year or as specific profit levels are achieved. (Example I: basic fee—3% each year; incentive fee: none first two years, 4% next two years, 8% each year thereafter. Example II: basic fee—3% each year; incentive fee—none first two years, 4% first $800,000 IBFC; 8% all amount over $800,000 IBFC.

[5]Subordination provisions vary significantly. Usually when inadequate cash flow is available to pay incentive fees, they are deferred until such time as cash flow is available; when deferred, fees are usually but not always subject to interest (fixed or floating rate). Occasionally incentive fees are waived in the early years of a project's life if cash flow is not available.

before fixed charges (gross operating profit) to: **(a)** cash flow available for debt service but after property taxes, insurance, and reserve for replacement; or **(b)** cash flow after debt service and, sometimes, after a stipulated return on equity. Three considerations have fostered the shift. First, owners want operators to reduce property taxes and insurance expenses, which many operators state they have the expertise to influence. Second, owners want to place the management of furniture, fixture, and equipment-replacement expenditures above the incentive-fee base to ensure effective management of replacement expenditures and to eliminate disagreements regarding allocation of funds for repair, maintenance, and replacement. Third, when owners' bargaining power is strong or when lenders insist, owners can negotiate an incentive fee that is earned only if debt service and sometimes a return on equity are covered. As the basis of the incentive fee is shifted further down the cash-flow priority, the operator's percentage of that base must increase to offset the smaller base and to increase the operator's total return commensurate with the additional risk the operator assumes. When a negotiated incentive fee is subordinated to debt service, or to debt service and a return on equity prior to the establishment of the actual debt-service or equity amounts (e.g., for a to-be-built property), a negotiated "reasonable" level for each is included in the contract, and that amount is used in the calculation of the incentive fees, regardless of the actual debt service incurred or the actual equity investment made.

— To match the fee structure with the ability of the property to pay fees, the incentive fee occasionally does not take effect until a negotiated stabilized year. For instance, the *basic* fee would be earned and paid beginning in the first year of operation, but the *incentive* fee would be calculated and earned only after the second or third year of operation and would continue throughout the remaining term of the contract.

— Incentive fees that are based upon a percentage of income before fixed charges or cash flow before debt service are usually deferred until such time as there is cash flow after debt service and, sometimes, cash flow after a negotiated return on equity to pay the incentive fees. When inadequate cash flow is available to pay incentive fees, incentive fees are usually deferred but sometimes waived. If deferred, they usually bear interest at a negotiated flat rate (eight to 12 percent) or on a floating rate (prime to prime-plus-three points). Deferred incentive fees become due and payable upon the termination of the contract or from proceeds available from refinancing of the property.

— The tiering of management-fee and investment-return payouts, whereby the operator and the owner receive their respective fees and returns on an alternating basis is becoming more prevalent. This mechanism represents the owners' attempts to ensure that operators and owners share equitably in operating and financial returns (when these returns occur). Examples of typical tiering mechanisms are illustrated in Exhibit III-7.

EXHIBIT III-7

Tiering Management Fees with Owner's Returns: Cash-Flow Priority Alternatives of a 3% Gross-Revenue Basic Fee, Plus a 10% Income Before Fixed Charges Incentive-Fee Formula

Payments are made as follows from available cash flow:	Alternate A	Alternate B	Alternate C	Alternate D
1. To operator (not deferred or waived)	3% gross revenue	3% gross revenue	3% gross revenue	2% gross revenue
2. To owner	50% debt service	Debt service	Debt service	Debt service
3. To operator	5% IBFC	10% IBFC	5% IBFC	1% gross revenue plus 5% IBFC
4. To owner	50% debt service	Balance of cash flow	10% return on equity	10% return on equity
5. To operator	5% IBFC	—	5% IBFC	5% IBFC
6. To owner	Balance of cash flow	—	Owner and operator divide remaining cash flow (70% to owner; 30% to operator)	Owner and operator divide remaining cash flow (50% to owner; 50% to operator)

Also to be negotiated:

a. If cash flow is not available in any given year, are unrealized fees or returns deferred or are they waived?
b. If fees or returns are deferred, will the deferred amounts bear interest? If so, what is the rate basis?
c. Is the debt service amount used to calculate the fee an actual or a negotiated amount?
d. Is the basis for a return on equity calculated as a negotiated amount, the beginning equity, or the adjusted equity (beginning plus additions)?

Tying basic and incentive management fees to project performance requires the owner and the operator to analyze the project's initial cost, operating-fund requirements, and cash-flow returns given a number of operating outcomes. The ability of both parties to work together through a variety of expected outcomes and to negotiate fee structures based upon their "best-guess" probabilities of these outcomes results in a fee structure that is usually considered to be as equitable as possible given the specific characteristics of the project.

Computer modeling can assist in assessing the returns to both operator and owner under a variety of fee-structure, operating, and financing scenarios. With an agreed-upon operating and financing scenario, the two parties can test a variety of management-fee structures to determine the magnitude and timing of cash flows each will receive. Also, given a specific management-fee structure, sensitivity analyses can be conducted to determine the effects on management-fee revenue and equity returns when changes occur in room rate, occupancy percentage, inflation rate, or other major assumptions in the projections. The testing of management-fee structures under various operating and financing scenarios can assist both the owner and the operator in arriving at a fee structure tailored to the economics of the particular project. In Chapter V, a computer-model example for the "Century 21 Hotel" project illustrates how operator and owner returns vary under different management-fee structures and when changes occur in operating and financing assumptions.

5. Operator System-Reimbursable Expenses

System-reimbursable expenses are paid by the owner to the operator for centralized services provided by the operator as part of his system-wide efforts in support of the owner's property. Chain-operator system-reimbursable expenses include expenditures for system-wide advertising and national and regional sales offices; centralized reservations systems; centralized accounting and management information systems; centralized purchasing and procurement services; centralized educational and training programs; and additional services such as life safety, energy management, insurance and risk management, preventative maintenance, auditing, preparation of owner tax returns, and special on-going project consultation. Independent operators offer system services but usually on a less comprehensive basis than chain operators. Exhibit III-8 summarizes system services offered by domestic and international chain operators and for independent operators as well as the reimbursement or cost basis for each service.

Two areas of contention concerning system-reimbursable expenses often arise during the term of the contract. The first involves disagreements as to which of the operator's corporate expenses can legitimately be billed to a property. The second involves the mechanism for verifying legitimate expense totals and the accurate apportionment of these to the properties in the system. A contract should state clearly which specific operator corporate expenses are and are not reimbursable expenses and should make disagreements subject to arbitration. The contract should also provide for an annual verification of the operator's total reimbursable expenses and the *pro-rata* calculation by independent means (usually by the owner's or operator's audit firm).

Since chain and independent operators use a variety of formats and formulas in calculating their management fees and system-reimbursable charges, the owner must make side-by-side comparisons of these packages if he is to assess them systematically. Different operators' costs (management fees and system-reimbursable charges) can be weighed against their benefits.

6. Conditions for Contract Termination

Specific termination rights granted to the owner and to the operator are outlined in the contract. These rights vary depending upon the original intent of the contract and upon the relative bargaining strengths of the owner and the operator. By virtue of its intent, a contract between an owner-in-foreclosure and an operator, under which the operator acts as a caretaker for the property, has more liberal termination provisions than a contract between a developer-owner and an operator, where the intent is to establish a long-term property investment by the owner and a long-term management investment by the operator.

EXHIBIT III-8

***Operator System-Reimbursable Expenses*[1]**

System Service	Chain Operator: Domestic	Chain Operator: International	Independent Operator with Developer-Owner
System-Wide Advertising and Sales Offices:			
Percentage of operators offering	100%	100%	14%
Bases:			
Percentage of property's revenues	34% ranges from 1% room sales to 2% gross revenues	40% ranges from 1% room sales to 1.8% gross revenues	50% ranges from 1–2% room sales
Direct cost pro-rated by number of rooms in system	50%	35%	50%
Direct cost pro-rated by number of properties in system	10%	14%	—
Direct cost pro-rated by number of rooms in system and average room rate	6%	11%	21%
Centralized Reservations System:			
Percentage of operators offering	100%	100%	21%
Bases			
Dollar amount per confirmed room-night[2]	38% ranges from \$10–\$14	45% ranges from \$10–\$16	—
Percentage of property's revenues	27% ranges from 1% room sales to .5% gross revenues	26% ranges from 1–2% room sales	—
Direct cost pro-rated by number of rooms in system	10%	14%	—
Direct cost pro-rated by number of confirmed room-nights	—	15%	100%
Centralized Accounting and Management Information Systems:			
Percentage of operators offering	100%	80%	64%
Bases:			
No charge	72%	50%	66%
Percentage of property's revenues	ranges from .5–.8% of gross revenues	—	ranges from .6–1.0% of room sales

EXHIBIT III-8, Operator System-Reimbursable Expenses[1] (continued)

System Service	Chain Operator: Domestic	Chain Operator: International	Independent Operator with Developer-Owner
Dollar amount per available room[2]	—	—	$150
Direct cost pro-rated by number of rooms in system	—	50%	22%
Purchasing and Procurement (for fixed assets):			
Percentage of operators offering	100%	72%	68%
Bases:			
Percentage of invoice	80% ranges from 5–7½%	90% ranges from 6–10%	90% ranges from 5–8%
Direct cost or other method	20%	10%	10%
Training and Educational Programs:[3]			
Percentage of operators offering	100%	100%	94%
Bases:			
No charge	80%	70%	76%
Direct cost pro-rated by number of properties	10%	10%	—
Direct cost pro-rated by number of participants	10%	20%	24%
Percentage of operators offering the following additional services:[4]			
Life safety	90%	80%	70%
Energy management	90%	75%	50%
Insurance and risk management	92%	80%	42%
Preventative maintenance	78%	80%	58%
Auditing	70%	80%	36%
Preparation of owner tax returns	50%	20%	22%
Special project consultation: (layout and design, remodeling, laundry)	100%	100%	80%

[1]Since operators charges for system-reimbursable expenses are uniform for managed properties and owned properties, data are not presented in the "no equity" and "equity interest" categories.
[2]Stated in 1986 dollars.
[3]Properties always assume expenses for travel, room, and board of property participants.
[4]Usually there is no charge for these additional services, except expenses incurred for travel, room, and board of operator's regional and corporate personnel while engaged on the project. For special project consultation, operators usually charge the property direct payroll cost of operator personnel working on the project.

a. Typical Termination Provisions. All contracts contain three provisions for termination, regardless of the contract's term or the relative bargaining strengths of the two parties. These provisions allow either the owner or the operator to terminate the contract if **(a)** the other party fails to keep, observe, or perform any material covenant, agreement, or provision, and the default continues for a period of 30 days after that party is given notice to cure the default; **(b)** the other party files a petition for bankruptcy or reorganization or assigns his property on behalf of creditors; or **(c)** the other party causes the property's licenses to be revoked or suspended.

Most contracts also permit the operator to terminate the contract if **(a)** the owner fails to maintain an agreed-upon minimal balance in the property's operating bank account; **(b)** the property is significantly damaged or destroyed by fire or other casualty; or **(c)** the property is condemned in whole or in part.

The intent of the above provisions is clear. Both the owner and the operator wish to protect their positions if the other party defaults on any contract provision or becomes unable to function as an economic entity. In addition, the operator wants to protect his position in the venture by having the right to terminate the contract if the owner is unable to meet his financial obligations in providing working capital or rebuilding a damaged property.

Three other provisions for contract termination usually require negotiation. These are **(a)** the owner's desire for the option to terminate the contract without cause; **(b)** the operator's concern about the contract in the event of the property's sale; and **(c)** the owner's desire to include an operator-performance provision in the contract.

b. Option of Owner to Terminate Without Cause. A provision permitting the owner to terminate the contract without cause is a part of 77 percent of contracts involving owners-in-foreclosure, but far fewer contracts with developer-owners. Exhibit III-9 summarizes the frequency of this termination clause, required notice periods, and penalty fee amounts to be paid to operators should owners exercise their option to terminate without cause. With owner-in-foreclosure contracts, both parties realize that the contract will likely be in effect for a short, indeterminate period of time and that the owner-in-foreclosure needs to maintain as many options as possible to improve profitability and sell the property. If the provision appears in a developer-owner's contract, it shows that the developer-owner has significant bargaining power relative to the operator.

In all contracts providing the owner an option to terminate without cause, owners are required to pay the operator a penalty fee if the owner exercises the option. The penalty amounts are usually a multiple of the most recent 12-month management-fee amount or projected management-fee amounts (based upon the agreed-upon *pro forma*) for a specified period of time. The basis of the penalty fee usually decreases as the remaining portion of the contract term decreases. While operators historically have strongly opposed provisions permit-

EXHIBIT III-9

Option of Owner to Terminate Without Cause

Provision	Chain Operator with Developer-Owner	Independent Operator: Developer-Owner	Independent Operator: Owner-in-Foreclosure
Without cause, at any time:			
Frequency of occurrence in contracts	19%	26%	77%
Required notice period	90–120 days	30–90 days	30–90 days
Penalty-fee amounts (in relation to management fees):	3–5 yrs.	1–5 yrs.	2 mos.–2 yrs.
Without cause, after a predetermined period:			
Frequency of occurrences in contracts	11%	27%	14%
Required notice period	60–120 days	30–90 days	30–90 days
Penalty-fee amounts (in relation to management fees):			
—After 6 months	3–5 yrs.	1–5 yrs.	2 mos.–1 yr.
—After 1 to 2 years	3–5 yrs.	3 yrs.	2–4 mos.
—After 3 to 4 years	2–4 yrs.	2 yrs.	2–4 mos.
—After 5 years	1–3 yrs.	1 yr.	2–4 mos.

ting owners to terminate without cause, they have recently been somewhat more willing to consider the provision when it spells out the specific cost to the owner to terminate—thereby sparing both parties the expense of litigation and the uncertainties regarding a settlement upon unilateral termination by the owner. When this provision occurs in the contract, the lender holding the first mortgage usually requires that the owner obtain the lender's approval before the option can be exercised.

c. Termination in Event of a Sale. When an owner wishes to sell his property, an operator wants to protect his position in the following ways: **(a)** by requiring that the new owner assume the existing contract; **(b)** by negotiating a specific termination fee to be paid to the operator should the buyer not assume the contract; and **(c)** by including in the contract the provision for a right of first refusal or a right of first offer.

Operators usually negotiate for a provision that requires the buyer to assume the existing contract, but which allows the operator to terminate the contract if the buyer does not meet net-worth or other specified criteria (e.g., must not be another hotel operator or have alleged connections with organized crime). Operators argue that they have been instrumental in developing the business value of the hotel and should have the right to continue operating it. For the most part, buyers want to retain a chain operator who can provide an identity to the property. When the property is managed by an independent operator, the owner more frequently replaces the operator.

EXHIBIT III-10

Provisions for Termination on Sale of Property

		Independent Operator	
	Chain Operator Developer-Owner	**Developer-Owner**	**Owner-in-Foreclosure**
Operator option to purchase property (frequency of occurrence):			
Right of first refusal	42%	38%	6%
Right of first offer	18%	16%	12%
Operator option to continue contract with new owner (frequency of occurrence)	54%	14%	0%
Termination fee paid to operator if new owner does not continue contract:			
Frequency of occurrence	24%	45%	86%
Fee amounts (in relation to management fees):[1]	2 to 5 times most recent 12-month operating period.	½ to 2½ times most recent 12-month operating period; fixed dollar amount.	⅙ to 1 times most recent 12-month operating period; fixed dollar amount.

[1]Most termination-fee amounts are graduated amounts based upon the number of years remaining in the initial term of the contract. (Example: in a ten-year contract term, three times the management fees of the most recent 12-month operating period if contract is terminated in years 2–4, two times the amount if terminated in years 5–7, and one times the amount if terminated in years 8–9.) Fixed-dollar amounts include a termination fee and occasionally relocation expenses for key management personnel.

When the buyer has the option to terminate the contract, the operator usually collects a termination fee, based upon a multiple of the management fees of the most recent 12-month operating period or upon a fixed dollar amount that decreases as the remaining period of the contract term decreases. Exhibit III-10 outlines the frequency of provisions giving the operator the option to require continuation of the contract with a new owner, the frequency of termination clauses, and the bases of termination fees.

Operators also wish to protect their position in the event of a potential sale by including in the contract an option to purchase the property either with a right of first refusal or with a right of first offer. Operators prefer to have the right of first refusal, while owners prefer that operators have the right of first offer. The right of first refusal gives the operator the option to purchase the property on the same terms offered to the owner by a prospective third-party buyer as long as the equivalent offer is made within a 30- to 60-day period. Owners often object to the right-of-first-refusal provision since it may inhibit their ability to sell the property; they fear potential buyers will not make the effort to negotiate a transaction if they know the operator will be given the right to match the offered price.

In more recent years, stronger owners have replaced the right-of-first-refusal provision with a right-of-first-offer provision that gives the operator the right to make the first offer to purchase the property. In this case, the owner can only sell the property to a third party if, within a specified period of time, the third party makes an offer that surpasses the one made by the operator. The right-of-first-offer provision eliminates the disadvantages to the owner inherent in the right-of-first-refusal provision. Exhibit III-10 illustrates the frequency of occurrence of these two provisions. Although the right-of-first-refusal provision is still the more prevalent, right-of-first-offer provisions are being negotiated more frequently.

d. Operator Performance Provisions. During the 1970s, management contracts rarely included operator-performance provisions. In the past several years, however, performance provisions have become more common, due to the increased competition among operators and to the insistence of strong owners. Operators are usually willing to agree to an operator-performance provision if it is reasonable and flexible. The provision must be based upon an agreed-upon, achievable measure, and allowances must be made for unexpected and uncontrollable economic circumstances.

Negotiations on operator-performance provisions center upon the following seven points: **(1)** the performance-criteria base; **(2)** the point when performance amounts are developed using the agreed-upon criteria; **(3)** the length of the operating period (number of years) before the performance period begins; **(4)** the allowable shortfall deviation (the allowable difference between the actual and the agreed-upon performance levels); **(5)** the number of consecutive years in which an allowable shortfall deviation can occur before the owner may exercise his option to terminate or before the operator may exercise his option to cure the shortfall; **(6)** the right of the operator to cure shortfalls and the method of cure; and **(7)** the test criteria for economic conditions that would allow downward revision of the performance levels. Exhibit III-11 summarizes the findings for each of the above factors.

The most common and most preferable performance-criteria base is the agreed-upon ten-year operating *pro forma* generated jointly by the owner and the operator that was used as the basis for negotiating the management-fee structure. This *pro forma* is preferred because it is the common basis from which the owner and the operator have negotiated other provisions of concern and have calculated their individual returns. The criteria base used is usually the amount of income before fixed charges (IBFC) for each year because this amount best represents the operator's ability to generate revenue and to manage operating expenses. The ten-year amounts are usually agreed to at the time of the contract signing, with an allowance sometimes made for the *pro forma* to be

EXHIBIT III-11
Operator-Performance Provisions

	Chain Operator			Independent Operator with Developer-Owner	
	Domestic				
	No Equity	Equity Interest	International	No Equity	Equity Interest
Percentage of properties managed in which operator-performance provisions occur:					
Prior to 1982	6%	4%	0%	3%	4%
1982 to 1984	18%	10%	8%	14%	8%
Since 1985	36%	18%	14%	28%	18%
Performance-criteria base:					
Income before fixed charges	usually	usually	usually	usually	usually
Cash flow after debt service	sometimes	sometimes	sometimes	sometimes	sometimes
Cash flow after debt service and return on equity	sometimes	occasionally	seldom	occasionally	seldom
Occupancy percentage	seldom	—	—	sometimes	—
When amounts are developed using agreed-upon criteria:					
At signing of contract	often	usually	sometimes	often	usually
Immediately prior to opening	usually	often	usually	usually	often
Annually	sometimes	sometimes	often	sometimes	sometimes
Operating period (number of years) before performance period begins:					
Start-up property:					
Minimum	none	none	2	none	none
Median	3	2	3	1–2	2
Maximum	6	5	8	3	3
Existing property:					
Minimum	none	none	none	none	none
Median	1	1	1	1	1
Maximum	2	2	3	1	1
Shortfall allowance:					
None	seldom	seldom	—	seldom	seldom
less than 10%	sometimes	usually	seldom	sometimes	usually
10–15%	usually	sometimes	sometimes	usually	sometimes
16–20%	sometimes	seldom	usually	sometimes	seldom
Number of consecutive years in which shortfall can occur before owner may exercise option:					
Any year	—	seldom	—	seldom	seldom
Any two consecutive years	sometimes	sometimes	seldom	sometimes	sometimes
Any three consecutive years	sometimes	sometimes	sometimes	sometimes	sometimes
Two of any three consecutive years	often	often	sometimes	sometimes	often
Three of any five consecutive years	sometimes	sometimes	seldom	seldom	sometimes

EXHIBIT III-11, Operator-Performance Provisions (continued)

	Chain Operator			Independent Operator with Developer-Owner	
	Domestic				
	No Equity	Equity Interest	International	No Equity	Equity Interest
Right to cure by operator	usually	always	always	usually	always
Method of cure:					
Outright cash contribution	usually	usually	sometimes	usually	usually
Contribution of current basic and/or incentive fees	sometimes	sometimes	sometimes	sometimes	seldom
Contribution of deferred incentive fees	occasionally	seldom	occasionally	occasionally	occasionally
Loan					
Interest bearing[1]	usually	sometimes	usually	usually	usually
Non-interest bearing	sometimes	sometimes	sometimes	seldom	seldom
Economic tests for unfavorable market conditions:					
Percentage of contracts with continuing tests	75%	68%	35%	44%	64%
Test criteria:					
Performance of competitive properties	100%	100%	100%	100%	100%
Comparison of projected and actual inflation rates	40%	25%	33%	30%	28%

[1]Interest rates were usually based upon a floating rate (prime to prime + 1½); fixed rates ranged from 10 to 13%.

updated immediately prior to the hotel's opening to provide a more accurate projection.

For a new property, the owner and the operator often negotiate a specified period of time between the property's opening and the start of the measured performance. Most owners wish not to include this grace period believing that the agreed-upon projections in the first few years should be measured even though both parties expect income before fixed charges to be inadequate for covering debt service. Operators argue that the first several operating years can be unpredictable and therefore want their performance to be measured beginning in an agreed-upon stabilized year. When the performance measure is adequate cash flow available for debt service rather than income before fixed charges, a "reasonable" debt-service amount is specified in the contract, since the operator wants the protection in case the owner highly leverages his property or later refinances with a significantly higher economic-value base. In addition, a specific year after opening is negotiated in which the performance measure takes effect.

Since the agreed-upon *pro formas* are developed long before actual operation and both parties acknowledge that economic conditions may deviate from projected assumptions, allowance for shortfalls and the length of time over which the shortfall may occur are subject to negotiation. Allowable deviations usually range from eight to 15 percent below the agreed-upon performance level. Also, the time frame during which shortfalls may occur is usually negotiated to be two or more consecutive years to allow the operator time to adjust to a rapid economic or market shift that may occur. The time frame for assessing a deviation, then, may be any one year, any two consecutive years, two of any three consecutive years, two of any four consecutive years, any three consecutive years, or another agreed-upon time frame.

When a performance provision is negotiated, operators usually want the option to cure the shortfall by paying the owner the difference between actual performance and the projected performance (less the shortfall-deviation allowance). By curing this difference, the operator eliminates the owner's option to terminate the contract, because the year for which the cure is made no longer can be considered a deficient year.

The operator cure is sometimes mandatory. In such a contract provision, the operator must cure a deficiency or be in default of the contract. Most owners favor a mandatory-cure provision, but some owners would rather grant an operator the option to make a cure and retain their option to terminate if the operator fails to cure. This arrangement provides the owner with greater flexibility to change operators.

The method of cure is also subject to negotiation. The cure can consist of any one of the following: an outright cash contribution; a contribution of current basic and/or incentive management fees; a contribution of deferred incentive management fees; or an interest- or noninterest-bearing loan. In most cases, the negotiated method of cure is an outright cash contribution; owners prefer this method, because it provides cash without an obligation to repay the amount. Operators, on the other hand, prefer cures to take the form of loans or contributions of deferred incentive management fees.

Operators usually insist that operator-performance criteria clearly identify the occurrence of unfavorable market and economic conditions that were not accurately predicted and included in the agreed-upon operating projections. Two such mechanisms exist. The first provides for a measurement of the property's operating performance compared with other identifiable competitive properties sharing the property's market. Some contracts will list three or four specific properties in the local market area for the comparison, while other contracts will permit an expert or arbitrator to choose the properties for the comparison. The test involves comparing business-volume data (usually average room rate multiplied by occupancy percentage) and, occasionally, profitability data (usually income before fixed charges as a percentage of gross revenues), if obtainable, from each of the specified properties with that of the contract property. If the contract property's performance level is equal to or greater than the average of the other properties' results, the operator is adjudged to be not deficient in his operating performance. If the contract property's performance level is less than the average of the other properties' results, the originally agreed-upon performance level is adjusted downward to reflect market performance that could reasonably be achieved given the actual market and economic conditions, and this revised achievement level would serve as the performance level for that year. The operator would then be subject to cure this adjusted shortfall.

The second mechanism to test for unfavorable market and economic conditions is the recasting of the agreed-upon operating projections using the actual inflation rate and revising the performance levels to reflect the actual room rate. Performance-level amounts may be significantly reduced if the estimated inflation rates used to develop the agreed-upon projections were higher than inflation rates that actually occurred. With either performance measure, comparable property performance or inflation rate, contracts provide only for downward, and not upward, revision of performance levels.

The person or firm to perform the tests for unfavorable market or economic conditions should be identified in the contract. Contracts state that the tests will be performed by one of the following: a specific hotel-consulting or -accounting firm named in the provision; a firm to be agreed upon by both parties and chosen at the time the operator requests the test; or the individual or firm specified in the contract's arbitration provision.

Exhibit III-12 shows an example of an operator-performance provision with the following provision terms: **(a)** a performance-criteria base using agreed-upon income before fixed charges amounts; **(b)** a two-year start-up exclusion period before the performance standards take effect; **(c)** a shortfall deviation allowance of ten percent of income before fixed charges; **(d)** a shortfall time frame of two of any three consecutive years after the start-up exclusion period; **(e)** a mandatory operator cash cure; **(f)** a test for unfavorable economic conditions based upon comparable property performance; and **(g)** an operator contract-renewal option based on performance measured by achieved income before fixed charges over the ten-year period.

To sum up, operators are usually willing to agree to performance provisions that are reasonable and flexible. If recent trends continue, the majority of contracts negotiated in the future will contain operator-performance provisions based upon reasonable and flexible performance criteria.

7. Personnel

Six personnel-related provisions in the contract form typically presented by the operator are of concern to the owner. These provisions are enumerated below.

EXHIBIT III-12

Example of an Operator-Performance Provision

	Year										Ten-Year
	1	**2**	**3**	**4**	**5**	**6**	**7**	**8**	**9**	**10**	**Total**
Agreed-upon IBFC (000s)	$2,610	$3,979	$5,401	$6,455	$7,214	$7,901	$8,663	$8,795	$8,443	$ 7,703	$67,235
Allowable IBFC with 10% shortfall deviation (000s)	2,349	3,581	4,861	5,810	6,493	7,111	7,797	7,916	7,599	6,933	
Adjusted allowable IBFC due to test for unfavorable economic conditions (000s)	—	—	—	—	6,300	7,000	—	—	—	—	
Achieved IBFC (000s)	2,300	3,500	4,800	5,700	6,300	6,950	8,800	9,300	9,800	10,000	67,450
Performance deficiency (000s)	49	81	61	110	—	50	—	—	—	—	
Operator cure (000s)	—	—	—	61	—	110	—	—	—	—	

Terms:

1. Performance criteria base: income before fixed charges
2. Start-up exclusion period: first two operating years
3. Shortfall deviation allowance: 10% of projected income before fixed charges
4. Shortfall time frame: 2 of 3 consecutive years after the start-up exclusion period
5. Cure and type: mandatory cash contribution
6. Test for unfavorable economic conditions: yes—comparable property performance
7. Renewal of contract: operator option to renew if achieved income before fixed charges equals or exceeds projected income before fixed charges for the ten-year period

Commentary:

Years 1 and 2: Performance deficiencies not subject to operator cure, due to exclusion of performance standards for first two operating years.

Year 3: No operator cure since first two years of operation are excluded from performance standards.

Year 4: Performance deficiencies of Years 3 and 4 represent deficiencies in two of three consecutive years; therefore Year 3's deficiency of $61,000 must be cured.

Year 5: Allowable IBFC adjusted due to test for unfavorable economic condition resulting in no performance deficiency.

Year 6: Allowable IBFC adjusted due to test for unfavorable economic condition resulting in a reduced-performance deficiency. Year 4's deficiency of $110,000 must be cured since deficiencies exist for two of the last three consecutive years. Earliest year in consecutive year time frame must be cured.

Years 7–10: Achieved IBFC exceeds allowable IBFC resulting in no performance deficiencies.

End of Year 10: Operator maintains option to renew contract since achieved IBFC for the ten-year period, $67,450,000, exceeds the agreed-upon IBFC of $67,235,000.

(The numerals and letters in parentheses following each provision indicate the location of that provision in Appendix A.)

— All employees shall be on owner's payroll, and operator shall not be liable to such employees for their wages or compensation (II:D.2).

— Operator will hire, promote, discharge, and supervise the work of the executive staff of the property (II:D.1).

— Operator may change or replace the general manager of the property at any time. The decision in regard to any change or replacement shall be at the sole discretion of operator (II:D.10).

— Owner shall not interfere or give orders or instructions to personnel employed at the property (II:D.9).

— The general manager shall be an employee of operator, and owner shall reimburse operator monthly for the manager's salary and fringe benefits (II:D.7).

— Owner agrees that if the general manager of the property leaves the employ of the operator for any reason, owner shall not hire the general manager in any capacity for at least one year following such termination (II:D.11).

Neither the owner nor the operator wishes to carry the employees of the property on his payroll. Each is reluctant to assume the continuing business obligations for keeping payroll and pension records and for negotiating and adhering to labor agreements. Also, neither wants to be liable for potential tort actions or EEOC claims.

In most cases, property employees are on the owner's payroll. However, they are employed by the operator in the following cases: **(a)** when the ownership entity is an insurance company or a real-estate investment trust that is prohibited by law from managing and operating properties; **(b)** when the ownership entity is a government, and it is in the best interest of both parties not to have civil-service rules governing hotel employees; and **(c)** when owners are in strong bargaining positions and are able to demand that property employees work for the operator. In each of the above cases, the operator's relationship to the owner changes from one of an agent to one of an independent contractor. In some states, state law requires that persons selling and serving alcoholic beverages be employees of the property owner. In such cases, all employees except beverage personnel may be employed by the operator. If the operator assumes the role of employer, he charges back to the owner the payroll and related expenses of the property personnel.

Payroll expenses of the operator's regional- or corporate-office personnel are not considered to be property expenses. Only when a regional or corporate employee fills a property line-item employee position can that person's salary be considered as a property expense. This situation may occur when an operator temporarily transfers a regional or corporate employee to a property to fill a vacancy while the operator searches for a permanent replacement.

The owner's second personnel-related concern is to influence or control the selection and the dismissal of the property's general manager and executive-staff members, since the owner is prohibited from interfering with or giving instructions to personnel employed at the property. Owners want to prevent operators from staffing their positions with inexperienced managers or from unilaterally replacing capable managers who are performing well.

In most cases, operators do not relinquish their sole discretionary rights in the selection, replacement, or termination of the general manager and key departmental personnel. However, in recent years, negotiated contracts more frequently contain provisions that permit some ownership influence in management selection. In approximately 25 percent of chain-operator contracts, the owner has the right to interview and to provide input to the operator on prospective general managers. The operator, however, reserves the right to make the selection. In slightly fewer cases, the owner has the right to review and provide input on other key personnel usually to include the director of marketing, the food and beverage director, the property controller, and the resident manager. In approximately eight percent of chain operator contracts and 17 percent of independent-operator contracts, the owner has the right to approve or to disapprove the general manager selected by the operator. In these contracts, that right seldom extends to other key employees. When the property owner is an equity syndication, the syndication's general manager often has the right to approve the general manager, since the general partner has the obligation to his limited partners to exercise judgment in overseeing operations.

In all contracts, operators reserve the right to transfer or to terminate property personnel, including the general manager and key department managers. They are adamant about retaining this right because they want maximum flexibility in placing management personnel to obtain maximum system-wide benefits and to provide adequate career ladders necessary to develop and hold effective management personnel.

Owners in some cases are able to negotiate payroll guidelines for key management personnel. These guidelines usually occur in contracts with independent operators for smaller properties where management salaries represent a substantial percentage of payroll expenses. Usually a maximum dollar amount indexed to inflation is specified for the general manager's salary. The operator must secure the owner's approval owner if he wishes to increase salary amounts beyond the negotiated limit. Most contracts do not include such limitations, since operators claim they need maximum flexibility to set competitive salary, bonus, profit-sharing, and benefit packages for key employees. When required to pay relocation expenses for personnel assigned to their property, some owners will negotiate to receive a prorated refund of those expenses if the employee is transfered to another property within a two-year period.

Owners who employ independent operators question the legality of provisions requiring the owner to refrain from hiring the general manager for one year following termination of the contract. Independent operators defend their right to require this provision in the contract because it discourages an owner from terminating the contract and hiring away a capable general manager. Most operators who include this provision in their contracts require their general managers to sign a similar clause in their employment contracts.

8. Budgeting and Spending Limitations

During negotiations, owners attempt to limit the operator's discretion in the area of budgeting and spending. Three types of budgets are usually identified: operating, reserve for replacement expenditures, and capital improvements/ additions expenditures. Each budget should be identified separately because each has a different purpose and a different approval mechanism.

The annual operating budget should be prepared by the operator and submitted to the owner for owner approval at least 60 days prior to the start of the fiscal year. A detailed market plan that serves as the basis for activity projections should accompany the operating budget and substantiate the revenue projections. Owners have three basic concerns relating to the operating budget. These are owner-approval rights, spending limitations, and establishment of proper account allocations. These concerns and typical owner-operator settlements on negotiated contracts are summarized in Exhibit III-13.

The budget for reserve for replacement expenditures is submitted annually by the operator to summarize expected expenditures to replace existing furniture, fixtures, and equipment inventory items. Owner concerns include: the annual dollar amounts to be placed in the reserve fund; notification and justification procedures for the expenditure; owner-approval rights; the funding mechanism; and the disposition of the interest earned and of the account balance at contract termination. These concerns and typical owner-operator settlements are summarized in Exhibit III-13.

The budget for capital improvements and additions expenditures is submitted annually by the operator to request funds for capital improvements and additions expenditures that are not replacements of existing inventories covered in the reserve for replacement budget. Owners want advance notification and justification from operators for these expenditures, the right to approve or disapprove expenditure items, and the right to monitor approved expenditures. Typical settlements for these concerns are also found in Exhibit III-13.

Agreement on the classification of expenditures is an on-going problem during the term of the contract unless category definitions are included in the contract or in an appendix to the contract. Differences of opinion often occur because an expenditure's classification can significantly affect the base amount upon which the incentive management fee is calculated. For instance, if an

EXHIBIT III-13

Budgeting and Spending Provisions: Concerns and Typical Settlements

Operating Budget: Annual operating budget is prepared and submitted by operator to owner.

Concern	Typical Settlement
1. Owner wants ability to approve or disapprove budget, based upon his judgment or upon lack of documentation.	1. If settlement is not reached, dispute may be taken to arbitration. Until settlement is determined, past year's budget is utilized. If operator is under a performance clause, owner will not have operating-budget approval rights.
2. Owner wants to establish spending limitations and to require operator to obtain owner's written approval prior to making deviations from approved budget.	2. Specific limitations may be negotiated on marketing, administrative and general, and repair and maintenance expenses. Bases for and limits on operator system-reimbursable expenses are established and reimbursable expenses are made subject to audit. Operator may deviate by line item but not on budget total unless appropriate volume change occurs.
3. Owner wants to ensure that proper account allocations are made for the calculation of management fees (e.g., repair and maintenance expenses are not calculated as replacement expenditures; complimentary rooms are not recorded in room revenue).	3. Specific definitions of repair and maintenance items and replacement items are included in contract or in contract appendix. Adjustments to revenue are clearly stated.

Reserve for Replacement Expenditures: Operator establishes adequate reserve for replacement fund from which expenditures are made to replace furniture, fixtures, and equipment.

Concern	Typical Settlement
1. Owner wants to influence amount of reserve for replacement funding.	1. Amounts are negotiated. Usually in the first several years of operation, a fixed dollar amount or a below-average percentage of gross revenues (1–2%) is used. Then a fixed percentage of gross revenues (3–4%) is used for the remaining term of the contract.
2. Owner wants advance notification and justification from operator for replacement expenditures.	2. Operator prepares annual replacement-expenditure budget, submits with annual operating budget, and includes justification for expenditures. Disputes may be subject to arbitration.

EXHIBIT III-13, Budgeting and Spending Provisions: Concerns and Typical Settlements (continued)

Reserve for Replacement Expenditures, *continued*

Concern	Typical Settlement
3. Owner wants to approve or to monitor replacement expenditures.	3. Operator usually has the right to expend funds up to the accumulated fund limit without owner approval. Owner has right to review competitive-bidding procedures.
4. Owner wants funding amounts to be "on call" rather than to be placed in escrow accounts.	4. Funds usually placed in escrow account. Maximum accumulation limit may be established with excess funds being subject to "call."
5. Owner wants interest revenue excluded from revenues for management fee calculation.	5. Interest revenue excluded in basis since interest revenue in replacement accounts is not classified as operating revenue.
6. Owner wants to receive balance in fund at termination of contract.	6. Balance in fund reverts to owner's control at termination of contract.

Capital Improvements and Additions Expenditures: Operator budgets for and supervises necessary capital improvements and expenditures.

Concern	Typical Settlement
1. Owner wants advance notification and justification from operator for capital improvements and additions expenditures.	1. Operator prepares annual capital-improvements and additions expenditures, submits with annual operating budget, and includes justification for expenditures.
2. Owner wants right to approve or disapprove expenditure items and to monitor approved expenditures.	2. Expenditure requests are classified as emergency and non-emergency expenditures. Owner usually has the right to approve or disapprove any non-emergency expenditure request. Operator has right to make emergency expenditures up to a specific dollar amount without owner's approval. Owner has right to review competitive bids. Disputes may be subject to arbitration.

expenditure is categorized as a repair and maintenance item, it will decrease income before fixed charges (or another profit line) and therefore decrease the incentive management fee. If, on the other hand, the expenditure is categorized as a reserve for replacement or capital-improvement expenditure item, income before fixed charges will not be affected, thereby resulting in a higher incentive management fee than previously would have been the case.

The following definitions are those generally recognized by experienced owners and operators as appropriate classifications in various categories:

— Repairs and Maintenance: Expenditures made for the purpose of maintaining any asset or for the purpose of maintaining the volume of business are classified as repair and maintenance expenses. These expenditures are necessary to keep the property and equipment used in the operation of the hotel in clean and presentable condition, regardless of the timing or magnitude of each expense, and including expenses made for extending the property's useful life. Minor replacements of vinyl, carpet, furniture repair, reupholstery, and mechanical-system maintenance and repair are considered repair and maintenance expenses.

— Furniture, Fixtures, and Equipment: All furniture, furnishings, and equipment required for the operation of the hotel, including, without limitation, office furniture, duplicating and communications equipment, and specialized hotel equipment, including equipment required for the operation of kitchens (stoves, refrigerator, ovens, etc.), laundries (dryers, washers, flat irons, folders, etc.), dry-cleaning equipment, and all other fixtures, equipment, apparatus, and personal property needed for such purposes, other than operating equipment. Items defined as operating equipment are generally considered to be expensed in the operating budget unless their cost per item exceeds $500 to $1,000, in which case their expenditure is classified as a furniture, fixture, and equipment replacement. Operating equipment includes all chinaware, glassware, linens, and silverware for the operation of the hotel, provided that these items are used for the day-to-day operations and are subject to general replacements, substitutions, and additions. Other items specifically included in operating equipment includes sundry kitchen equipment, maids' carts, vacuums, and other specified rolling stock. Portable equipment, such as calculators, blenders, and sundry individual items that are considered to be general replacements, substitutions, and additions are also operating equipment.

— Capital Improvements and Additions: Capital improvements include any revisions or alterations to or rebuilding of the property itself, the cost of which is not charged to repairs and maintenance in the property-operations and maintenance account. A test of whether an expenditure is a capital item is whether making the improvement will either increase the earning capacity or materially prolong the useful life of the property, or whether the project is of a one-time nature. Permanent additions or other such alterations in the hotel building are capital expenses. Capital improvements include major changes to the structure, or are items that are permanent or of an non-recurring nature; they do not include repairs, replacements, or redecoration. Examples may include enhanced life safety devices or building of a health facility. Disagreements as to the appropriate classification of a specific expenditure once the contract has been negotiated should be made subject to arbitration.

9. Banking, Accounting, and Financial Reporting

Owners do not balk at placing funds in an account in the operator's name, but they are concerned that their monies not be mingled with funds belonging to the operator or to owners of other properties managed by the operator. When the operator manages more than one property for the owner, the owner does not object to the operator's request to use one central account for all the owner's properties. Pooling of monies in these cases permits the operator to manage the combined properties with smaller cash balances. Owners also want to minimize the cash-balance amounts in the account and to withdraw excess funds from the account at their discretion. Operators with substantial bargaining strength remit excess funds to the owner only on a quarterly basis; operators with minimal bargaining strength automatically remit excess funds to the owner as the money becomes available.

Knowledgeable owners evaluate the operator's ability to perform the accounting services necessary to maintain adequate operational controls and demand that the operator furnish accurate and timely monthly operating statements, balance sheets, and, often, statments of changes in financial position. Many owners want actual-versus-budgeted comparisons of all revenue and expense accounts for use in monitoring operator performance, as well as a written management analysis commenting on reasons for variations and on operating adjustments the operator will make in the upcoming period.

Exhibit III-14 outlines the annual, quarterly, and monthly financial reporting mechanisms found in typical management contracts. The quality and complexities of reporting have increased significantly due to the growing sophistication of operators and demands of owners. These improvements include the inclusion of a detailed market plan that serves as the basis of the annual operating budget, justification analyses for projected reserve for replacement and capital improvement and addition expenditures, management analysis of operating performance, and audited calculation and reconciliation of operator system-reimbursable expenses. Since many contracts describe financial-reporting systems in general terms, it is recommended that the above reporting requirements be specifically stated in the contract.

One operator who provides a detailed financial-reporting system commented: "Good communication and reporting, with every willingness to disclose fully all relevant information, has eliminated any significant disputes between us [owner

EXHIBIT III-14

Financial Reporting by Operator to Owner

Financial-reporting mechanisms found in typical management contracts:

Annually:

Budgets:

Annual operating budget and market plan: revenue, expenses, and cash-flow projections shown on monthly break-down.

Projected reserve for replacement expenditures to include justification analysis.

Projected capital-improvement/addition expenditures to include justification analysis.

Financial Statements:

Audited financial statements: balance sheet, income statement, replacement and capital-improvement/addition-expenditure reports, statement of changes in financial position.

Management-analysis report: overview of performance to include analysis of variations from budget.

Reconciliation of annual basic and incentive management fees.

Calculation and reconciliation of operator system-reimbursable expenses (audited).

Quarterly:

Financial Statements:

Unaudited financial statements: balance sheet, income statement, replacement and capital-improvement/additions-expenditures reports, statement of changes in financial position.

Management-analysis report: review of past quarter's performance to include analysis of variations from budget and overview of upcoming quarter's management plan to achieve projections.

Calculation of incentive management fee (paid quarterly).

Calculation of operator system-reimbursable expenses (paid quarterly).

Monthly:

Financial Statements:

Unaudited financial statements; balance sheet, income statement, statement of changes in financial position.

Management-analysis report: review of past month's performance to include analysis of variations from budget; overview of upcoming month's management plan to achieve projections.

Calculation of basic management fee (paid monthly).

Other:

Additional reports often required include weekly revenue reports, daily or weekly cash deposit/withdrawal reports, and, if applicable, franchisor property-inspection reports.

and operator]. When adverse conditions affect the property, advance notice to the owner, with recommendations by us [operator], has improved the owner's satisfaction."

10. Dispute-Settlement Procedures

Arbitration provisions appear in the majority of chain-operator contracts and in about half of the independent-operator contracts. Owners negotiating long-term contracts in which their ability to terminate the contract is limited want an arbitration clause included.

Most contracts that include arbitration provisions employ American Arbitration Association (AAA) guidelines to speed a settlement, reduce costs, produce a final and non-appealable decision, and ensure confidentiality (since no public record of the dispute or of the settlement is established). About 60 percent of the contracts with arbitration provisions specify that the arbitrator be a member of the American Arbitration Association, while the remainder state that the arbitrator be a nationally recognized hotel-accounting or -consulting firm. In the latter case, a specific firm or a listing of specific firms is often stipulated in the contract provision. In most cases, the arbitrator must be mutually acceptable to both the owner and the operator. If both parties cannot agree on a single arbitrator, each chooses an arbitrator, and these two persons select a third arbitrator. Their choice of the third party to arbitrate is binding on the owner and the operator. In several cases of properties managed by independent operators, the property's franchisor is named as the arbitrator.

Most owners and operators interviewed recommended that the arbitration clause state clearly whether all contract provisions should be subject to arbitration or whether arbitration should be limited to specific disputes such as management-fee calculations, operator system-reimbursable expense allocations, determination of unfavorable economic conditions for operator-performance provisions, repair and maintenance/reserve for replacement/capital improvement allocation decisions, and specific budget disputes. It is also recommended that if a dollar amount is disputed, the owner and the operator each submit his best offer and that the arbitrator choose one of the offers and not elect a compromise position. This mechanism encourages each side to submit a reasonable settlement proposal, since each wants the arbitrator to choose its position.

In international contracts, the arbitration process falls under local arbitration rules unless the contract stipulates that arbitration be conducted in accordance with rules of the International Council of Commercial Arbitration (ICCA) or AAA. Several international chain operators insist that disputes regarding some financial matters, such as inflation factors for costs that are to be indexed, be subject to binding determination of independent auditors.

Although a growing number of owners and operators insist that arbitration provisions be included in their contracts, most are reluctant to use the mechanism. "A concerted effort to work out disagreements ourselves is the best solution," states a large institutional owner, "since this process inherently involves some compromise. If this effort doesn't work, we would then submit the dispute to arbitration." Most owners and operators interviewed reported that they had not initiated the arbitration mechanisms in their contracts but believed that the existence of the mechanism is an important factor in encouraging agreement between both parties.

11. Restrictive Covenants

In a restrictive covenant, the operator agrees he will not own, manage, or be affiliated with another property within a specified geographical area of the owner's hotel. During negotiations, the owner wants to expand the geographical area of the restriction to gain the exclusive benefit of the operator's ability to attract any type of business to the hotel. The operator, on the other hand, wants to negotiate a covenant that provides maximum flexibility to expand his ability to manage additional properties in what may be a growing and changing market. Consequently, the operator attempts to structure the covenant to: **(a)** minimize the geographical area; **(b)** permit additional properties within the area if they are targeted to identifiably different market segments; **(c)** obtain the right of first refusal to manage future additional properties developed in that area by the owner; **(d)** obtain the right to own or manage additional properties that will not materially affect business at the owner's hotel; and **(e)** negotiate a specific time limitation on the restrictive covenant.

If the area of the restrictive covenant is specified in miles, the provision should state whether the distance is in air miles or road miles. Emerging operating companies are more willing to offer larger geographical areas than established operators to gain a competitive advantage in negotiations. In their former eagerness to gain properties, several operators made what they now find are too-liberal covenants that restrict their ability to expand within a specific market area. "You need to be somewhat visionary," stated one chain operator, "and consider what your position will be five to ten years from now, especially with the industry developing market-segmented properties."

With the increasing emphasis on market segmentation, operators in recent negotiations have attempted to exclude from the restrictions properties of different types or those oriented toward different markets. Owners agree, however, that in only rare cases can a legitimate case be made that different types of properties (full-service, all-suites, economy, or budget) do not draw from somewhat overlapping markets and that exceptions made on this basis would not detrimentally affect the volume of business in their hotels. If the market segmentation efforts continue, owners will be under increasing pressure by operators to exclude other types of properties from the restrictions. Before agreeing to such an exclusion, an owner should feel relatively certain that these properties will not draw from his property's market.

Most owners will agree to offering the operator the right of first refusal to manage future additional properties constructed in the restricted area but will not agree to a provision that prohibits the owner from developing an additional property if the operator chooses not to manage it.

In some contracts, owners and operators have negotiated market tests to determine whether an operator can manage another property within the restricted area. These tests establish volume criteria (usually the hotel's or the market area's occupancy percentage) and a time period (usually a specific number of consecutive years) that are used to determine whether the growth in the market area can support additional properties, and if additional properties are not permitted, the operator will suffer a relative setback in his ability to maintain his market share.

Specific time limits on restrictive covenants generally range between ten and 20 years and often coincide with the intial term of the contract.

Because restrictive-covenant provisions are location- and market-specific, caution should be exercised in comparing these provisions from contract to contract. The negotiated provision for a specific contract must ultimately provide protection for the owner's investment and some flexibility for the operator as markets expand over time.

B. Negotiated Provisions Affected by Bargaining Strength

The effects of bargaining strength on negotiated provisions of concern for four operator-owner relationships are presented in Exhibits III-15 through III-18: **(1)** domestic contracts between chain operators and developer-owners; **(2)** domestic contracts between independent operators and developer-owners; **(3)** domestic contracts operators and owners-in-foreclosure; and **(4)** international contracts between operators and developer-owners. As bargaining strength shifts toward the owner, the following trends in the negotiated provisions tend to occur:

— Nature of the contractual arrangement: Concept of independent operator replaces the concept of agency. Indemnification of owner by operator is included. Operator's sole and exclusive right to manage remains unchanged, but owner gains additional options and approval rights in other contract provisions.

— Operator loan and equity contribution: The operator offers a nominal loan contribution that is increased in amount if necessary. An operator equity contribution may be substituted depending upon mutually agreeable objectives of both parties. The amount may first cover working capital, but may be

EXHIBIT III-15

The Effect of Relative Bargaining Strengths on Provisions of Concern for Domestic Contracts Between Chain Operators and Developer-Owners

	Relative Bargaining Strength			
Provision	**Heavily Favors Operator**	**Slightly Favors Operator**	**Slightly Favors Owner**	**Heavily Favors Owner**
Nature of contractual arrangement:				
Agency-independent contractor	Agency[1]	Agency[1]	Usually agency[1]	Usually independent contractor
Indemnification of	Operator	Operator	Operator	Operator and owner
Sole and exclusive right	Unaffected	Unaffected	Unaffected	Unaffected
Operator contribution:				
Loan	None	Occasionally	Working capital	Working capital, inventories, or furniture and fixtures
Equity	Seldom	Seldom	Occasionally	Occasionally
Term of contract:				
Initial term length	20 years	15–20 years	10–20 years	5–15 years
Number of renewal terms	2–3	1–2	1–2	1–2
Length of each renewal	10 years	5–10 years	5–10 years	5 years
Management fees:				
Technical assistance	Not negotiable	Not negotiable	Often negotiable	Usually negotiable
Pre-opening management	Not negotiable	Occasionally negotiable	Occasionally negotiable	Often negotiable
Post-opening management:				
Basic-incentive mix	3% gross + 10% IBFC	3% gross + 10% IBFC	3% gross + 10% IBFC	3% gross + 10% IBFC; 3% gross + 25% CFADS and 10% ROE
Subordination/waiver	Occasionally	Usually	Usually	Most always subordination; occasional waiver

Operator system-reimbursable expenses	Not negotiable	Not negotiable	Not negotiable	Usually not negotiable
Contract termination by owner:				
Without cause	None	None	Seldom but with termination fee	Occasionally but with termination fee
Event of sale	Right of first refusal	Right of first refusal	Right of first offer	Right of first offer
Operator-performance provision	None	Seldom	Often	Usually
Personnel:				
Employer	Owner[1]	Owner[1]	Usually owner[1]	Usually operator[1]
Owner approval of manager	None	None	Occasionally	Often
Budgeting and spending:				
Owner approval	Seldom	Often[2]	Usually[2]	Most always[2]
Deviation from budget	Operator discretion	Usually operator discretion	Usually operator discretion	Owner right to disapprove[2]
Escrow requirements on replacement reserve	Always	Usually	Often	Occasionally
Banking—working capital balances	Not negotiable	Not negotiable	Sometimes negotiable	Usually negotiable
Dispute-settlement procedures	Seldom	Occasionally	Usually	Usually
Restrictive covenants	Minimal	Specific market area	Specific geographical or market area	Specific geographical area

[1]Except when prohibited by law.
[2]Except when operator-performance provision exists.

EXHIBIT III-16

The Effect of Relative Bargaining Strengths on Provisions of Concern for Domestic Contracts Between Independent Operators and Developer- Owners

	Relative Bargaining Strength			
Provision	**Heavily Favors Operator**	**Slightly Favors Operator**	**Slightly Favors Owner**	**Heavily Favors Owner**
Nature of contractual arrangement:				
Agency-independent contractor	Agency	Agency	Agency	Often independent contractor
Indemnification of	Operator	Operator	Operator	Operator and owner
Sole and exclusive right	Unaffected	Unaffected	Unaffected	Unaffected
Operator contribution:				
Loan	None	None	Seldom	Often
Equity	None	None	Seldom	Seldom
Term of contract:				
Initial term length	10–20 years	5–10 years	5–10 years	3–8 years
Number of renewal terms	2–3	1–2	1–2	0–2
Length of each renewal	3–5 years	2–3 years	2–3 years	1–2 years
Management fees:				
Technical assistance[3]	Not negotiable	Occasionally negotiable	Occasionally negotiable	Often negotiable
Pre-opening management	Not negotiable	Occasionally negotiable	Occasionally negotiable	Often negotiable
Post-opening management:				
Basic-incentive mix	3% gross + 10% IBFC	3% gross + 8% IBFC	2½–3% gross + 6–8% IBFC	2½–3% gross + 6% IBFC; 3% gross + 25% CFADS and 10% ROE
Subordination/waiver of incentive fee	Occasional subordination	Usually subordination	Usually subordination	Most always subordination; occasional waiver

Operator system-reimbursable expenses	Not negotiable	Not negotiable	Usually not negotiable	Usually not negotiable
Contract termination by owner:				
Without cause	None	Seldom but usually with termination fee	Occasionally but with termination fee	Occasionally but with termination fee
Event of sale	Right of first refusal	Occasionally right of first refusal	Occasionally right of first offer	Occasionally right of first offer
Operator-performance provision	None	Occasionally	Often	Usually
Personnel:				
Employer	Owner[1]	Owner[1]	Usually operator	Usually operator
Owner approval of manager	None	Occasionally	Often	Usually
Budgeting and spending:				
Owner approval	Occasionally[2]	Often[2]	Usually[2]	Most always[2]
Deviation from budget	Operator discretion	Usually operator discretion	Usually operator discretion	Owner right to approve[2]
Escrow requirements on replacement reserve	Most often	Often	Occasionally	Seldom
Banking—working-capital balances	Not negotiable	Sometimes negotiable	Sometimes negotiable	Usually negotiable
Dispute-settlement procedures	Seldom	Occasionally	Usually	Usually
Restrictive covenants	Minimal	Specific market area	Specific geographical area	Specific geographical area

[1]Except when prohibited by law.
[2]Except when operator-performance provision exists.
[3]When offered.

EXHIBIT III-17

The Effect of Relative Bargaining Strengths on Provisions of Concern for Domestic Contracts Between Operators and Owners-in-Foreclosure

	Relative Bargaining Strength			
Provision	**Heavily Favors Operator**	**Slightly Favors Operator**	**Slightly Favors Owner**	**Heavily Favors Owner**
Nature of contractual arrangement:				
Agency-independent contractor	Usually independent contractor	Usually independent contractor	Independent contractor	Independent contractor
Indemnification of	Operator	Operator	Operator	Operator
Sole and exclusive right	Unaffected	Unaffected	Unaffected	Unaffected
Operator contribution:				
Loan	None	None	None	None
Equity	None	None	None	None
Terms of contract:				
Initial term length	½–3 years	½–1 year	½–1 year	½ years
Number of renewal terms	1–2	1–2	0–2	0–1
Length of each renewal	½–2 years	½–2 years	½–1 year	½–1 year
Management fees:				
Technical assistance[1]	Negotiable	Negotiable	Negotiable	Negotiable
Pre-opening management[2]	Occasionally negotiable	Negotiable	Negotiable	Negotiable
Post-opening management:				
Basic-incentive mix	3–4% gross + 5% IBFC	3% gross; Fixed amount	2½–3% gross; Fixed amount	2½–3% gross; Fixed amount
Subordination/waiver	None	—	—	—
Operator system-reimbursable expenses	Not negotiable	Not negotiable	Not negotiable	Seldom negotiable
Contract termination by owner:				
Without cause	Occasionally but with termination fee	Occasionally but with termination fee	Often but with termination fee	Usually but with termination fee
Event of sale				
Operator-performance provision	None	Seldom	Occasionally	Occasionally
Personnel:				
Employer	Operator	Operator	Operator	Operator
Owner approval of manager	None	None	None	Occasionally
Budgeting and spending:				
Owner approval	Often	Usually	Usually	Usually
Deviation from budget	Usually operator discretion	Usually operator discretion	Often owner right to approve	Usually owner right to approve
Escrow requirements on replacement reserve	None	None	None	None
Banking—working-capital balances	Sometimes negotiable	Negotiable	Negotiable	Negotiable
Dispute-settlement procedures	Occasionally	Occasionally	Occasionally	Occasionally
Restrictive covenants	Occasionally	Seldom	None	None

[1]When offered.
[2]If operator assumes responsibility to manage prior to opening date..

EXHIBIT III-18

The Effect of Relative Bargaining Strengths on Provisions of Concern for International Contracts Between Operators and Developer-Owners

Provision	Relative Bargaining Strength: Heavily Favors Operator	Slightly Favors Operator	Slightly Favors Owner	Heavily Favors Owner
Nature of contractual arrangement:				
Agency-independent contractor	Agency[1]	Agency[1]	Agency[1]	Occasionally indpendent contractor
Indemnification of	Operator	Operator	Operator	Operator
Sole and exclusive right	Unaffected	Unaffected	Unaffected	Unaffected
Operator contribution:				
Loan	None	None	None	Occasionally working capital or inventories
Equity	None	None	None	Occasionally
Terms of contract:				
Initial term length	20–30 years	20 years	20 years	10–15 years
Number of renewal terms	2–5	2–3	2	0–2
Length of each renewal	5–10 years	5–10 years	5–10 years	5 years
Management fees:				
Technical assistance	Not negotiable	Not negotiable	Seldom negotiable	Occasionally negotiable
Pre-opening management	Not negotiable	Not negotiable	Seldom negotiable	Occasionally negotiable
Post-opening management:				
Basic-incentive mix	3–4% gross + 10–15 IBFC	3% gross + 10% IBFC	3% gross + 10% IBFC	3% gross + 8–10% IBFC
Subordination/waiver	No subordination	Seldom subordination	Seldom subordination	Occasional subordination
Operator system-reimbursable expenses	Not negotiable	Not negotiable	Not negotiable	Not negotiable
Contract termination by owner:				
Without cause	None	None	None	Seldom but with termination fee
Event of sale	Right of first refusal	Right of first refusal	—	—
Operator-performance provision	None	None	None	Occasionally
Personnel:				
Employer	Owner[1]	Owner[1]	Owner[1]	Occasionally operator
Owner approval of manager	None	None	None	Seldom
Budgeting and spending:				
Owner approval	Seldom	Seldom	Occasionally[2]	Often[2]
Deviation from budget	Operator discretion	Operator discretion	Usually operator discretion	Owner occasionally has right to disapprove[2]

EXHIBIT III-18, The Effect of Relative Bargaining Strengths on Provisions of Concern for International Contracts Between Operators and Developer-Owners (continued)

	Relative Bargaining Strength			
Provision	**Heavily Favors Operator**	**Slightly Favors Operator**	**Slightly Favors Owner**	**Heavily Favors Owner**
Escrow requirements on replacement reserve	Always	Usually	Usually	Usually
Banking—working-capital balances	Not negotiable	Not negotiable	Seldom negotiable	Occasionally negotiable
Dispute-settlement procedures	Seldom	Occasionally	Usually	Usually
Restrictive covenants	Minimal	Specific market or geographical area	Specific geographical area	Specific geographical area

[1]Except when prohibited by law.
[2]Except when operator-performance provision exists.

expanded to include inventories, furniture, fixtures, and equipment, or a specified amount to be applied to operating deficits.

— Term of the contract: Initial term length, number of renewal terms, and length of renewal terms generally decrease. Option to renew sometimes shifts to owner or is tied to the operator achieving specified performance goals.

— Management fees: Technical assistance and pre-opening management fees become negotiable. Incentive management fees play a greater role in the mix of basic and incentive fees. Incentive fees are subordinated to a predetermined cash flow or are tiered with debt-service obligations and, sometimes, an owner's return on equity.

— Operator system-reimbursable expenses: Systematic monitoring of expenses increases. Dollar limitations may be placed upon specific items.

— Contract termination by owner: Operator-performance provisions are often included. Owner occasionally obtains right to terminate without cause for a termination fee. Right of first offer is substituted for right of first refusal in event of a sale.

— Personnel: Property employees may become employees of the operator. Owner may obtain the right to review and approve selection of general manager.

— Budgeting and spending limitations: Owner's approval rights for approving operating, reserve for replacement, and capital improvements/additions budgets increase. Replacement funds are "on-call" rather than in escrow accounts.

— Banking, accounting, and financial reporting: Cash-balance amounts required by operators become negotiable. Requirements for financial reporting become more specific and include submission of market plan, management analysis of operations, cash-flow projections, and audited reconciliation of operator system-reimbursable expenses.

— Dispute-settlement procedures: Dispute-settlement or arbitration provisions are added, and provisions subject to arbitration increase.

— Restrictive covenants: Geographical area in which operator is restricted from operating may be enlarged. Exclusions from restrictions may decrease.

It should be noted that this listing indicates only general tendencies. The reader should refer to Exhibit III-15, which pertains to the applicable owner-operator relationship between the parties' relative bargaining strengths and the outcome of their negotiations.

Contract negotiations give the owner an opportunity to minimize his concerns before the contract's term begins. If irreconciable differences exist, the owner can terminate negotiations and sever relations with the operator. If the owner feels his concerns are manageable, however, he signs the contract.

Once the contract is put into effect, another set of concerns arises. Many of these result from unresolved owner concerns that return to haunt both parties; others are initiated by the operator. In either case, difficulties usually stem from financial problems affecting one or both parties. Financial concerns can rapidly expand to operational and legal concerns if appropriate action is not taken. The concerns arising during the contract term are identified and analyzed in the next chapter.

IV

Provisions of Concern during the Term of the Contract

Concerns arising during the term of the contract usually escalate if the owner and the operator do not take remedial action. This chapter will describe concerns that occur if either the owner's or the operator's objectives for the project are not met. Three major factors influencing these will be analyzed: the compatibility of owner and operator objectives; the owner-operator working relationship as defined in the contract; and the quality of communication established between the owner and the operator during the term of the contract. Since the original intent of the contract is to establish a relationship of reasonable duration between a developer-owner and an operator, the description and analysis concentrate on management contracts involving developer-owners and operators.

A. Financial, Operational, and Legal Concerns

The provisions of concern to owners and operators are summarized in Exhibit IV-1.

1. The Hierarchy of Concerns

In the course of interviews with owners and operators, the author observed the following:

— If the financial goals of both parties are being achieved, owners and operators generally do not express financial, operational, or legal concerns.

— An inadequate financial return to either party creates concern relating to financial provisions. If the disappointed party perceives the inadequate return as a product of factors beyond the control of the other party—for example,

EXHIBIT IV-1

Owner and Operator Concerns During the Term of the Contract

OWNER CONCERNS:

FINANCIAL

Owner maintains minimal working-capital balances.*

Owner funds replacement-reserve and repairs-and-maintenance escrow accounts.*

OPERATIONAL

Quality of service:

- Operator provides services customarily provided in properties of comparable class and standing.
- Owner has access to property and records for inspection and review.
- Operator informs owner of policy matters and obtains owner's approval of policy changes.

Ability of operator:

- Operator is qualified in supervision, operation, and management of hotels and motor inns.
- Management fees: owner is receiving value of fee paid for supervisory and referral services.
- Group-services fees: owner is receiving value of fee paid for group services.

- **Operator exercises sole and exclusive right to manage without interference of owner:**
- Owner shall not interfere or give orders or instructions to employees on property.
- Operator maintains right to change or replace the general manager at any time.
- Operator maintains right to deviate from budget when necessary.*

LEGAL

Owner indemnifies operator for any act or omission in the performance of the contract.*

Operator is agent and shall not be held liable for payment of liabilities incurred in behalf of the owner.*

Owner may terminate agreement if operator fails to observe any material covenant.*

For at least one year following termination, owner shall not hire general manager if general manager leaves the employ of the operator.

Arbitration and litigation procedures, if any.

OPERATOR CONCERNS:

FINANCIAL

Owner maintains minimal working-capital balances.*

Owner promptly pays management fee.

OPERATIONAL

Operator exercises sole and exclusive right to manage without interference of owner.*

Operator maintains control of general manager even though salary is paid by owner.*

Within limitations established during negotiations, operator maintains control of budgeting process.

LEGAL

Owner indemnifies operator for any act or omission in the performance of the contract.*

Operator has the right to terminate contract subject to owner's inability to fund losses.

Owner has the right to terminate contract if operator is subject to performance provision.*

Arbitration and litigation procedures, if any.

*Major concerns

increased construction costs, an economic downturn, or overbuilding—the concern usually remains in the financial category.

— If the inadequate financial return is considered attributable in part or in whole to the acts or omissions of the other party in the operation or management of the property, the first party's concern is expanded to include operational provisions, as well as financial provisions.

— If satisfactory operational adjustments are not made to correct financial concerns, the party's concerns expand to include legal provisions, as well as operational and financial provisions.

— If satisfactory legal adjustments are not made, the dissatisfied party terminates the contract. In cases where termination is within the contractual rights of the dissatisfied party, or if the termination of the contract is accomplished by mutual consent, no further action occurs; if termination is protested by the other party, litigation ensues.

— Satisfactory resolution of any one category of concern is not achieved until the concerned party perceives an improvement in the original concern.

Exhibit IV-2 illustrates this five-step hierarchy of concerns. If the financial goals of each party are met, the level of concern within the contractual relationship is at **Level I.** Concerns develop and expand, moving to higher levels, if either party is unable to resolve concerns on a lower level. Inadequate financial returns produce concern over the contract's financial provisions, thus extending the level of concern to **Level II.** The inability to resolve financial concerns leads the concerned party or parties to reconsider provisions relating to operational aspects of the property—**Level III**—in an attempt to effect operational changes, increase financial returns, and consequently decrease concern on Level II. The inability to improve financial returns from action taken at Level III expands concern into provisions in the legal category—**Level IV.** If concerns on Level IV are not settled, contract termination—**Level V**—is the result. If the parties resolve or lessen the concerns on a lower level by making changes on a higher level, the concern moves back to the lower level.

The relative bargaining strengths of the parties affect each party's ability to influence changes on a higher level to minimize or eliminate a concern at a lower level. The party with the greater bargaining power has usually negotiated the contract to secure for itself maximum flexibility of action within the negotiated provisions. Consequently, that party has increased the ease with which it may move to the next higher level of concern to resolve the initial concern and concomitantly reduced the other party's ability to move to a higher level of concern.

Either the owner or the operator can initiate movement from one level to the next higher level. However, this expansion of concern is usually initiated by the owner, since he generally bears a greater financial risk than does the operator. The following sections describe the typical sequence of events following the

EXHIBIT IV-2
The Hierarchy of Concerns

If concerns on one level are not resolved, concerns expand to the next higher level. If concerns on one level are resolved to the satisfaction of the parties, concerns contract to the next lower level.

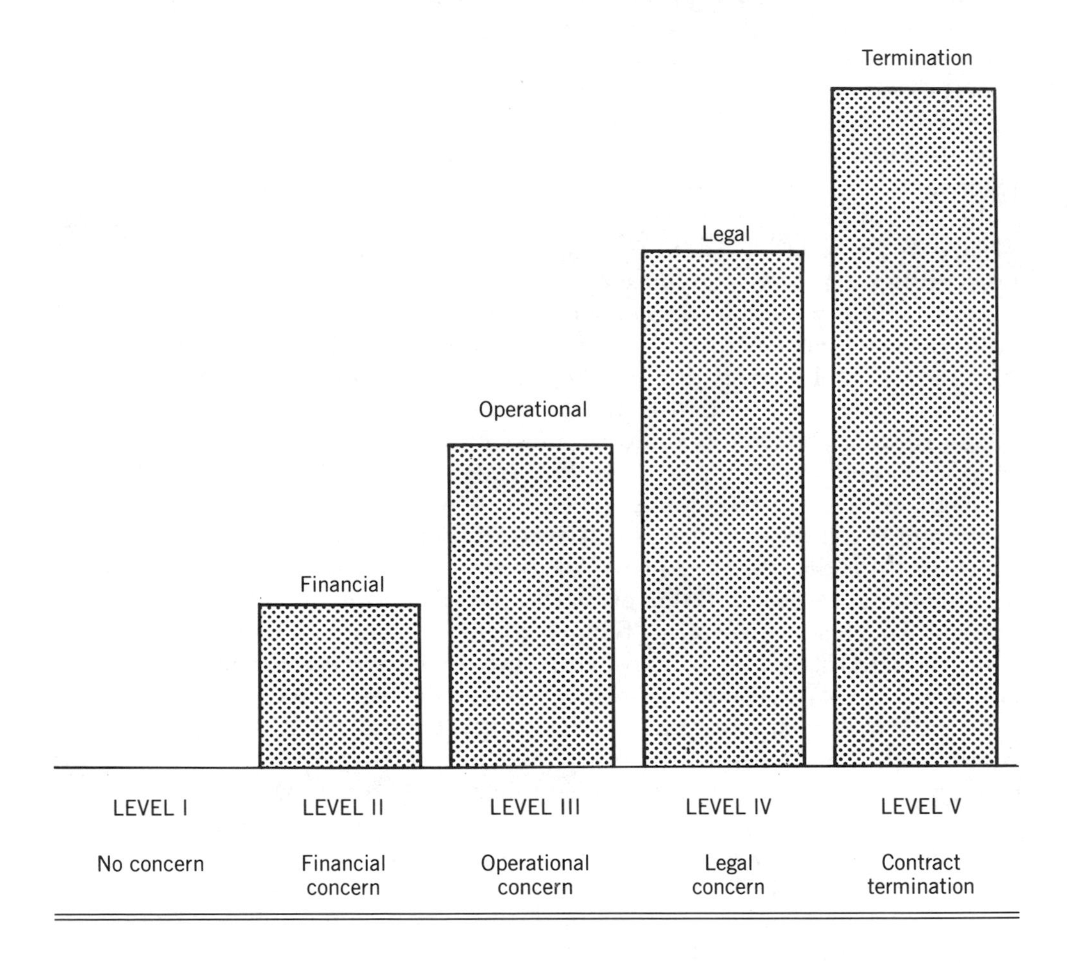

acknowledgment of an area of concern. They illustrate the manner in which owners and operators attempt to remedy one concern by focusing attention on the next higher level of concern.

2. Owner-Initiated Concerns

An owner's first concern typically develops when the cash flow generated by the operation falls below projected levels. If the owner has minimal financial reserves, he wants the operator to reduce the specified working-capital balances. If the owner is required to maintain reserve-for-replacement escrow accounts, he wants the operator to release these funds for use as working capital. Although continued losses may be the result of economic and market factors outside of the operator's control, the owner's doubts about the operator's ability, aggressiveness, and conscientiousness are heightened because the operator bears little or no risk. As a result, the owner's concerns expand into the operational area, and the owner becomes critical of three specific aspects: the quality of service provided by the operator; the ability of the operator to promote and manage the property effectively; and the operator's sole and exclusive right to manage without interference from the owner.

The owner begins to scrutinize the operator's market plan, marketing efforts, pricing structure, quality of service, and housekeeping and maintenance standards. The owner begins making suggestions to the general manager to improve the services. The owner also demands that the operator's home office provide additional regional and corporate staff support to improve operations.

The extent to which the operator will tolerate the owner's suggestions is a function of the relative bargaining strengths of the two parties. Operators are more receptive to suggestions from owners with extensive lodging experience, often entertaining these suggestions and ultimately incorporating them in their procedures. If the owner perceives the operator as unresponsive to suggestions, he may question the operator's ability and commitment to his project and attempt to expand his own influence in the property's operation. The owner makes more frequent visits to the property and spends considerable time evaluating such areas as advertising and promotional efforts, employee training, rate and pricing structures, and menu offerings, while attempting to persuade the general manager and the operator's staff to adopt his suggestions.

In an effort to improve the operating results, the owner may request or demand that the operator replace the general manager or members of the manager's staff. Frustrated by his continued inability to achieve his financial goals while the operator receives regular management fees, the owner questions the operator's ability and sincere interest in his project. The owner openly questions the value he is receiving for the management fees and group-service fees being paid to the operator.

At this point, the operator has two alternatives. The first is to adopt the owner's suggestions, thus including the owner to some degree in operational decision-making. The other choice is to adhere strictly to the sole-and-exclusive-right contract provision and to ignore the owner's suggestions. Again, the operator is influenced by the owner's relative bargaining power. If the owner can terminate the contract without cause, the operator attempts to incorporate owner suggestions or demands. If the owner is in a weak bargaining position or if the contract contains an operator-performance provision, the operator warns the owner against interfering with the property's operation. Most owners who have operator-performance provisions in their contracts are aware that owner interference may weaken their position in arbitration or litigation proceedings if the agreed-upon operator-performance levels are not met.

Owner concern generally diminishes if one or more of the following occurs: the owner finds the operator receptive to suggestions; the operator keeps the owner informed of the operator's attempts to improve the property's financial results; and the financial results improve due to the operator's efforts or to an improvement in the economy.

If none of the above three occurs, the owner's concerns usually expand to include the legal issues—Level IV. If the contract contains an arbitration or dispute settlement provision, and the concern is included as one under the jurisdiction of the provision, the dispute is reviewed and adjudged by the arbitrator in favor of the owner or of the operator, and both parties are obliged to accept the settlement. If the contract contains provisions permitting termination without cause or for the operator's failure to meet specified standards of performance, the owner may exercise his option and terminate the contract—Level V. If the contract does not contain unilateral termination provisions except for due cause, the owner may attempt to substantiate suspected gross negligence or fraud as the cause. If the owner is unsuccessful in substantiating the above, he often assumes occupancy of the property and ejects the operator. In this case, most employees remain since they are usually the employees of the owner. Key managerial personnel often resign and take positions at other operator-managed properties. The owner and the operator then settle through litigation the extent of the damages and the amount of the award. A methodology for determining an award settlement is presented later in this chapter.

In recent years, a number of owners and operators have developed a hotel policy committee as part of their contracts to discuss, and if possible, settle disputes prior to their being referred to arbitration. The committee comprises three members appointed by the owner (usually the owner himself or his managing general partner, his asset manager, and another designee) and three members appointed by the operator (usually the operator's president or appropriate vice-president, the property's general manager, and another designee). The committee's initial chair is usually the operating company's president. The committee's scope of operational authority is outlined in the contract and usually is limited to the review and approval of the annual budget and market plan, additional funds necessary to maintain working capital and inventories at levels necessary to satisfy the needs of the hotel, expenditures for replacement of furniture, fixtures, and equipment, and expenditures for major capital improvements. To act, the committee requires a unanimous vote of representatives present and entitled to vote at the meeting. In the event of a deadlock in any vote of the committee, the issue is immediately submitted to the owner's president (or designated representative) and to the operator's president (or designee) for resolution. In the event they are unable to resolve the issue, either party shall then be free to submit the issue to arbitration.

3. Operator-Initiated Concerns

Operator-initiated concerns usually develop as a result of owner-initiated concerns. The operator's first concern is financial (Level II), which arises if the owner is unable to fund negative cash flows adequately during the operation's start-up phase. This concern affects the operator in two ways. First, the cash shortage cripples the operator's ability to promote the property aggressively and to maintain it sufficiently. This handicap usually results in a lower-than-anticipated business volume. Since the operator receives the bulk of his fees during the start-up period from the basic management fee that is calculated on the basis of gross revenues, the operator realizes lower fee revenues that expected. Second, the inability of the owner to fund the operation may force the operator to make a financial contribution, usually in the form of a loan, in an effort to sustain the operation until a positive operating cash flow is realized.

The operator expands his concern into contract provisions dealing with operational matters—from Level II to Level III—in reaction to the owner's expansion of operational concerns. As the owner attempts to influence the general manager, the operator must decide to what degree he will accept the owner's influence. Operators interviewed stated that their willingness to be influenced by owners depends upon the owner's bargaining power and level of expertise. Most operators are extremely reluctant to concede to any operational change against their better judgment for fear of setting a precedent or of jeopardizing their operating results if the contract contains an operator-performance provision.

Expansion of operator concern from the operational category (Level III) to the legal category (Level IV) occurs only if the owner cannot contribute adequate funding to maintain the operation or other dispute-settlement provisions in the contract. If, in the first case, the operator believes the property still has the potential to generate a profit, he will attempt to influence the owner or the property's mortgagor to sell the property to a new owner better able to fund the operation. The operator may then be able to continue to manage the property with the hope of earning the expected return. If, on the other hand, the operator feels the property is a burden, he will unilaterally terminate the contract on the grounds that the owner was unable to fund the operation.

4. Existing Contracts and the Hierarchy of Concerns

Using the hierarchy-of-concerns model, Exhibit IV-3 illustrates the status of the contractual relationships between participating developer-owners and operators

EXHIBIT IV-3
Extent of Concerns in Existing Contracts

Level of Concern		Percentage of Contractual Relationships: 1976	1979	1986
I	No Concern	20%	32%	35%
II	Financial Concern	35	28	34
III	Operational Concern	30	26	20
IV	Legal Concern	12	10	8
V	Termination	3	4	3

during the 1975, 1979, and 1986 studies. Note that more contracts were reasonably free of concerns during the more recent periods.

Two comments are in order concerning the categorizations in the exhibit. First, the author frequently determined the status of a given contract, because owners generally reported their contracts being at a higher level of concern than did operators. Second, the categorization represents an attempt to describe a fluid situation in a static manner. Movement between levels occurs constantly, as working relationships are altered and economic activity accelerates or decelerates.

Exhibit IV-3 shows that owners and operators expressed financially initiated concern in 80 percent (Levels II through V) of the contractual relationships existing in the 1976 period. By 1979, this figure had dropped to 68 percent, and in 1986 the percentage decreased further to 65 percent. The table also shows that concern relating to the operator's sole and exclusive right to manage without interference by the owner existed in 45 percent (Levels III through V) of the contractual relationships in 1976 and decreased to 40 percent in 1979 and to 31 percent in 1986. The reader must take care in drawing conclusions on the basis of these data because the market and economic factors giving rise to financial concerns affected most properties built during the late 1960s and 1970s, regardless of their operational arrangements. What was unique under management-contract agreements was the owner's sense of helplessness, stemming from his inability to influence the operator or remedy his own financial concerns.

When an owner is dissatisfied with the operator's performance and the contract contains no provisions relating to operator performance, the owner often unilaterally removes the operator from the property and refuses to pay further management fees. The operator responds by suing the owner for breach of contract, followed by an owner countersuit against the operator for negligence. To date, such suits and countersuits have resulted in out-of-court settlements. Negotiated settlements have generally included an award amounting to one or two years' worth of management fees to the operator for resettlement expenses and the loss of future management fees. If a chain operator was involved, the settlement has also entailed replacing the management contract with a franchise agreement to maintain some support systems for the property. The outcome of any particular settlement, however, depends entirely upon the circumstances affecting the case.

B. Factors Contributing to Owner and Operator Concerns

Three underlying factors were identified as contributing to the owner and operator concerns expressed during the term of the contract: failure of the owner and the operator to evaluate proposed projects critically; the owner-operator relationship as defined by the management-contract agreement; and lack of adequate or effective communication between the owner and the operator during the term of the contract.

1. The Critical Evaluation of Proposed Projects

Two questions should be answered when evaluating a proposed project in which two parties must work together: **(1)** are the objectives of the two parties compatible and jointly attainable? and **(2)** can the proposed project achieve these objectives? The project can be successful only if the answer to both questions is yes.

a. The Compatibility of Owner and Operator Objectives. In the late 1960s and early 1970s when contracts were first introduced, both owners and operators were under pressure to construct and operate new hotel projects. Owners sought ways to invest funds as a hedge against inflation, and operators felt pressure to increase their market shares by expanding the number of rooms they operated. Owners who had little or no experience in the hospitality field were dependent upon the operators' abilities to manage their properties successfully. The following comments made by an executive with an independent operating firm are representative of both owners' and operators' statements regarding the lack of project evaluation by both parties to a contract.

> Looking back, we were greedy. We were both [owners and operators] in a hurry to capture a share of the expanding market and shifts within the existing market. We felt that if we didn't move quickly, other developers and operators would benefit at our expense. Investors were looking for any way to invest their money without first making a proper financial analysis. We [operators] were usually very willing to oblige them. Looking back, this approach has hurt both of us [owners and operators].

When developers, taking advantage of the tax-shelter benefits of the Economic Recovery Tax Act of 1981, initiated another hotel-construction boom in the early 1980s, both owners and operators had by that time gained experience in utilizing contracts and in negotiating new ones. The resulting negotiated contracts achieved a more balanced set of provisions compatible with their respective objectives than had existed the decade before. Owner objectives can be categorized into one of the following three "sets":

1. to maximize cash flow as soon as possible and sell the property as soon as major refurbishing is required;
2. to maintain a break-even cash-flow status but carry a net operating loss as a tax shelter for income from other business sources and consider sale of the property when the benefit of the tax shelter expires; and
3. to expect and to fund cash-flow losses during the early years, and to keep the property as a long-term investment for future cash flow and capital appreciation.

Operators basically had one set of objectives: to realize immediate fee revenues and increased market penetration, and to build a stable base for these revenues and this market penetration over an extended period of time.

Exhibit IV-4 categorizes owner and operator objectives as short-, intermediate-, or long-term, and notes the compatibility of each set with the other party's objectives. Owner and operator objectives were wholly compatible when both parties expected to maintain the contractual relationship on a long-term basis and the owner was capable of funding the property to maintain its competitive status. Owner and operator objectives were compromised when the owner planned to use the project as a tax shelter and consider sale of the property when the tax-shelter benefits expired. Owner and operator objectives were incompatible when the owner invested in the project to realize maximum cash flow in the early years and to sell the property prior to making any major refurbishing.

b. The Project's Ability to Achieve the Parties' Objectives. Assessment of a proposed project's ability to achieve owner and operator objectives is based upon realistic market and financial analyses to determine the probable operating results of the project and upon an evaluation of whether owner and operator objectives will be achieved from the projected operating results.

The general inability of owners and operators to assess economic and market conditions realistically during the real-estate booms and to predict the unexpected recessions that followed affected owners in different ways. Owners with objective sets #1 or #2 who relied heavily upon their projects' short-term cash-flow results were extremely vulnerable and registered financial concerns almost immediately after their properties opened. As the recessions deepened, their concerns quickly expanded to include operational and legal aspects of the contract. Most of these owners and operators recorded concerns on Level III, IV, or V. Owners whose primary objectives were long-range (objective set #3) and who had the ability to fund negative cash flows were less vulnerable to the

EXHIBIT IV-4
The Compatibility of Owner and Operator Objectives

Objectives	Short Term (1–5 years)	Intermediate Term (6–10 years)	Long Term (10–20 years)	Reaction of Other Party to Objectives
Owner Set #1	Maximize cash flow by putting minimal cash back into operation. Recapture investment within 3–5 years.	Sell property prior to making major refurbishings and repairs for possible although not expected capital appreciation.	Not applicable	Not consistent with operator's short-, intermediate- or long-term objectives. Cash drain prohibits maintenance of property's competitive status.
Owner Set #2	Break-even cash flow with net operating loss as tax shelter against income from other business sources.	Consider sale of property after benefit of tax shelter expires for possible capital appreciation.	If property not sold prior to this, sell for capital gain.	Not consistent with operator's intermediate- or long-term objectives. Consistent with operator's short-term objectives only if break-even cash flow is achieved.
Owner Set #3	Fund cash-flow losses to promote and maintain property in competitive status.	Realize positive cash flow but continue to fund promotion and refurbishing to maintain property's status.	Realize positive cash flow but continue to fund promotion and refurbishing. Realize increased value through capital appreciation.	Consistent with operator's short-, intermediate-, and long-term objectives if owner is financially capable of providing continuous funding as necessary.
Operator	Adequate fee revenues from basic and incentive fees to provide projected financial return. Maintain market share.	Adequate fee revenues from basic and incentive fees to provide projected financial return. Maintain market share.	Adequate fee revenues from basic fee to cover up-front expenses and minimal financial return. Increase market penetration.	Wholly consistent only with owner set #3. May be consistent with owner set #2 if owner can fund unexpected negative cash flow during short-term period and if owner holds property into long-term period. Wholly incompatible with owner set #1.

recessions. They recorded, along with their operators, concerns on Levels I, II, and occasionally III, but they seldom terminated their contracts.

2. The Owner-Operator Relationship Defined in the Contract

When the concerns of either owners or operators escalated from Level II to Level III because their financial objectives were not being achieved, the owner-operator relationship as defined in the management contract came under close scrutiny. Exhibit IV-5 illustrates the relationship of the three decision-making entities (the owner, the operator's corporate office, and the general manager) as outlined in the contract. The contract stipulates little or no ownership involvement in operations.

The distance between entities and the width of the connecting links in Exhibit IV-5 represent the relative degree of influence or control in the individual relationships. Where the relationship is characterized by strong influence or control, the two entities are shown close to each other and connected by a wide link. Weak influence in a relationship is represented by a greater distance between the entities and a narrower connecting link.

The services and forms of remuneration provided by each entity to the other two entities are listed along the solid lines. The operator's corporate office provides support, guidance, and employment to the general manager, who in turn is responsible to the operator corporate office for the property's operating results. The operator corporate office strongly influences the general manager. The operator corporate office provides a financial return to the owner, communicated primarily through financial statements, and the owner provides the operator's management fees. The influence between these two entities is considered moderate. The owner finances the salaries of the general manager and property employees, while the general manager determines the quality of services the operation provides, which the owner observes during on-site visits. The contract, through its noninterference-by-owner provisions, defines a minimal or negligible link of influence between the owner and the general manager.

The positions of and distances between each pair of entities are significant. The operator positions himself between the owner and general manager to minimize owner influence over the general manager and to delineate the division of operating responsibilities outlined in the contract. Operators state that this separation emphasizes the value of the management contract; the owner is paying for a management and supervisory service (and a national trade name and reservations system, in the case of a chain operator) greater in value than the services an owner with his own general manager could provide. As a result, the operator corporate office should control and coordinate all managerial affairs of the property. An owner can exert some indirect influence on the operation, but he may do so only through the operator corporate office, which may then relay the information to the general manager.

EXHIBIT IV-5

Contractual Relationships (Minimum Ownership Involvement in Operations)

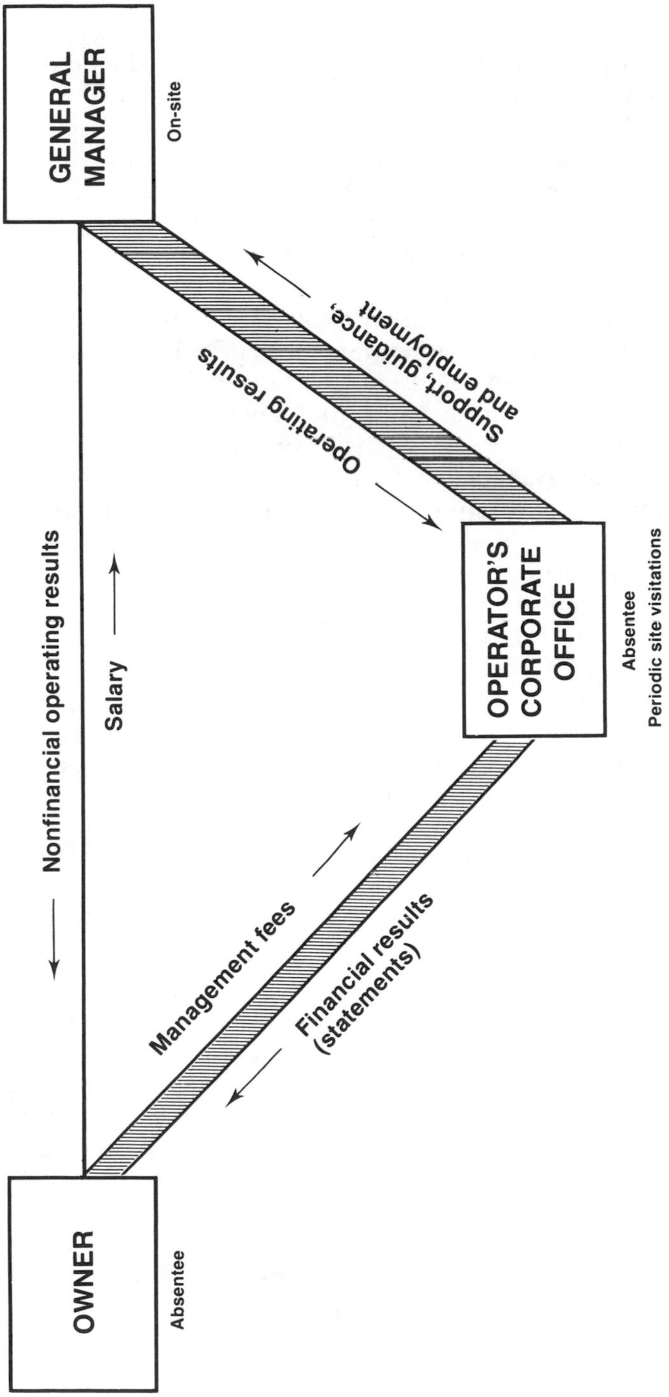

OWNER

Absentee

GENERAL MANAGER

On-site

OPERATOR'S CORPORATE OFFICE

Absentee

Periodic site visitations

← Nonfinancial operating results

Salary →

Operating results →

← Support, guidance, and employment

Management fees →

← Financial results (statements)

This route permits the operator to judge the worth of the owner's suggestions before accepting or rejecting them. If, however, the owner is able to influence the general manager directly or if the general manager operates the property independent of the corporate office, the operator's control of the property diminishes, and the owner does not receive the full value of the services for which the management fee is paid. Ownership influence on the general manager subverts the effectiveness of the operator in providing his company's services and contravenes the intent of the agreement.

Exhibit IV-6 illustrates the divisions of operating and legal responsibilities as outlined in the contract. The division of legal responsibilities does not coincide with the division of operating responsibilities. As a result, the position of general manager (which also represents the on-site management of the property) lies within the quadrant in which the operator maintains complete operating responsibility and the owner maintains complete legal responsibility. Owners consider this arrangement an unnatural relationship because the operator is responsible for operating the property but is not legally accountable for the outcome of his actions.

An owner with substantial bargaining power is able, with the operator's consent, to shift the relative positions of the three entities and correspondingly shift the control. For instance, an institutional owner with significant lodging holdings and an experienced operations-analysis staff to monitor his investments can discuss more freely with a general manager a property's operating results and possible solutions to operational problems as long as the owner coordinates this effort with the operator corporate office. In such a case, the general manager's position in Exhibit IV-6 would shift toward the owner to indicate greater owner influence, but only with the operator's consent would it cross the line representing the division of operating responsibilities.

As discussed earlier, the owner's financial concern expands into operational concern when the property does not achieve the expected financial return. As a result, the owner attempts to alter the owner-operator relationship depicted in Exhibit IV-5 to gain more control of the operation. In addition to trying to resolve the operational concerns stemming from financial concerns, the owner tries in good faith to influence the operation via the general manager when he does not fully understand the owner-operator relationship laid out in the contract. This situation most often occurs when the owner resides near the property or is an entrepreneur, rather than an institutional owner. The operator can usually reestablish the owner and operator roles defined in the contract through tactful but firm reiteration of the contractual relationship as long as the owner does not have financial concerns.

An attempt by ownership without operator consent to influence the general manager directly or to participate in operations of the property produces a significant shift in the relationships outlined in the contract and depicted in

EXHIBIT IV-6

Contractual Responsibilities (Minimum Ownership Involvement)

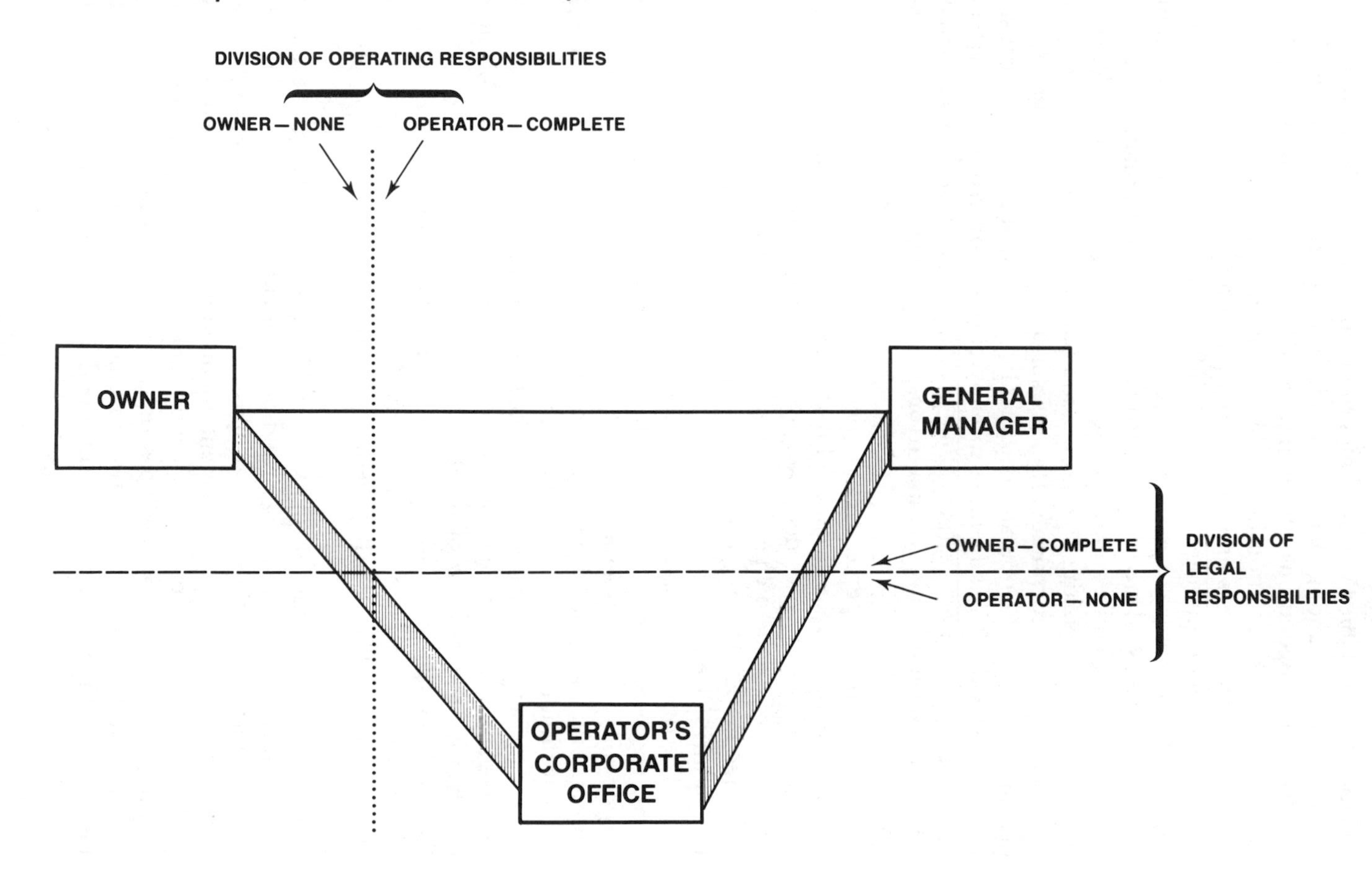

Exhibit IV-5. Exhibit IV-7 illustrates the relationship of the owner, operator's corporate office, and general manager resulting from concerted ownership involvement in operations. Owner intervention in operations creates the following changes in the relationship established by the contract.

— The owner moves on-site to direct operations.

— The general manager's position shifts toward the owner's position and replaces the operator corporate office as the central entity of the relationship.

— The owner's influence and control over the general manager increase; the owner offers incentives and bonuses to gain the manager's allegiance; the manager begins reporting operating and financial results directly to the owner.

— The operator corporate office loses its influence over the general manager; employment by the operator becomes less important to the manager since the owner is providing management incentives; operator group services continue and, if they are effective (providing a chain name, reservations system, and accounting services), they counter to some degree the manager's shift toward the owner.

— As the owner perceives the operator's services to be less effective than originally expected, the strength of the relationship between the owner and the operator corporate office decreases accordingly, and the relationship is further strained because the owner feels he is not receiving full value for the management fee he pays. Strong operator group services counter to some degree this loss of influence.

— The division of operational responsibilities shifts. With increased involvement, the owner has unilaterally, though informally, reallocated most or all responsibility of the operational duties from the operator corporate office to himself and the general manager, and the owner now considers the general manager under his influence and control.

The division of legal responsibilities is unchanged. Increased ownership involvement shifts the division of operating responsibilities to coincide more closely with the division of legal responsibilities as outlined in the contract. Exhibit IV-8 illustrates the repositioning of the division of operating responsibilities brought about by heavy ownership involvement in operations and the resulting parallel relationship between the divisions of operating and of legal responsibilities.

The relationship shown in Exhibit IV-5 represents strict adherence to the roles of owner, general manager, and operator corporate office as delineated in the contract, while Exhibit IV-7 illustrates the changes brought about by determined ownership involvement in operations. They represent extreme positions at opposite ends of a continuum of ownership involvement. Most existing contracts are of the types represented in Exhibits IV-5 and IV-7. A contract can fall between these two extremes if the owner and the operator can mutually accommodate informal shifts in their relationships. Satisfactory mutual

EXHIBIT IV-7
How Maximum Ownership Involvement in Operations Affects Relationships

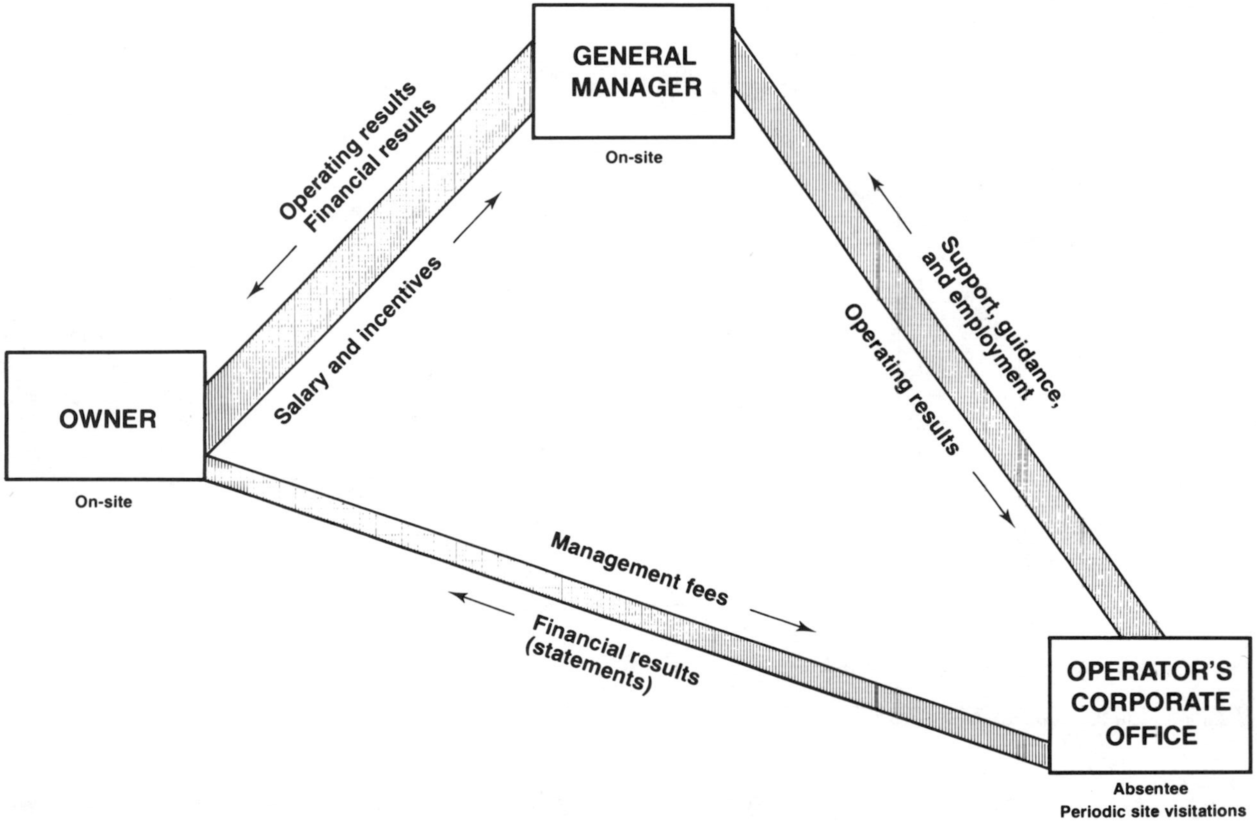

GENERAL MANAGER
On-site

OWNER
On-site

OPERATOR'S CORPORATE OFFICE
Absentee
Periodic site visitations

Operating results
Financial results

Salary and incentives

Support, guidance, and employment

Operating results

Management fees

Financial results (statements)

EXHIBIT IV-8
How Maximum Ownership Involvement in Operations Affects Responsibilities

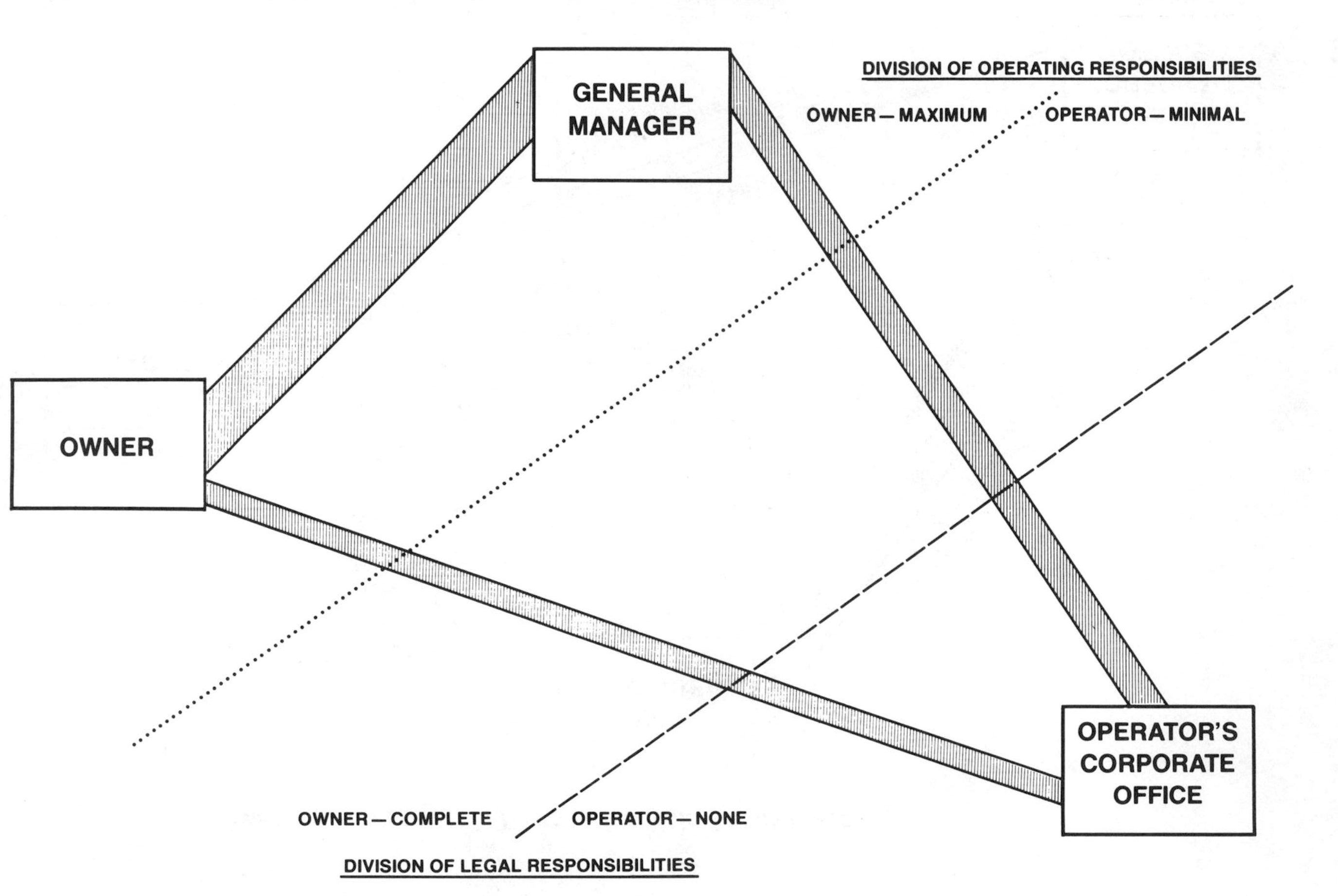

EXHIBIT IV-9

Adherence to the Owner-Operator Relationship Outlined in the Contract

	Operator Control of Operation		
	Complete	Compromise (closer to complete than to minimal)	Minimal
Operators:			
Chain	60%	35%	5%
Independent	40%	35%	25%
Owners:			
Entrepreneurial	30%	30%	40%
Institutional	45%	45%	10%
Quality of communication:			
Effective	50%	40%	10%
Ineffective	10%	30%	60%

accommodations, however, tend to be closer to the strict-adherence extreme (Exhibit IV-5) than to the owner-dominated extreme (Exhibit IV-7). Under a contract in the owner-dominated extreme, the owner's concerns encompass those at the legal level, and the owner will probably terminate the contract unilaterally.

Owners are less likely to adhere to the owner-operator relationship as outlined in the contract if the owner is an entrepreneurial owner rather than an institutional owner, the operator is an independent operator rather than a chain operator, or the quality of communication between operator and owner is considered inadequate by the owner. Exhibit IV-9 indicates the degree to which existing contracts adhere to the owner-operator relationship outlined in the contract.

Entrepreneurs entering the hotel field via management contracts sought ways to invest funds they earned as successful entrepreneurs in other fields of endeavor. They had records of achievement and confidence in their business judgment. They were experienced in analyzing a business, in determining what steps should be taken to correct problems, and in implementing those steps to maximize the success of the business. Because an entrepreneur believed that his personal involvement accounted for the success of previous endeavors not connected with the hotel business, he was likely to regard his personal involvement as an ingredient of success when entering into management contracts. He tended to monitor operations at the property and took liberties in attempting to influence the general manager and the property's operating policies. In short, the entrepreneurial spirit preempts the owner-operator roles specified in the contract.

An institutional owner, on the other hand, is more likely to respect the owner-operator contractual relationship because this type of owner has a less personal view of the project. The investment generally represents a staff or committee decision, and the primary criterion for that decision is an expected financial return. The personal detachment of an institutional owner is less likely to infringe upon predetermined roles than the personal involvement an entrepreneur may wish to maintain.

A chain operator is less likely to encounter owner interference than an independent operator for two reasons. First, chain operators manage larger properties, most of which belong to institutional, rather than to entrepreneurial, owners. Second, because of the chain operator's established reputation and apparent strength its trade name and reservations system to attract business, owners have a higher regard for a chain operator's abilities. If the property is managed by a chain operator, owners will defer taking action for a longer period before attempting to influence operations. However, if financial concerns are not alleviated, owners are ultimately as likely to get as involved with chain operators as with independent operators.

3. Communication Between Owner and Operator

The third factor influencing the degree of owner concern during the contract term is the quality of communication established between the owner and the operator. As a relatively passive party in the contract, the owner relies upon the accuracy and timeliness of communications generated by the operator—and is understandably sensitive to his dependence.

Owners and operators agree that the operator has the following four responsibilities in establishing a communications network:

— To educate the owner about the lodging business and the factors that affect performance.

— To provide the owner with realistic projections of expected revenues, expenses, and cash flows; to outline the strategies and programs he will implement to achieve these projections; and to explain the economic and market factors that may affect the outcome of the projections.

— To keep the owner informed of actual performance through timely reports and meetings.

— To apprise the owner of problems, variances from budgeted figures, and steps being taken to remedy problems and variances. To accomplish these functions, operators have established formal communications networks, as summarized in Exhibit IV-10. These networks are designed to maximize communication between the owner and the operator and to minimize communication between the owner and the general manager.

An owner grows concerned if he believes that the operator is not providing accurate information or honest opinions in the four areas above. Owner

EXHIBIT IV-10

Communication among Entities in Existing Contracts

	Communication Between:			
	Operator & Developer-Owner	**Operator & Owner-in-Foreclosure**	**Operator & General Manager**	**General Manager & Owner**
Oral				
Telephone access at any time	100%	100%	100%	60%
Meetings:				
Weekly	—	10%	—	—
Monthly	50%	80%	90%	—
Quarterly	90%	100%	100%	30%
Only as Needed	10%	—	—	80%
Written				
Projections:				
Weekly	—	10%	30%	—
Monthly	70%	100%	100%	—
Quarterly	100%	100%	100%	—
Annually (annual plan and budget)	100%	100%	100%	—
Financial Statements:				
Weekly	—	—	—	—
Monthly	80%	90%	100%	—
Quarterly	100%	100%	100%	—
Annually	100%	100%	100%	—
Other:				
Manager's daily report	20%	70%	100%	20%
Revenue report (weekly)	30%	90%	100%	—
Cost-percentage report (weekly)	30%	80%	100%	—

concerns most often develop when actual operating results consistently fall short of the projections provided by the operator; when the owner receives information from the general manager that conflicts with information provided by the operator; or when the owner receives information about his property from a third party (his lender, a business associate, or a guest) before receiving that information from the operator. The placard prominently displayed on the desk of one owner sums up the ownership concerns involving communication. The placard reads: "Don't bring me any surprises."

The above situations are usually caused by the operator's reluctance to report disappointing results to the owner; by the operator's failure to coordinate communication procedures between himself and the general manager, resulting in the premature release of information to the owner; and by the failure of each party to designate the specific person or persons within his organization to provide and receive information and to represent the party in all discussions involving policy matters and contract concerns. The triangular nature of the owner-operator-general manager relationship will continue to cause difficulties in communication, but it is necessary that owners and operators fine tune their communication procedures to provide better communication than has been achieved in the past.

The ability of owners and operators to deal with the concerns identified in the study will influence the future use of management contracts. The next chapter outlines a negotiating process designed to identify and address owner and operator concerns and discusses the underlying causes for dissatisfaction once the contract has been implemented.

V

Preparing for Successful Negotiations

This chapter presents guidelines for an orderly, efficient approach to negotiations between owners and operators. The model proposed here is designed to encourage effective communication between the two parties from the outset of their relationship—and to ensure that both parties hold realistic expectations of the project's financial return. Exhibit V-1 sets forth recommended steps for owners and operators throughout the process. Although the diagram shows only one owner and one operator, the owner may well duplicate the same process with several owners until a negotiated contract is signed. Developing a project's concept (step 1) and initiating contact with prospective operators (step 2) are largely self-explanatory, preliminary steps. This chapter's discussion emphasizes the evaluations conducted concurrently by each party (step 3), the development of realistic operating projections and financial returns for the project (step 4), and the development of negotiating strategies by each party (step 5).

A. Self-Evaluations

The successful negotiation of a management contract depends as much on the owner's and the operator's preparation as it does on the decisions reached when the parties face each other across the bargaining table. After the initial contact between an owner and operator, each party should evaluate his position, define the goals he wishes to achieve through the hotel project, and identify the specific concerns raised by the prospect of working with the other party. It is essential that these considerations be evaluated exhaustively in writing so that the resulting document can be used as the basis for assessing the other party and, later, for developing "going-in" and "fall-back" positions to be used during the contract negotiations. The categories of considerations reviewed by each party to the contract are discussed below.

EXHIBIT V-1

The Process of Negotiating a Management Contract

1 *Owner* proposes project:
- Evaluation of project's suitability to firm's objectives
- Market study performed
- Preliminary discussions with prospective lenders

2 *Owner* contacts prospective operators:
- Presentation of general plans to operators
- Operators' expression of varying levels of interest in project

3 *Owner:*
- Assesses own position and basic concerns
- Assesses operator
- Develops operating and financial projections

Operator:
- Assesses own position and basic concerns
- Assesses owner
- Develops operating projections

4 *Owner and Operator:*
- Discuss projections
- Develop agreed-upon projections

5 *Owner:*
- Develops going-in and fall-back negotiating positions

Operator:
- Develops going-in and fall-back negotiating positions

6 *Owner and Operator:*
- Negotiate
- Sign negotiated contract if both parties are satisfied

1. Owner Self-Assessment

The owner should identify the following critical factors: **(1)** his financial objective for the investment; **(2)** his relative bargaining power as he enters negotiations; and **(3)** the concerns raised by the contract forms provided by each management company at the initial meeting with the owner.

The owner's definition of the project's financial objectives should be expressed both in terms of specific quantitative measures (e.g., maximum cash flow from operations, appreciation of the real estate, earnings per share, tax-shelter benefits) and his view of the project as a short-, intermediate-, or long-term investment. Non-quantitative objectives—diversification, image enhancement, support for related products or services, employment of family members—should also receive explicit evaluation as part of the process.

As discussed in Chapter II, the owner's bargaining position when he enters contract negotiations depends on seven factors. The operator must realistically assess his bargaining power in light of these factors and the related particulars of the project, adjusting each evaluation to reflect the individual circumstances of each operator with whom he expects to negotiate.

The owner's review of the standard contract provided by each prospective operator leads inevitably to his identification of provisions that cause him concern. It is imperative that the owner identify these concerns and incorporate his questions about them in his formal request for information from the operator.

2. Operator Self-Assessment

The operator should analyze his own position, defining **(1)** how the proposed project fits his strategic objectives and corporate resources; **(2)** his relative bargaining power, based on the bargaining-power factors outlined in Chapter II; and **(3)** his concerns regarding the owner.

In defining the objectives of his involvement in the project, the operator should identify the anticipated impact of the project on his financial performance, as well as the likely effects participation in the project will have on the operating firm's reputation and market position. In addition, the operator should analyze how the proposed hotel will be integrated into his group of properties, estimating the commitment of management time and energy required by the proposed venture. Finally, if an equity contribution to the project is indicated, the operator should specify the financial objectives he expects to achieve from his investment.

Like the owner, the operator has gathered preliminary information about this counterpart, both during their initial meeting and from other sources. As a result of this exposure, the operator may be concerned, for example, about the owner's ability to manage the construction of the hotel or his readiness to fund cash-flow deficits during the project's start-up phase. The operator should conclude his self-assessment by identifying these concerns explicitly, using this review to formulate questions to be posed as part of this evaluation of the owner (discussed below).

B. Assessing the Other Party

The cross-assessment by the two negotiating parties requires each party both to solicit and to provide detailed information. Outlined below is a procedure recommended to owners for their evaluation of operators, followed by the recommended procedure for operators' evaluations of owners.

1. Owner Evaluation of Operators

Because the owner initiates the negotiating process, he should take the lead in developing an orderly evaluation procedure and providing a structure that requires each interested operator to respond thoroughly and candidly to a single set of questions. Moreover, the structure should incorporate a specific timetable for the completion of each step, from the initial solicitation of information through the signing of the management contract that concludes the process. The author has found that when a carefully prescribed procedure confers the following several benefits on both parties.

— The owner must conduct a rigorous self-assessment to prepare the questionnaire submitted to prospective operators.

— The timetable of the formal structure makes each operator aware of the time available for compiling the required information, thus permitting each operator to decide early whether it wishes to pursue negotiations.

— Questions posed by the owner are designed to cut through the sales pitches made by operators, address more critical concerns, and require operators to declare how they would deal with problems inherent in the specific project.

— Operators' responses to a common set of questions provide the owner with uniform data sets, facilitating comparison among the operators contending for the contract.

— Providing thoughtful, complete responses to an owner's questions requires a major commitment of time from the operator and therefore acts to eliminate those operators who are only marginally interested in the project.

— The owner's willingness to conduct a time-consuming, painstaking analysis puts operators on notice that the owner demands highly professional responses and performance.

The full structure of the evaluation by the owner and the subsequent steps of the negotiating process are documented in Exhibits V-2 and V-3. The letter of invitation to operators (Exhibit V-2), which also serves as a cover letter to the owner's request for the operator's responses to key questions, outlines the five phases and specifies the timetable for the complete process. The reader will note that the main categories of the inquiries contained in the owner's request for information (Exhibit V-3) correspond to areas identified in the letter of invitation. The questions contained in Exhibit V-3 were developed by the author for an owner evaluating chain operators, but the same format is applicable when evaluating independent management companies. In either application, it may be desirable to add or delete queries, depending on the financial, operational, and marketing attributes of the individual property.

The cost of responding to the owner's request for information, including time and out-of-pocket expenses, can range from $5,000 to $15,000, depending on the type of hotel contemplated and the operator's prior knowledge of the market area. The costs are usually absorbed by chain operators, but their allocation is often subject to negotiation when independent operators are involved. If they are awarded the contract, independent operators commonly charge the costs against the pre-opening budget or the first year's operating expenses.

EXHIBIT V-2
Letter of Invitation to Operators

Mr. H. J. Kay
Vice President for Development
XYZ Hotel Management Company
Corporate Offices
XYZ Hotel
New York, NY

Dear Mr. Kay:

We are preparing to evaluate and select a hotel operating company to manage our _____ property under a management contract. XYZ is one of the four operating companies we are seriously considering.

Our evaluation process consists of the following phases and timetable:

Phase I: Our request to operators, described further in the accompanying outline, to provide:

a) a statement of selected operating procedures;
b) your corporate development strategy in the _____ region;
c) your proposed marketing plan for the _____ project;
d) an assessment of personnel, recruiting, and training requirements;
e) the average room rates and occupancy percentages for the past five years for each of your properties;
f) your operating and financial projections for the _____ project; and
g) your response to our position on the major contract provisions enumerated in the outline.

Phase II: Operators provide written responses to the above. Deadline for submission of responses: _____

Phase III: Our evaluation of operators' responses completed by _____

Phase IV: Negotiations with operators to commence _____

Phase V: Selection of operator and signing of management contract concluded by _____

Our objective is to follow an orderly selection process resulting in an owner-operator agreement of mutual benefit to the parties involved. Because our project development schedule is firmly established, we expect strict adherence to the deadlines specified above.

Please contact me as soon as possible to let me know of your intent to be included in the above selection process.

Sincerely yours,

P. Q. Owner

EXHIBIT V-3
Owner's Request for Information from Operator

A. Selected Operating Procedures

1. ***Technical-assistance services***
a. Outline the specific technical services provided by you during the development of a property.
b. In which of the above services do you consider yourself the strongest?
c. In which of the above services do you consider yourself the weakest?

2. ***Pre-opening services***
a. Outline a typical schedule you might utilize when providing pre-opening services for a property. Include the services performed and the timing of these services in relation to the opening date.
b. What do you consider to be the major constraints affecting your accomplishment of the above?

3. ***Marketing services***
a. What is the present structure of the chain and regional marketing organization supporting your individual properties?
b. What changes, if any, do you plan to make in the above structure during the next five years?
c. Outline what you consider to be the strongest areas of your corporate marketing strategy.
d. Outline what you consider to be the weakest areas of your corporate marketing strategy.
e. Outline your group advertising program. What is the basis for your pro-rata distribution of program costs to managed properties?
f. What major criteria do you use to select an individual property's marketing staff?

4. ***Supervision and controls***
a. Outline the supervisory structure utilized to provide guidance and control to your management-contract properties.
b. Under what circumstances does the above structure work well? Under what circumstances do problems arise with the above structure?
c. What do you consider to be the major problem in maintaining an effective supervisory structure?

5. ***Reimbursable expenses to operator***
a. List all expenses, other than the management fee, incurred by the operation that are reimbursable to you under a management contract.
b. What are the bases (percentage of sales, dollar amount per room, etc.) for each of the above?

6. ***Other comments***
Comment briefly on any other services you perform or benefits you provide that you feel will be helpful to us in making our selection of an operator.

B. Corporate Development Strategy in the ________ Region

1. Briefly outline your overall ten-year corporate-development strategy in the ________ region.
2. What new properties (provide location and approximate size) do you plan to open during this ten-year period?
3. What specific operating problems do you foresee in your expansion program?
4. How do you plan to approach these problems outlined above?

C. Proposed Marketing Plan for the Project

1. Outline your forecasts of specific sources and composition of the expected demand for guest rooms and food and beverage facilities for the ________ project.
2. What portion do you expect to attain from present demand? What portion do you expect from new business brought into the market area?
3. Outline briefly your strategy for attracting and holding the expected composition of demand.

EXHIBIT V-3, Owner's Request for Information (continued)

D. Assessment of Personnel, Recruiting, and Training Requirements

1. What do you expect to be the major sources of recruitment for each of the following classifications of personnel required for the ________ project: **(a)** managerial; **(b)** supervisory; and **(c)** non-supervisory personnel?

2. What specific problems do you foresee in recruiting reliable individuals in each of the above three classifications during the next ten years, as both your organization and other hotel operating companies expand?

3. How, specifically, do you plan to deal with the above problems?

4. Outline your corporate training resources and describe specifically how they will be employed to train property personnel.

5. Based upon your concept of the hotel's operation, prepare a staffing schedule to approximate the personnel requirements of the ________ property.

E. Past Operating Results

For each of your properties located in the ________ area, indicate the property's opening date and the average room rate and occupancy percentage for the past five years. Comment on any of the above figures if you feel they need clarification.

F. Operating and Financial Projections for Subject Property

1. Project operating cash flows through gross operating profit, but before management fees, for ten years beginning with the opening year of ________ . The project will consist of ________ guest rooms. Include both projected occupany percentage and average room rate statistics. Food and beverage revenue, minor operated department revenue, and other income should be based upon estimates of restaurant, coffeeshop, bar, lounge, and banquet-space allocations you propose for the property.

2. Prepare an estimated pre-opening budget using cost estimates for the year prior to opening.

3. Estimate inventory cost levels for all china, glass, silver, linen, and consumables using cost estimates for the year prior to opening.

G. Postion on Major Contract Provisions

Outlined below is our position on those contract provisions of major concern to us. Please respond separately to each item listed.

1. ***Operator's contribution and loans***

a. The operator will contribute free of charge all technical assistance services rendered by the operator's staff.
b. The operator will finance, through a loan to the owner, fees incurred by the outside consultants used by the operator to provide technical services.

c. The operator will finance, through a loan to the owner, all pre-opening expenses.

d. The operator will finance, through a loan to the owner, the operation's initial working capital.

e. The operator will purchase, own, and maintain at his own expense all linen, china, glass, and silver inventories necessary for the operation of the property. Owner will reimburse operator for a reasonable percentage of the annual maintenance costs.

f. The operator will finance, through a loan to the owner, a portion of the property's furniture, fixtures, and equipment.

2. ***Term of the contract***

a. The initial term of the contract will be ________ years.

b. Renewal terms agreed upon will be at the option of the owner.

EXHIBIT V-3, Owner's Request for Information (continued)

3. ***Management fees***

a. The management-fee structure will provide the largest portion of the fee revenues from the incentive portion of the fee.

b. Based upon our ten-year operating projections for the project, several acceptable fee-structure variations have been derived by us. After reviewing the operating projections you will provide to us, we will review—and, if necessary, adjust—our proposed fee structures before our negotiations with you. Our objective is to negotiate an equitable fee for both parties.

4. ***Termination by owner***

Owner will have the option of terminating the contract if cash flow from the operation is inadequate to cover the annual debt service for any three consecutive years.

5. ***Personnel***

a. Owner must approve the operator's selection of a general manager prior to the assignment of the general manager to the property. Owner has the right to reject the general manager proposed by the operator.

b. All hotel employees will be the employees of the operator, with payroll and related expenses reimbursed to the operator by the owner.

6. ***Budgeting and spending limitations***

a. The bases for the owner's portion of the operator's centralized services (group advertising, reservation-system expenses, etc.) must be defined in the contract. No changes in the formulas to determine these bases will be made by the operator without the owner's approval.

b. Owner has the right to approve or disapprove the annual operating budget and the annual capital-expenditure budget.

c. Repairs and maintenance expenses each year will be limited to three percent of budgeted revenues for the year with no carry-forward of unused portions of the amount to subsequent years.

d. Reserves for replacement will be limited to 2½ percent of budgeted revenues for the year. Unused amounts will be accumulated in a balance which the owner will produce on demand but which will not be held in escrow.

e. Renovation proposals must be approved mutually by the owner and operator prior to undertaking such renovations.

7. ***Financial statements and reporting***

a. Owner has the right to inspect all books and accounting records at any time.

b. An audit, the expense of which will be assumed by the operation, will be performed annually by an independent accounting firm.

c. Operator will provide on a monthly basis: **(1)** an operating statement; **(2)** a balance sheet; **(3)** a statement of changes in financial position; **(4)** a report of pertinent hotel operating statistics, the precise contents of which are to be agreed upon by the owner and the operator; **(5)** a written narrative discussing the month's operations; and **(6)** a cash-flow projection by month for the upcoming 12 months.

d. Operator will meet with the owner no less than quarterly to present **(1)** an analysis of the most recent operating results and
(2) the management plan for the upcoming quarterly period.

8. ***Restrictive convenant***

Owner has the right of first refusal to develop and own any other property that the operator plans to manage in the ________ area.

2. Operator Evaluation of Owners

During the period in which the management company is responding to the owner's request for information, it should be addressing its own set of questions to the owner. Exhibit V-4 lists questions operators commonly ask an owner to determine his financial strength and commitment to the project. (Although the responses elicited by Exhibit V-4 are designed to permit the evaluation of an existing property, the same areas of inquiry apply for hotels yet to be developed.) An operator may ask the owner to respond in writing to some or all of the queries appearing in that exhibit, and may reasonably prescribe that the responses be submitted to him by the deadline imposed by the owner for the completion of Phase I.

C. Financial Evaluation of the Proposed Project

The financial evaluation of the proposed project (whether it is an existing property or one to be constructed) requires a thorough, demanding analysis, incorporating three components: **(1)** a *market profile* that includes an estimate of the subject property's projected market share; **(2)** a *long-term capital-investment analysis* that establishes the equity investor's rate of return on invested capital and permits comparison to his "hurdle" rate (the return he requires); and **(3)** *short-term cash-flow projections* for the critical pre-opening and post-opening periods, when the project is most susceptible to default. Both the owner and the operator look for evidence in the market-profile projections that the project will not only achieve the necessary long-term return on equity, but will also sustain itself during the critical pre- and post-opening period.

These three basic components of a financial evaluation are explained in detail on the following pages using as an example the Century 21 Hotel project—a 300-room, center-city, convention-oriented hotel with an estimated turn-key project cost of $38 million.

1. The Market Profile

The purpose of the market profile is to summarize information developed by the feasibility analyst and documented in the detailed market study. The market profile is presented in the form of projected occupancy levels at a period five years from the completion of the market study. (The end of the five-year period would normally be the third year of the property's operation, assuming a lead time of two years from the completion of the study to the opening of the property.) The reliability of the summary market profile depends upon accurate projections of market data. The following estimates are essential: **(1)** the present room-night demand; **(2)** the average growth rate of that demand, specified for each of the area's identifiable market segments; **(3)** the current room-night supply, provided by existing competitive properties; **(4)** expected changes in that

EXHIBIT V-4
Operator Evaluation of Owner

A. Owner Profile and Preferences

1. Describe your experiences in real-estate development. Which projects were successful and why? Which projects were not successful and why?

2. How long do you intend to maintain ownership? Are ownership goals and objectives short-term or long-term? Is ownership a result of a voluntary decision?

3. Describe current associations and affiliations which led you to purchase this property or will be beneficial to its future.

4. Describe the financial return (return on investment, cash flow, return on equity) projected for this property for a ten-year period. Will the project be expected to stand on its own as an investment? Tax shelter? A means of diversifying an investment portfolio?

5. What are the proposed investment and capital-additions schedules and provisions? How were they formulated? On what assumptions were they based?

6. Provide an outline of related investments (i.e., hotel properties), other management contracts, and the decision procedure utilized to select the management companies.

7. What specific attributes are you looking for in a management-contract team?

8. What is your management philosophy?

B. Financial Profile

1. Provide, if available, a balance sheet, income statement, and changes-in-financial-position statement for the past five years. Describe your future financial investment strategy and objectives.

2. Provide, if available, an appraiser's report of the property. Provide a copy of a loan agreement made in acquiring this property. The loan agreement should include the payment schedule, interest rate, term, restrictions, etc.

3. Describe expected financial returns from other investments, as well as other sources of revenue.

4. What insurance policies do you have or intend to have for this property?

5. What was the price paid for the subject property? What is its current valuation? Do you expect to make additional investment and capital expenditures?

6. Do you own or lease the land? If leased, who is the lessor? Do you own or lease the building? If leased, who is the lessor?

7. Describe the depreciation policies and other tax savings derived from the subject property.

8. Are there other equity participants?

9. What percentage of your assets are liquid? How critical is working capital to you in the near future?

10. What are the area's property tax policies, likely future assessments, etc.?

C. Property Description

1. Please provide descriptions and drawings of the property's location, age, size, land area, building layout, and design.

2. Describe the major attributes of this property. List major weaknesses.

3. Does the property have potential for alternate uses? If so, what are they?

EXHIBIT V-4, Operator Evaluation of Owner (continued)

4. Describe the property's visibility and accessibility characteristics.

5. List the furniture, fixtures, and equipment provided; identify food and beverage facilities, public facilities, rental spaces.

6. Please provide, if available, current market analysis, site analysis, competition analysis. What is the area's growth potential? Who compiled this material, and when was it compiled?

7. Were there any project cost overruns, anticipated overruns, labor troubles, delays? What is the completion date?

8. Describe future problems the property might encounter. What is its present condition? Are improvements planned?

9. Who were the former property owners? Why did they sell the property?

10. Describe the property's original use and past financial history.

D. Contract Obligations

1. Please indicate anticipated contract term.

2. Will performance evaluations be tied to contract termination clauses?

3. What management-fee structures are you willing to discuss?

4. Do you have any areas of concern with other existing management contracts?

5. Do you anticipate equity contributions? If so, what type or form do you suggest?

6. What procedures will be required regarding banking, accounting, and the generation of management information reports?

7. What qualities do you seek in a general manager?

E. Operational Considerations

1. Describe anticipated budgeting and spending restrictions.

2. List, if available, the property's average room rate, average occupancy, and operating profit before fixed charges for the past five years.

3. Will technical assistance in areas of training, marketing, engineering, and pre-opening be required? Which areas are, in your view, the most critical?

4. What are your expected average room rate and occupancy?

5. Describe the qualities and strengths a management team needs to operate the subject property.

6. What communication network is the most desirable for discussion between the operator and yourself?

7. How soon do you need a management team? What amount have you budgeted for achieving the management capabilities required for the property?

F. Legal Considerations

1. Are there any existing legal restrictions that might limit the property's operating performance (i.e., easements, litigations, restrictive covenants)?

2. Has the property obtained the necessary liquor licenses, zoning rights, building permits, etc.?

3. Will the management-contract operator have right of first refusal should you decide to sell the property?

4. Please provide name and address of your lawyer, construction manager, architect, and other consultants serving on the project.

EXHIBIT V-5

Projection of Market Demand Growth, 1987–1992

Estimated room-night demand in 1987, based upon estimated occupancies of currently competitive properties = 25,600 rooms × 68% occupancy × 365 days = 6,353,920 room-nights demanded

Projected growth rate, 1987–1992

Market Segment	Est. % of Market, 1987	Proj. Growth of Market, 1987–1992	Composite Projected Growth
Individual business traveler:			
Domestic	36%	8 %	.0288
International	4	20	.0080
Conference-convention business:			
Local	8	2	.0016
Regional	22	6	.0132
National	13	5	.0065
Tourist and vacation business:			
Not tour:			
Domestic	3	5	.0015
International	2	15	.0030
Tour:			
Domestic	4	(2)	(.0008)
International	3	25	.0075
Government:			
State	1	—	—
Federal	4	—	—
	100%		.0693 or 6.93%

Estimated room-night demand in 1992, based upon 1987 room-night demand and estimated five-year growth rate = 6,353,920 room-nights × 1.0693 = 6,794,250 room-nights demanded

supply over the next five years; and, consequently, **(5)** the projected occupancy of the proposed property for its third operating year.

Exhibits V-5 and V-6 illustrate how projected activity levels are established. In Exhibit V-5, the estimated present room-night demand is projected five years forward into the stabilized year of the property. For the Century 21 project, the stabilized year is estimated to be the third operating year. The present room-night demand is estimated from the results of a survey of properties currently attracting the market segments defined for the project. The properties surveyed

EXHIBIT V-6

Projection of Annual Occupancy for Stabilized Year—Century 21 Hotel Project

Existing competitive guest rooms available in the market area, 1987:	25,600
Plus: New competitive rooms expected to enter the market by 1992:	
Century 21: 300 rooms (proposed)	
Hotel A: 450 rooms (under construction)	
Hotel B: 350 rooms (under construction)	
Hotel C: 107 rooms (proposed addition)	
Hotel D: 220 rooms (proposed: financing not yet obtained)	1,427
Expected number of guest rooms in 1992	27,027
Less: Present competitive rooms expected to lose competitor status by 1992:	
Hotel E: 310 rooms	
Hotel F: 500 rooms	810
Expected number of competitive rooms available in 1992:	26,217

Estimated number of competitive room nights available in 1992:

26,217 rooms × 365 days = 9,569,200

Projected average annual occupancy for competitive properties in market area in 1992:

$$\frac{\text{Estimated room-night demand}}{\text{Estimated room-nights available}} = \frac{6{,}794{,}250}{9{,}569{,}200} = 71\% \text{ occupancy}$$

Assuming that the Century 21 Hotel will share equally in the market area's demand for competitive rooms, the property should achieve a 71-percent occupancy in 1992.

should include those considered to be the proposed project's competitors as well as properties that are not truly competitive but that, due to an inadequate supply of competitive rooms, are accommodating customers the proposed project hopes to attract. The demand estimate shown in Exhibit V-5 is derived from several sources: information on existing market segments whose members would be attracted to the proposed project; the projected growth rate of each identified segment; and the composite projected growth rate, based upon the weighted averages of the component market segments. In the example, the composite growth rate is estimated at 6.93 percent. In the final step of the projection, the estimated room-night demand is determined by multiplying the base-year room-night demand by the composite projected growth rate—yielding a figure, in this case, of 6,794,250 room-nights demanded.

In Exhibit V-6, the projected room-night demand is used to estimate the annual occupancy for the project's third year of operation. The first step in this procedure is to identify the number of existing competitive guest rooms in the market area. This rooms inventory is then projected five years into the future by adding the number of competitive guest rooms expected to enter the market during the period and subtracting the number of currently competitive guest rooms that are expected to lose their competitive status during that period. The resulting figure is multiplied by 365 (days) to determine the estimated number of competitive room-nights available during the project's third year of operation. In this case, 9,569,200 room-nights will be available in 1992. The last step is to compute the projected market-wide occupancy percentage by dividing the estimated room-night demand (from Exhibit V-5) by the estimated room-night supply. As noted in Exhibit V-6, the project should achieve a 71-percent occupancy in its third year of operation—assuming that the estimates used in the calculations are realistic and that the property as developed is competitive. This third-year occupancy percentage becomes the basis for projections of activity levels in the long-term capital-investment analysis described in the next section.

2. The Capital-Investment Analysis

The objective of the capital-investment analysis is to determine whether the project's expected financing package can provide a long-term return on equity (after management fees) greater than the equity hurdle rate demanded by the equity interests. It is vital that the owner and the operator concur in regard to the assumptions and judgments used in developing the projections as well as to the outcome of the analysis. The analysis then serves as a vehicle to ensure that the owner's expectations are compatible with the operator's. If the parties are able to agree on what constitutes a realistic and attainable projection, the owner-operator working relationship begins on a good footing. A project may be considered feasible by both parties when the analysis indicates that the project will provide **(1)** sufficient income to compensate the operator for achieving the projections and **(2)** a return on equity greater than the equity-hurdle rate.

In the capital-investment analysis, the expected cash-flow return to the equity, on a discounted cash-flow basis, is compared with the initial equity investment. In the present example, we assume the owner has negotiated the most favorable mortgage package available. What must be established is whether, under the terms of this package, the return available to the owner is adequate for him to proceed with the project. In this analysis, the equity investment consists of the nondebt-financed portion of the total project cost, and the equity return consists of **(1)** the annual cash flows available to the equity after meeting all obligations, including management fees, debt service and reserves for replacement, and **(2)** the residual value of the business, less the mortgage and tax liabilities, measured at some point in the future—usually ten to 12 years after opening.

Since these cash flows occur over an extended period, they are discounted to reflect their differences in timing and the risk associated with hotel investment.

A specific example will illustrate the various steps in the capital-investment analysis. Although the figures pertain only to this specific case, the procedures are applicable to all such analyses. Four tables will be used to document the analysis: Exhibit V-7, which provides the ten-year revenue and operating-expense projections through income before fixed charges; Exhibit V-8, which uses the figures from Exhibit V-7 to illustrate the deduction of fixed charges and the conversion of profits (or losses) to positive (or negative) cash flows after debt service and reserves for replacement; and Exhibit V-9, which is a summary of cash flow generated from sale of the property; and Exhibit V-10, which summarizes projected inflows and outflows.

a. The Ten-Year Operating Projections. The ten-year operating projections (Exhibit V-7) form the basis of the capital-investment analysis, and the owner and operator must agree that these estimates are both realistic and attainable. The estimated business volume is based upon the projected annual occupancy for the first normal operating year, as determined in the project's market profile (Exhibits V-5 and V-6); here, the 71-percent occupancy determined in Exhibit V-6 becomes the base for the third year (1992) projections in Exhibit V-7. Projected occupancy begins at 61 percent, reflecting both the difficulties of the opening year and the ability of the operator to market the property properly at opening; occupancy increases in steps to 76 percent (considered, in this case, a realistic annual occupancy during the project's strong years); and it decreases to 73 and 72 percent respectively during the ninth and tenth years, reflecting the property's slightly decreased ability to compete as newer hotels enter the market.

The projections for departmental sales are based upon projected occupancy and anticipated activity in the restaurant, telephone, and other income-producing areas. These sales figures are calculated for each year to reflect expected changes in volume levels and the estimated effect of inflation. Projected departmental expenses and undistributed operating expenses are based upon levels of service commensurate with the type of property; they too are adjusted annually for increased and decreased activity levels and for expected inflationary effects. The expense projection for the management fee should at first be estimated using a typical fee structure—with the understanding, of course, that the fee structure is subject to negotiation, depending upon the outcome of the return-on-equity analysis and upon the relative strengths of the owner's and the operator's bargaining positions.

A list of the assumptions used to calculate each line item in the projections should be prepared to ensure that both parties are fully mindful of the bases of the projections. The following list, used in developing the Century 21 ten-year projections, is illustrative of the kinds of assumptions requiring explicit mention.

EXHIBIT V-7

Ten-Year Operating Projections—Century 21 Hotel Project (1990–1999)

	Year 1 (1990)		Year 2 (1991)		Year 3 (1992)		Year 4 (1993)		Year 5 (1994)	
	$	%	$	%	$	%	$	%	$	%
Activity level:										
Average room rate	$87	—	$96	—	$102	—	$115	—	$124	—
Occupancy percentage	61%	—	66%	—	71%	—	72%	—	73%	—
Rooms sold	66,795	—	72,270	—	77,745	—	78,840	—	79,935	—
Departmental revenues:										
Rooms	$ 5,806,000	39.4%	$ 6,903,000	37.8 %	$ 7,963,000	36.5%	$ 9,058,000	35.7%	$ 9,948,000	35.0%
Food	4,452,000	41.5	7,869,000	42.9	9,553,000	43.7	11,271,000	44.5	12,753,000	44.9
Beverage	1,659,000	11.3	2,151,000	11.7	2,626,000	12.0	3,075,000	12.1	3,479,000	12.3
Public Rooms	233,000	1.6	301,000	1.6	366,000	1.7	431,000	1.7	487,000	1.7
Telephones	303,000	2.1	369,000	2.0	447,000	2.0	509,000	2.0	579,000	2.0
Rental and other income	607,000	4.1	738,000	4.0	892,000	4.1	1,016,000	4.0	1,158,000	4.1
Total	14,723,000	100.0	18,331,000	100.0	21,847,000	100.0	25,360,000	100.0	28,404,000	100.0
Departmental expenses:										
Rooms	1,354,000	23.3	1,510,000	21.9	1,645,000	20.7	1,847,000	20.4	2,019,000	20.3
Food and beverage	6,616,000	85.1	7,826,000	78.1	9,293,000	76.3	10,760,000	75.0	12,174,000	75.0
Telephone	273,000	90.1	333,000	90.2	402,000	89.9	457,000	89.8	520,000	89.8
Total	8,243,000	56.0	9,669,000	52.8	11,340,000	51.9	13,064,000	51.5	14,713,000	51.8
Departmental profit:										
Rooms	4,452,000	76.7	5,393,000	78.1	6,318,000	79.3	7,211,000	79.6	7,929,000	79.7
Food and beverage	1,391,000	14.9	2,495,000	21.9	3,252,000	23.7	4,017,000	25.0	4,545,000	25.0
Telephone	30,000	9.9	36,000	9.8	45,000	10.1	52,000	10.2	59,000	10.2
Rental and other income	607,000	100.0	738,000	100.0	892,000	100.0	1,016,000	100.0	1,158,000	100.0
Gross Operating Income	6,480,000	44.0	8,662,000	47.30	10,507,000	48.1	12,296,000	48.5	13,691,000	48.2
Undistributed operating expenses:										
Administrative and general (excluding management fees)	1,060,000	7.2	1,210,000	6.6	1,311,000	6.0	1,522,000	6.0	1,704,000	6.0
Marketing	957,000	6.5	770,000	4.2	917,000	4.2	1,065,000	4.2	1,193,000	4.2
Energy	604,000	4.1	660,000	3.6	765,000	3.5	888,000	3.5	994,000	3.5
Property operation and maintenance	736,000	5.0	807,000	4.4	765,000	3.5	888,000	3.5	994,000	3.5
Total	3,357,000	22.8	3,447,000	18.8	3,758,000	17.2	4,363,000	17.2	4,885,000	17.2
Income before fixed charges and management fees	3,123,000	21.2	5,215,000	28.4	6,749,000	30.9	7,933,000	31.3	8,806,000	31.0
Management fees paid (3% gross revenue plus 10% IBFC subordinated to debt service and reserve for replacement)	442,000	3.0	1,236,000	6.7	1,348,000	6.2	1,478,000	5.8	1,592,000	5.6
Income before fixed charges	$ 2,681,000	18.2%	$ 3,979,000	21.7 %	$ 5,401,000	24.7%	$ 6,455,000	25.5%	$ 7,214,000	25.4%

	Year 6 (1995)		Year 7 (1996)		Year 8 (1997)		Year 9 (1998)		Year 10 (1999)	
	$	%	$	%	$	%	$	%	$	%
Activity level:										
Average room rate	$133	—	$143	—	$153	—	$159	—	$161	—
Occupancy percentage	75%	—	76%	—	76%	—	73%	—	72%	—
Rooms sold	82,125	—	83,220	—	83,220	—	79,935	—	78,840	—
Departmental revenues:										
Rooms	$10,951,000	34.9%	$11,887,000	34.6%	$12,773,000	34.0%	$12,694,000	31.9%	$12,707,000	31.0%
Food	13,972,000	44.6	15,217,000	44.4	16,767,000	44.7	18,618,000	46.8	19,431,000	47.4
Beverage	3,901,000	12.5	4,361,000	12.7	4,941,000	13.2	5,322,000	13.4	5,552,000	13.5
Public Rooms	539,000	1.7	616,000	1.8	701,000	1.9	693,000	1.7	752,000	1.8
Telephones	695,000	2.2	767,000	2.2	829,000	2.2	862,000	2.2	904,000	2.2
Rental and other income	1,291,000	4.1	1,474,000	4.3	1,514,000	4.0	1,588,000	4.0	1,648,000	4.0
Total	31,349,000	100.0	34,322,000	100.0	37,485,000	100.0	39,777,000	100.0	40,994,000	100.0
Departmental expenses:										
Rooms	2,219,000	20.3	2,402,000	20.2	2,568,000	20.0	2,572,000	20.3	2,599,000	20.4
Food and beverage	13,405,000	75.0	14,684,000	75.0	16,281,000	75.0	18,194,000	76.0	19,487,000	78.0
Telephone	615,000	88.5	679,000	88.5	729,000	88.0	759,000	88.0	796,000	88.0
Total	16,239,000	51.8	17,765,000	51.8	19,578,000	52.2	21,525,000	54.1	22,882,000	55.8
Departmental profit:										
Rooms	8,732,000	79.7	9,485,000	79.8	10,166,000	80.0	10,122,000	80.0	10,108,000	79.6
Food and beverage	5,007,000	25.0	5,510,000	25.0	6,128,000	25.0	6,439,000	24.0	6,248,000	22.0
Telephone	80,000	11.5	88,000	11.5	99,000	12.0	103,000	12.0	108,000	12.0
Rental and other income	1,291,000	100.0	1,474,000	100.0	1,514,000	100.0	1,588,000	100.0	1,648,000	100.0
Gross Operating Income	15,110,000	48.2	16,557,000	48.2	17,907,000	47.8	18,252,000	45.9	18,112,000	41.2
Undistributed operating expenses:										
Administrative and general (excluding management fees)	1,881,000	6.0	2,060,000	6.0	2,249,000	6.0	2,466,000	6.2	2,624,000	6.4
Marketing	1,316,000	4.2	1,510,000	4.4	1,874,000	5.0	2,028,000	5.1	2,173,000	5.3
Energy	1,097,000	3.5	1,201,000	3.5	1,312,000	3.5	1,512,000	3.8	1,722,000	4.2
Property operation and maintenance	1,097,000	3.5	1,202,000	3.5	1,575,000	4.2	1,671,000	4.2	1,804,000	4.4
Total	5,391,000	17.2	5,973,000	17.4	7,010,000	18.7	7,677,000	19.3	8,323,000	20.3
Income before fixed charges and management fees	9,719,000	31.0	10,584,000	30.8	10,897,000	29.1	10,575,000	26.6	9,789,000	23.9
Management fees paid (3% gross revenue plus 10% IBFC subordinated to debt service and reserve for replacement)	1,818,000	5.8	1,921,000	5.6	2,102,000	5.6	2,132,000	5.4	2,086,000	5.1
Income before fixed charges	$ 7,901,000	25.2%	$ 8,663,000	25.2%	$ 8,795,000	23.5%	$ 8,443,000	21.2%	$ 7,703,000	18.8%

EXHIBIT V-8

Cash Flow Projections—Century 21 Hotel Project (1990–1999)

	Year 1 (1990)		Year 2 (1991)		Year 3 (1992)		Year 4 (1993)		Year 5 (1994)	
	$	%	$	%	$	%	$	%	$	%
Income before fixed charges	$2,681,000	18.2%	$3,979,000	21.7%	$5,401,000	24.7%	$6,455,000	25.5%	$7,214,000	25.4%
Fixed Charges:										
Property insurance	117,000	1.0	125,000	0.7	133,000	1.6	143,000	0.6	153,000	0.5
Property taxes	307,000	2.0	329,000	1.8	353,000	1.6	377,000	1.5	404,000	1.4
Interest	2,990,000	20.3	2,974,000	16.2	2,956,000	13.5	2,934,000	11.6	2,911,000	10.3
Interest kicker	—	—	—	—	—	—	272,000	1.0	298,000	1.0
Total interest	2,990,000	20.3	2,974,000	16.2	2,956,000	13.5	3,206,000	12.6	3,209,000	11.3
Depreciation	2,130,000	14.0	2,130,000	11.6	2,130,000	9.8	2,130,000	8.4	2,130,000	7.5
Total fixed charges	5,544,000	37.7	5,558,000	30.3	5,572,000	25.5	5,856,000	23.1	5,896,000	20.8
Income before taxes	(2,863,000)	(19.5)	(1,579,000)	(8.6)	(171,000)	(0.8)	599,000	2.4	1,318,000	4.6
Income taxes	—	—	—	—	—	—	—	—	—	—
Loss carry over	(2,868,000)	—	(4,442,000)	—	(4,613,000)	—	(4,014,000)	—	(2,696,000)	—
Income after taxes	(2,863,000)	(19.5)	(1,579,000)	(8.6)	(171,000)	(0.8)	599,000	2.4	1,318,000	4.6
Add: Depreciation	2,130,000	14.0	2,130,000	11.6	2,130,000	9.8	2,130,000	8.4	2,130,000	7.5
Cash flow from operations	(733,000)	(5.0)	551,000	3.0	1,959,000	9.0	2,729,000	10.8	3,448,000	12.1
Reserve for replacement	147,000	1.0	366,000	2.0	653,000	3.0	760,000	3.0	853,000	3.0
Principal repayment	168,000	1.1	185,000	1.0	204,000	0.9	225,000	0.9	248,000	0.9
Net cash flow from operations	($1,048,000)	(7.1 %)	$ 0	0.0 %	$1,102,000	5.1 %	$1,744,000	6.9%	$2,374,000	8.3%

	Year 6 (1995)		Year 7 (1996)		Year 8 (1997)		Year 9 (1998)		Year 10 (1999)	
	$	%	$	%	$	%	$	%	$	%
Income before fixed charges	$7,901,000	25.2%	$8,663,000	25.2%	$8,795,000	23.5%	$8,443,000	21.2%	$7,703,000	18.8%
Fixed Charges:										
Property insurance	163,000	0.5	176,000	0.5	188,000	0.5	201,000	0.5	215,000	0.5
Property taxes	433,000	1.4	463,000	1.4	496,000	1.3	537,000	1.4	575,000	1.4
Interest	2,885,000	9.2	2,856,000	8.3	2,824,000	7.5	2,789,000	7.0	2,751,000	6.7
Interest kicker	329,000	1.1	357,000	1.1	382,000	1.1	381,000	1.0	381,000	1.0
Total interest	3,214,000	10.3	3,213,000	9.4	3,206,000	8.6	3,170,000	8.0	3,132,000	7.7
Depreciation	958,000	3.1	958,000	2.8	958,000	2.6	958,000	2.4	958,000	2.3
Total fixed charges	4,768,000	15.2	4,810,000	14.0	4,848,000	12.9	4,866,000	12.2	4,880,000	11.9
Income before taxes	3,133,000	10.0	3,853,000	11.2	3,947,000	10.5	3,577,000	9.0	2,823,000	6.9
Income taxes	130,000	0.4	1,156,000	3.4	1,184,000	3.1	1,073,000	2.7	847,000	2.1
Loss carry over	—	—	—	—	—	—	—	—	—	—
Income after taxes	3,003,000	9.6	2,697,000	7.9	2,763,000	7.4	2,504,000	6.3	1,976,000	4.8
Add: Depreciation	958,000	3.1	958,000	2.8	958,000	2.6	958,000	2.4	958,000	2.3
Cash flow from operations	3,961,000	12.6	3,655,000	10.7	3,721,000	9.9	3,462,000	8.7	2,934,000	7.2
Reserve for replacement	942,000	3.0	1,029,000	3.0	1,124,000	3.0	1,193,000	3.0	1,228,000	3.0
Principal repayment	274,000	0.9	303,000	0.9	335,000	0.9	370,000	0.9	409,000	1.0
Net cash flow from operations	$2,745,000	8.8%	$2,323,000	6.8%	$2,262,000	6.0%	$1,899,000	4.8%	$1,297,000	3.2%

In order to clearly separate assumptions and later discussions about revenues, cost, and inflation, all dollar amounts in this list are expressed in constant dollars.

— The annual inflation rate during the projection period was estimated at 6 percent.

— The 1990 average room rate of $82 in the first year was increased to $96 in the eighth year to reflect the increased market penetration. The occupancy percentage is projected at 61 percent in the first year and increases up to 76 percent in the seventh year. At the end of the projection period, however, the projected average room rate and occupancy percentage are expected to decline slightly as a result of the age of the property and of newly constructed, more competitive properties entering the market.

— Considering the characteristics of the project, the restaurant sales are estimated to be higher than room sales. In later years, the restaurant becomes established in the local market and thus less dependent of hotel guests.

— The operating expenses of the rooms department were estimated at 23.4 percent of room sales in the first year. In later years this percentage is expected to decrease, since the fixed departmental cost as a percentage of total room sales decreases.

— The operating expense of the food and beverage department were estimated at 85 percent of restaurant sales in the first year. In later years this percentage is also expected to decline, since the portion of fixed departmental cost decreases due to the increasing departmental sales.

— Administrative and general expenses, excluding management fees, were estimated at 7.2 percent of total sales in the first year. In the stabilized year of operation, this percentage is expected to decrease due to the high portion of fixed costs in the department.

— Marketing expenses were estimated at 6.5 percent of total sales in the first year due to the necessarily higher cost of penetrating the market. For the stabilized year of operation the marketing expenses were estimated at 4.2 percent of total sales.

— Energy expenses were estimated at 4.1 percent of total sales in the first year and 3.5 percent of total sales in the stabilized year of operation.

— Property, operation, and maintenance expenses were estimated at 5 percent of total sales in the first year and at 3.5 percent in the stabilized year of operation.

— The management fee was based on a basic fee of 3 percent of gross revenue and 10 percent of income before fixed charges, subordinated to debt service and reserve for replacement. The unpaid incentive fees are accruing at an annual interest rate of 10 percent.

b. Determination of Operating Cash Flows. Exhibit V-8 illustrates the process of converting the income before fixed charges to cash flow after reserve for

EXHIBIT V-9

Calculation of Simulated Sale—Century 21 Hotel Project

A. Assumptions:

1. The hotel is sold at the end of the tenth year of operation.
2. The sale price is determined using the eleventh year's estimated cash flow capitalized at a rate of 10 percent.
3. Straight-line depreciation was utilized during the project's life.
4. Selling expenses are estimated to be six percent of the sale price.
5. The capital-gains tax rate is 30 percent.

B. Sale-Price Calculations:

Estimated cash flow in 11th year after management fees, property taxes and insurance, and reserve for replacement but before debt service: $5,835,000

Expected sale price:	$58,350,000
Selling expenses	3,500,000
Net sale proceeds	54,850,000
Less: outstanding mortgage balance	27,281,000
Before-tax equity reversion	$27,569,000

C. Adjusted Base Calculations:

Depreciation base	$28,460,000
Less: accumulation depreciation	15,437,000
Plus: land cost	3,000,000
Adjusted base	$16,023,000

D. Taxable-Income Calculations:

Expected sales price	$58,350,000
Less: selling expenses	3,500,000
Net sale proceeds	54,850,000
Less: adjusted basis	16,023,000
Total gain	38,827,000
Accelerated depreciation gain	—
Capital gain	38,827,000
Taxes payable (based upon 30% rate)	$11,648,000

E. Calculation of After-Tax Cash Flows From Sale:

Before-tax equity reversion	$27,569,000
Less: taxes payable	11,648,000
After-tax cash flow from sale	$15,921,000

replacement and principal repayment—the cash flow available to the equity each year.

Notes to the cash-flow projections, listing all assumptions, should accompany the statement. Listed below are the kinds of items that should be detailed in the notes, illustrated by the specific assumptions employed to determine the projected occupation and tax costs for the Century 21 project.

Property taxes and insurance were estimated at $400,000 in the first year. For the remainder of the projection period, this amount was increased by 1 percent net of inflation.

Depreciation and amortization of the project cost were broken down into the building, furniture, fixture, and equipment cost, as well as the capitalized soft construction costs. Straight-line depreciation with the following depreciation periods were used: building cost at 29 years; furniture, fixtures, and equipment at 5 years; and other capitalized at 10 years.

Interest expense and principal repayment were based on a $30 million mortgage amortized over 30 years at an annual fixed interest rate of 10 percent, plus an interest kicker of 3 percent of room sales after the third year of operation.

The income tax rate was estimated at 30 percent. Current loss carry-forward procedures were used in the computations.

Reserve for replacement expenses were estimated to be 1, 2, and 3 percent of total sales in the first, second, stabilized and later years of operation respectively.

c. Determination of Cash Flow from Sale of Property. In addition to the cash flow received for the first ten years of operation, the owner receives operating cash flow beyond the tenth year if he retains the property or net proceeds from the sale of the property if he elects to sell rather than continuing to own the hotel. In either case, a "forced" sale must be calculated to derive this value to the owner. For this calculation, an estimated sale price is determined based upon a reasonable capitalization rate. Net proceeds from the sale are determined by deducting from the sale price the selling expenses, the outstanding balances of existing mortgages, the capital gains tax incurred from the sale, and any accrued incentive management fees that may be due on sale of the property. Whether the owner plans to sell the property at the end of the tenth year is immaterial in the analysis; the "forced" sale on paper is used only to establish a value on the business, which is in fact a return on equity not included in the operational cash flows. To ignore this value would be to understate significantly the actual return on equity.

The following data were used to compute the value of the business accruing to the equity at the end of the tenth year. To provide a comprehensive analysis of the returns to the owner a forced sale was simulated at the end of the tenth year based on the income before fixed charges expected in the eleventh year, less the reserve for replacement, property taxes and insurance, and the management fees due in the eleventh year. The projected income before financing and depreciation was capitalized with a capitalization rate of ten percent to arrive at the expected sale price. To determine the after-tax sale proceeds to the owner, the following items were deducted from the expected sale price: selling expenses of six percent of the sales price; the outstanding mortgage balance; taxes due on sale; and accrued incentive management fees. The capital gains from the sale was taxed at a 30-percent rate. Exhibit V-9 presents the forced-sale calculations.

d. Return on Equity Analysis. After determining the cash outflows and inflows to the equity during the ten-year period, the project's long-term rate of return on equity is calculated with discounted cash flow analyses. Using the owner's required after-tax rate of return (equity hurdle rate), the cash inflows and outflows are discounted to determine whether the project's return on equity is greater than, equal to, or lesser than the required return. In addition, the exact project return is calculated to determine the magnitude of the deviation between the required rate of return and the project's return. If the project return is equal to or greater than the required return and the ownership entity is adequately comfortable with the assumptions upon which the projections were based, the project is accepted. If the project return is less than the required return, the ownership entity assesses **(1)** the validity of the assumptions which may be revised for subsequent return on equity calculations and **(2)** the possible existence of positive ripple effects that may provide benefits to ownership not calculated in the project return (i.e., a boost to existing real-estate projects owned by the ownership entity adjacent to or in close proximity to the proposed hotel, or a hotel location in a city necessary to strengthen the hotel chain's market presence and network). After the above considerations have been made, the rate-of-return analysis is recalculated to determine whether these factors will alter the decision's outcome. Present-value factor tables for discounting cash flows are in Appendix C.

For the Century 21 Hotel, the ownership entity required a 15-percent rate of return. Using the 15-percent discount factor, the net present value of the cash flows was calculated to be $1,574,000, revealing that the project return was greater than 15 percent. Exhibit V-10 illustrates the return-on-equity analysis for the Century 21 project. The second step is to determine the project's actual return using higher discount factors until the net present value is calculated to be zero. For the Century 21 project, a positive net present value is calculated using the 17-percent discount factor, and a negative net present value is calculated using the 18-percent discount factor revealing that the actual project return is between 17 and 18 percent. The actual return is calculated to be 17.58 percent. Since the return was above the equity-hurdle rate and the ownership entity was comfortable with the assumptions underlying the cash flows, the project was approved.

e. Short-Term Cash-Flow Projections. Performing the capital-investment analysis illustrated in the previous section will indicate whether, over the long term, the project will provide an adequate return to the owner and operator. The owner and the operator should also jointly develop short-term cash flow projections to determine whether adequate funding is available to cover cash outflows during the critical construction, pre-opening, and post-opening phases of the project. It is during this period that a significant number of foreclosures occur, due to inadequate funding of negative cash flows. The operator must provide adequate information concerning pre-opening expenses, inventory requirements, and working-capital levels. This information, together with the

EXHIBIT V-10

Rate-of-Return Calculations—Century 21 Hotel Project

			Net Present Value: 15%		Net Present Value: 17%		Net Present Value: 18%	
Year	Item	Inflow (Outflows)	Present Value Factor	Discounted Cash Flow	Present Value Factor	Discounted Cash Flow	Present Value Factor	Discounted Cash Flow
0	Equity investment (project cost less debt)	($ 8,000,000)	1.0000	($8,000,000)	1.0000	($8,000,000)	1.0000	($8,000,000)
1	Cash flow from operations	(1,048,000)	0.8696	(911,000)	0.8547	(896,000)	0.8475	(888,000)
2	Cash flow from operations	0	0.7561	0	0.7305	0	0.7182	0
3	Cash flow from operations	1,102,000	0.6575	725,000	0.6244	688,000	0.6086	671,000
4	Cash flow from operations	1,744,000	0.5718	997,000	0.5337	931,000	0.5158	900,000
5	Cash flow from operations	2,347,000	0.4972	1,167,000	0.4561	1,070,000	0.4371	1,026,000
6	Cash flow from operations	2,745,000	0.4323	1,187,000	0.3898	1,070,000	0.3704	1,017,000
7	Cash flow from operations	2,323,000	0.3759	873,000	0.3332	774,000	0.3139	729,000
8	Cash flow from operations	2,262,000	0.3269	739,000	0.2848	644,000	0.2660	602,000
9	Cash flow from operations	1,899,000	0.2843	540,000	0.2434	462,000	0.2255	428,000
10	Cash flow from operations	1,297,000	0.2472	321,000	0.2080	270,000	0.1911	248,000
10	Computed value of business	54,850,000	0.2472	13,559,000	0.2080	11,411,000	0.1911	10,480,000
10	Repayment of outstanding mortgage	(27,281,000)	0.2472	(6,744,000)	0.2080	(5,675,000)	0.1911	(5,212,000)
10	Taxes due on sale	(11,648,000)	0.2472	(2,879,000)	0.2080	(2,423,000)	0.1911	(2,226,000)
			Net Present Value	$1,574,000		$ 326,000		($ 225,000)

Actual Rate of Return is 17.58%

revenue and expense projections, provides the material for reasonable estimates of cash flows during the first year or two after opening. The results of the short-term projections will provide a guide to the owner for lining up his sources of funding to keep the operation alive during this critical period.

Exhibit V-11 illustrates one approach to drafting short-term cash flow projections. The period covered should begin at the time of the first cash outlays and should continue until adequate cash flow is available from operations to repay short-term loans taken out to cover operating deficits. In Exhibit V-11, the time span is 36 months. The negative cash flows from operations projected during the months following the opening are funded from the equity and short-term loans. When the project begins to generate a positive cash flow, the cash flow is used first to repay the short-term loans prior to any distribution to the equity.

If the capital-investment analysis indicates that the project will provide a long-term return on equity equal to or greater than the equity-hurdle rate and an adequate return in management fees to the operator, and if the owner is able to provide debt or equity funding throughout the critical pre- and post-opening periods, the project should be considered feasible and serious negotiations may begin.

D. Performing Sensitivity Analyses to Assist in Project Evaluation and in Contract Negotiation

As discussed in Chapter III, computer modeling can assist both owner and operator in performing sensitivity analyses for the purpose of evaluating various management-fee structures under various operating and financing scenarios. Exhibit V-12 illustrates the present values of operator and owner returns for the following types of scenarios: **(a)** a standard "three percent of gross revenue, plus ten percent of income before fixed charges" formula applying the four different cash priority alternatives (Alternatives A,B,C and D) illustrated in Exhibit III-7 applied to the Century 21 best-guess projections; **(b)** two additional management-fee structures applied to the best-guess projections in which the incentive fees are based upon cash flows after debt service and, in one case, a return on equity; and **(c)** a three percent of gross revenue plus a ten percent of income before fixed charges formula, for which the following operating and financial assumptions are varied: average room rate, occupancy percentage, mortgage-interest rate, and inflation rate. As one can see, the use of sensitivity analysis provides valuable information on the significant effect of different management-fee structures and key operating and financial assumptions on both operator and owner returns. It is important to be aware of these effects prior to finalizing one's negotiating strategy.

A quantitative model for analyzing project and management-fee returns is

EXHIBIT V-11

Pre- and Post-Opening Monthly Cash-Flow Projections—Century 21 Hotel Project (000s)

	Prior to −18	−18	−17	−16	−15	−14
Beginning cash balance	0	20	100	100	100	100
Cash in:						
Equity funds	100	3,130	40	30	20	20
Construction and interim loan proceeds		4,160				
Permanent mortgage proceeds						
Total cash in	100	7,290	40	30	20	20
Total cash available	100	7,310	140	130	120	120
Cash out:						
Development costs (preliminary studies, option on land, etc.)	50	40	20	10		
Land		3,000				
Construction cost and interest		4,160				
Furniture, fixtures and equipment						
Pre-opening expenses (marketing, training, salaries, management fees)	30	10	20	20	20	20
Inventories and working capital						
Repayment of construction/interim loans						
Total cash out	80	7,210	40	30	20	20
Ending cash balance	20	100	100	100	100	100

	Opening date	+1	+2	+3	+4	+5
Beginning cash balance	50	50	50	50	50	50
Cash in:						
Equity funds		400	200	150	100	75
Short-term loans		120	80			
Positive cash flow from operations[1,2]						
Total cash in		520	280	150	100	75
Total cash available		570	320	200	150	125
Cash out:						
Construction costs and interest		120	80			
Negative cash flow from operations[1]		400	200	150	100	75
Repayment of short-term loans						
Return of equity available[2]						
Total cash out		520	280	150	100	75
Ending cash balance	50	50	50	50	50	50

[1]After reserve for replacement and principal repayment

[2]When positive cash flow from operations occurs, repayment of short-term loans are first paid from the cash flow. After short-term loan obligations have been repaid, remaining cash flows become available as a return to the equity. For the Century 21 project, a net return on equity occurs near the end of the third year of operation.

−13	−12	−11	−10	−9	−8	−7	−6	−5	−4	−3	−2	−1
100	100	100	100	100	100	100	100	100	100	100	100	100
20	930	20	20	20	20	30	30	30	460	580	740	1,760
4,160	1,090			5,160				5,160	1,090	1,090	1,100	6,860
												30,000
4,180	2,020	20	20	5,180	20	30	30	5,190	1,550	1,670	1,840	38,620
4,280	2,120	120	120	5,280	120	130	130	5,290	1,650	1,770	1,940	38,720
4,160				5,160				5,160				5,160
	2,000								1,500	1,500	1,500	2,500
20	20	20	20	20	20	30	30	30	40	70	110	150
									10	100	230	860
												30,000
,180	2,020	20	20	5,180	20	30	30	5,190	1,550	1,670	1,840	38,670
100	100	100	100	100	100	100	100	100	100	100	100	50

+6	+7	+8	+9	+10	+11	+12	+13	+14	+15	+16	+17	+18
50	50	50	50	50	50	50	50	50	50	50	50	50
25	20	20	20	20	10	8	8	8	4			
										2	4	4
25	20	20	20	20	10	8	8	8	4	2	4	4
75	70	70	70	70	60	58	58	58	54	52	54	54
25	20	20	20	20	10	8	8	8	4			
										2	4	4
25	20	20	20	20	10	8	8	8	4	2	4	4
50	50	50	50	50	50	50	50	50	50	50	50	50

EXHIBIT V-12

Operator and Owner Returns Using Sensitivity Analysis for the Century 21 Project

	Present value of operator's fees[1]	Present value of owner's returns[2]
Using the best-guess projections[3] but varying pay-out schedules of the 3% gross plus 10% IBFC management-fee structure illustrated in Exhibit II-9:		
—Alternate A	$ 9,191,000	$13,721,000
—Alternate B	$ 9,135,000	$13,764,000
—Alternate C	$ 9,555,000	$12,649,000
—Alternate D	$ 9,836,000	$13,262,000
Using the best-guess projections[3] but with the following other management-fee structures:		
—3% gross plus 15% cash flow after debt service and reserve for replacement	$ 6,498,000	$17,944,000
—3% gross plus 25% cash flow after debt service, reserve for replacement and 10% on equity.	$ 7,522,000	$15,377,000
Using a 3% gross plus 10% IBFC management-fee structure (accruing incentive-fee portion subordinated to debt service and reserve for replacement) with the following variations to the best-guess projections[4]		
—Best-guess projections	$ 9,135,000	$13,764,000
—Average room rate		
5% decrease	$ 8,867,000	$11,712,000
5% increase	$ 9,402,000	$15,712,000
—Occupancy percentage		
5% decrease	$ 8,881,000	$11,964,000
5% increase	$ 9,389,000	$15,551,000
—Mortgage-interest rate[5]		
at 8%	$ 9,204,000	$16,309,000
at 12%	$ 9,202,000	$11,002,000
—Inflation rate[6]		
at 4%	$ 8,220,000	$ 9,024,000
at 8%	$10,158,000	$19,272,000

[1]Operator's basic fee, incentive fees, and interest on accrued fees discounted at 10 percent.

[2]Owner's return after annual operating expenses, management fees, debt service and reserve for replacement as well as the residual value from the sale in the tenth year have been calculated based on a discount rate of 10 percent.

[3]See Exhibit IV-7.

[4]Deferred incentive fee earned 10-percent annual interest.

[5]Mortgage-interest rate in projections is 10 percent.

[6]Inflation rate in projections is 6 percent.

presented in Appendix D. The appendix includes a description of the model and the effect that various changes in occupancy rate, room rate, mortgage interest rate, and inflation rate have on the Century 21 projections and on the subsequent owner and operator returns under four different management-fee structures.

E. Going-In and Fall-Back Positions for the Bargaining Table

Each project is unique, and the premise that an operator or an owner will agree only to a predetermined contract package is highly unlikely. The work done by the two parties in preparing financial projections will lead to some common ground for negotiating management fees commensurate with the project's ability to generate a return to its owners. The form that these fees take (e.g., basic-incentive mix, stand-asides, performance measures) will be determined by the relative bargaining power of the owner and the operator and by each party's willingness to participate in give-and-take bargaining on the other key provisions of the contract.

In negotiating these major provisions, many outcomes are possible, but only a few will be mutually acceptable. Each party views some provisions as more important than others. As a result, it is important that before formal negotiations begin, each side separately evaluate the relative importance of every provision of concern and develop preferred "going-in" positions—as well as acceptable "fall-back positions" on those provisions where compromise is possible, given reciprocal concessions from the other party.

Defining one's position on these provisions is the culmination of assessing the opposite party's relative bargaining strength and ability to perform his contractual obligations. The going-in and fall-back positions developed by an owner to deal with one operator, for example, may not be appropriate for another operator, because the relative bargaining strengths of the parties will differ.

Exhibit V-13 lists representative going-in and fall-back positions for an owner entering a typical negotiation. Some provisions are perceived as more negotiable than others, and a party's willingness to yield on a point will reflect the parties' relative bargaining strengths, as well as the opposite party's flexibility on other points.

F. Conclusions

An owner and an operator approach the negotiating process from different perspectives, each aware of the risks he faces in the proposed project. Each wants to minimize his own risks and maximize his influence to ensure a return commensurate with his efforts and the risks involved.

The procedures outlined above for analyzing the proposed project's financial

Exhibit V-13

Going-In and Fall-Back Positions for Negotiating Provisions of Concern (Owner)

Going-In Position	First Fall-Back	Second Fall-Back
Operator's contribution and loans:		
• Operator will contribute free of charge all technical-assistance services provided by the operator's staff.	• Operator will charge at cost those services.	• Operator will charge at going rate—2½ times cost—for those services.
• Operator will finance through a loan to owner fees incurred by outside consultants used by operator to provide technical services.	• Owner will finance fees.	
• Operator will finance through a loan to owner all pre-opening expenses.	• Owner will finance expenses.	
• Operator will finance through a loan to owner the operation's initial working capital.†	• Owner will finance working capital.	
• Operator will purchase, own, and maintain at own expense all linen, china, glass, and silver inventories; owner will reimburse operator for reasonable percentage of annual maintenance costs.	• Owner will own inventories and will pay only for reasonable percentage of annual maintenance costs; operator will pay for any costs beyond this.	• Owner will own inventories and pay all maintenance costs.
• Operator will finance through a loan to owner a portion (50%) of this property's furniture, fixtures, and equipment.*	• Same, except 20% of property's furniture, fixtures, and equipment.†	
Term of the contract:		
• Initial term 5 years	• Initial term 10 years.	• Initial term 20 years.
• Renewal terms at option of owner.	• Two 5-year renewal terms at option of owner.	• Two 5-year renewal terms by mutual consent.
Management fees (based upon agreed-upon financial projections):		
• 3% gross plus 10% IBFC with incentive fee deferred to debt service plus 10% return on equity.	• Same, except with incentive fee deferred for debt service.†	• 3% gross plus 5% IBFC plus 10% IBFC deferred to debt service.
Termination by owner:		
• If cash flow is inadequate to cover annual debt retirement for any three consecutive years.	• Same, except: after the first two years of operation.†	• Same, except: after the first three years of operation.

Personnel:		
• Owner has right to reject selection of general manager proposed by operator.		
• Hotel employees will be employees of operator.	• Hotel employees will be employees of owner.	
Budgeting and spending limitations:		
• No changes of centralized services formulas by operator without owner's approval.*	• Changes must be equitably applied.	
• Owner has right to approve or disapprove operating budget and capital-expenditure budget.		
• Repairs and maintenance limited to 3% gross with no carry-overs to subsequent years.*	• 3% gross with carry-overs.*	• As needed.
• Reserves for replacement limited to 2½% gross; unused amounts accumulated but not in escrow.	• Limited to 2½% gross; unused amounts accumulated in escrow.†	• Limited to 3½% gross; unused amounts accumulated in escrow.
• Renovation proposals must be approved mutually by owner and operator.		
Financial statements and reporting:		
• Owner has right to inspect all books and accounting records at any time.*	• At time mutually convenient to owner and operator.	
• Audit performed by independent auditor.		
• Operator will provide monthly operating statement, balance sheet, statement of changes in financial position, statistics, written analysis, and cash-flow projections by month for upcoming 12 months.	• All except cash-flow projections by month for upcoming 12 months.	
• Operator will provide quarterly review of operator results and management plan for upcoming quarter.		
Restrictive convenant:		
• Right of first refusal to develop or own any other property that operator plans to manage in greater metropolitan area.†	• Same but in city limits.†	

*Especially flexible position.
†Especially firm position.

viability will indicate what returns may be shared by the owner and the operator and allow each party to develop going-in and fall-back positions for negotiations. Following these procedures cannot guarantee the elimination of unrealistic expectations or of possible misunderstandings, but it does permit ample opportunity for potential problems to surface, allowing them to be identified and dealt with.

Successful negotiation depends to a large extent on the trust developed between the two parties before negotiations even begin. If both parties are candid and cooperative during the initial period of analysis, each will be able to judge with reasonable accuracy the positions the other party is likely to take when the negotiating process ensues; as a result, a mutually acceptable agreement is more likely to emerge. On the other hand, if the parties are not candid during the analysis, their opening positions may differ significantly, and negotiations will probably break down. In short, the success of the negotiation—and, indeed, of the contract's administration—is a function of the parties' willingness to perceive each other as partners, rather than as antagonists.

VI

Management Contracts for Commercial Restaurant Operations

Most commercial restaurant operations are managed by operators who own or lease the restaurant facilities. These methods of operation maximize the operators' freedom of control and the significant returns that can result from a well-promoted and -managed restaurant operation. Management-contract fees are usually less lucrative in comparison.

Management contracts for commercial restaurant operations generally are used in two specific types of situations. The first occurs when an owner develops a freestanding commercial restaurant and wishes to lease it to an operator, but the operator is not willing to assume the risk associated with a lease. The second occurs when an owner develops and operates a hospitality or other multipurpose facility (e.g., resort, hotel, conference center, amusement park, athletic club, or transportation center), but wishes to employ an operator to manage the food and beverage operations within the facility. In either case, the owner is seeking an experienced restaurant operating firm or restaurateur to manage the facility.

A. Operator and Owner Responsibilities

Operator and owner rights and responsibilities in restaurant management contracts parallel closely those in hotel contracts but involve more explicit agreements involving operating policies, especially in contracts that involve close cooperation, as in the case of an operator's managing the restaurant activities and the owner's managing other, closely-related activities.

The operator assumes responsibility for managing the restaurant on behalf of the owner. These responsibilities include:

— Recommending to the owner the theme and the decor of the operation;

— Determining and implementing operating policies;
— Establishing the menu and pricing structure;
— Developing and conducting all marketing, advertising, and public-relations programs;
— Hiring, training, and supervising all operational supervisors and employees as well as establishing their salaries and pay scales;
— Developing annual operating, replacement, and capital-improvement budgets for submission to the owner for approval;
— Negotiating, on the owner's behalf, service contracts required in the ordinary course of business, including contracts for electricity, gas, telephone, cleaning, vermin extermination, etc.;
— Purchasing, on the owner's behalf, inventories, provisions, supplies, and operating equipment necessary to properly maintain and operate the property;
— Making or causing to be made all necessary repairs, decorations, renewals, revisions, and alterations to the building, furnishings, and equipment;
— Applying for and obtaining and maintaining all licenses and permits required of the owner or operator in connection with the management and operation of the property;
— Depositing in a banking institution in accounts in the owner's or operator's name all monies furnished by the owner as working capital and received by the operator for or on behalf of the owner and disbursing and paying the same as required in connection with the ownership, maintenance, and operation of the property;
— Delivering to the owner financial statements showing the results of the property's operation; and
— Keeping on behalf of the owner full and adequate books and accounts reflecting the results of the operation.

The owner's responsibilities include providing the restaurant facility, together with adequate working capital and insurance coverage; granting the operator sole and exclusive right to supervise, direct, and control the management and operation of the property; compensating the operator through basic and incentive management fees; and reimbursing the operator for operator system-reimbursable expenses.

B. Provisions of Concern and Negotiated Outcomes

Contract negotiations tend to center on the following ten contract provisions: **(1)** the nature of the contractual arrangement; **(2)** determination and coordination of operating policies; **(3)** operator loan and equity contributions; **(4)** the term of the contract; **(5)** management fees and system-reimbursable expenses; **(6)** conditions for contract termination, including operator-performance provisions; **(7)** personnel; **(8)** budgeting and spending limitations; **(9)** dispute settlement; and **(10)** restrictive covenants.

1. Nature of the Contractual Arrangement

The issue of whether the operator is an agent or independent contractor arises in restaurant management-contract negotiations as it does in hotel management contracts. In the majority of the contracts negotiated for freestanding restaurants, the operator is an independent contractor, while in the majority of the contracts negotiated for restaurant operations within other facilities, the operator is an agent of the owner. Owners state that it is primarily through negotiating the other provisions of concern that they hope to gain some influence on operator decision-making, behavior, and performance.

2. Determination and Coordination of Operating Policies

Because restaurants do not usually operate on a 24-hour basis and often have the flexibility of offering expanded or contracted service, both the times of operation and the type and extent of services are of significant interest to the owner and the operator.

In contract negotiations, the owner attempts to gain influence or approval rights over the specific hours, days of the week, and seasons the restaurant will remain open. If the restaurant supports other facility operations, the owner wants to ensure that restaurant hours complement these operations. Structuring of the management fees in an effective basic-incentive mix can reinforce the trade-off between setting hours that will maximize revenues and hours that will maximize profits.

The owner also negotiates to gain influence or approval rights on the type and extent of services that will be offered. In a multi-purpose facility, such as a resort, hotel, or conference center, operating decisions involving the offering of room service, food and beverage group functions, or outside catering utilizing the kitchen facilities could beneficially or detrimentally affect other facility activities and overall profitability. The owner wants to ensure that restaurant services complement non-restaurant services.

A decision mechanism is also necessary in multi-purpose facilities in order to coordinate pricing (e.g., the relationship between room and restaurant prices and possible suboptimization of one for the benefit of the operation as a whole), as well as the respective room and restaurant revenue components on package pricing in which one combined price, usually one lower than the individual prices, is offered in order to generate business during slow operating periods.

3. Operator Loan and Equity Contributions

In the vast majority of the contracts, operators do not make loan or equity contributions. In situations where they do so, they negotiate for a lease arrangement. Operators will only make loans when the contract is viewed as a good long-term opportunity and when the length of the term reflects that opportunity. Most loans are negotiated at fixed interest rates and are amortized over the life of the loan. Loan amounts usually cover initial working capital, operating inventories, or occasionally, furniture and fixtures.

4. Term of the Contract

Owner and operator concerns with the initial length of the contract term and term-renewal options are similar to those in hotel management contracts. Most initial terms range from three to ten years with the median term being four years. When initial terms are short, contracts usually give the operator an option to renew for one to two renewal periods ranging from two to four years each. Operator performance criteria tied to the operator's right to renew occur in only a few contracts.

5. Management Fees and Operator System-Reimbursable Expenses

The owner's objective in negotiating fees is to develop a basic-incentive fee mix appropriate for the specific operation. The owner wants the fee structure to be one that the property can afford to pay, that will provide adequate incentive to maximize profitability, and that will encourage cooperation with and accommodation to other revenue-producing efforts that may exist in the facility.

Basic fees are usually structured in one of the following three ways: **(1)** a fixed dollar amount; **(2)** a fixed dollar amount plus a percentage of gross revenues above a specified revenue volume; or **(3)** a percentage of gross revenues. The fixed dollar amounts and specified volumes above are often indexed to inflation or the consumer-price index.

Incentive fees for free-standing restaurant contracts are usually based **(1)** upon a percentage of income before rent and other occupation costs (the line item equivalent to income before fixed charges for hotels), with the fee occasionally being subordinated to debt service; or **(2)** upon a percentage of profit after rent and other occupation costs but before depreciation and income taxes. Incentive fees for restaurant operations within a multi-purpose facility are based upon a percentage of restaurant departmental income less, in some cases, direct marketing and advertising expenses conducted specifically for the restaurant operation. Basic and incentive fee components exist in most contracts. When only one component exists, it is the basic fee component.

Because most restaurants are location- and market-specific, it is difficult to present representative basic- and incentive-fee ranges. In general, however, management-fee structures (combined basic and incentive components) equate to a range of from five to eight percent of gross revenues with most fee structures equating to a figure of six to seven percent of gross revenues.

Operator system-reimbursable expenses tend to be significantly less for restaurant contracts than for hotel contracts. Typical reimbursable expenses often cover the following centralized services: accounting and data processing, training, and procurement of furniture, fixtures, and equipment. System marketing and advertising expenses tend to be minimal or non-existent since marketing and advertising for restaurants are unit-specific and are arranged locally and charged to the operation as a direct marketing expense.

6. Conditions for Contract Termination

Restaurant management contracts usually contain the following termination rights found in hotel contracts. If either party fails to keep, observe, or perform any material covenant, agreement, or provision; if the other party files for bankruptcy; if the other party causes the property's licenses to be revoked or suspended; if the owner fails to maintain an adequate working-capital balance; and if the property is damaged, destroyed, or condemned.

Provisions giving the owner the right to terminate without cause or establishing operator performance standards are virtually nonexistent in restaurant contracts. Most owners attempt to compensate for the above by negotiating for shorter lengths of the term of the contract and for non-competition provisions if the contract is terminated due to the operator's breach of contract. The non-competition provision stipulates that other operators may not own or manage another or a similar restaurant within a specified geographical area for a specified number of years following contract termination. In a substantial number of contracts, the operator has either the right of first refusal or the right of first offer in the event the owner wishes to sell the property.

7. Personnel

Personnel issues in restaurant contracts are similar to the ones in hotel contracts. Owners usually want the employees to be employees of the operator and to have review or approval rights in the selection of the restaurant's general manager. In a slight majority of the contracts, employees are the employees of the operator. In most all contracts, the owner does not have review or approval rights of the restaurant's general manager. However, when the operator personally serves as the restaurant's general manager, the owner occasionally has approval rights if the operator desires to replace himself with another manager from his organization.

8. Budgeting and Spending Limitations

Most contracts require that the operator submit an annual operating budget and include in it capital expenditure requests for furniture, fixtures, and equipment replacements and capital improvements. Seldom is a reserve-for-replacement fund established as is done in hotel contracts. In most contracts, the owner has the right to approve the budget but his approval cannot be unreasonably withheld. Operators are not required to obtain owner approval for budget deviations except in the case when the budget's overall expendure amount is exceeded. Owners usually have the right to review the accounting procedures used to allocate operator system-reimbursable expenses to their properties.

9. Dispute-Settlement Procedures

Provisions providing for dispute settlement are absent in more than half of the restaurant contracts reviewed. Many owners interviewed stated that they regret not having this mechanism included, since they believe it would have increased their leverage in negotiating differences of opinion after the contract was signed. Those contracts that do contain dispute-settlement provisions use procedures similar to those contained in hotel contracts.

10. Restrictive Covenants

Restrictive covenant provisions are of major concern to owners of freestanding restaurants. These owners do not want their restaurants' trade names used within a given geographical area but are often willing to permit the operator to manage another restaurant within the restricted area if it differs significantly in theme, concept, and type of service from the owner's restaurant. A difference of opinion on an exception should be subject to the contract's dispute-settlement procedure. Geographical areas for restrictive covenants vary widely from as small as several city blocks to as large as eight to ten miles depending on the restaurant's concept and the nature of the local market.

Significant future growth in the number of restaurant management contracts is uncertain, because more profitable options and opportunities generally exist for operators to own or to lease restaurant that offer good value and are targeted well to existing adequate markets. The restaurant contract concept has, as has the hotel contracts concept, matured in recent years and can offer if negotiated astutely an equitable business agreement between owner and operator.

VII

The Future of the Management Contract

In this chapter the findings of the author's study are reviewed. The summary is then used as a foundation for discussing the future of the management contract.

A. The Adoption of Management Contracts

Nine major factors contributed to the rapid adoption of management contracts and thereby affected the goals and expectations of both owners and operators entering into contracts. These factors are:

— Competition increased among chain operators intent on expanding their earnings bases—the number of rooms managed.

— The availability of money for real-estate ventures, supplied primarily by real-estate investment trusts and limited partnerships, led to an increase in the number of owners with little or no lodging experience, overbuilding in most lodging markets, and the development of marginal properties heavily dependent upon achieving high volumes of business.

— Larger properties, and correspondingly larger investments, yielded higher fixed costs and debt-service commitments, significantly increasing the ownership risks of new hotels and motor inns.

— Most hotel chains made policy decisions to change from being real-estate companies to operating companies. This strategy permitted them to shift the investment risk to the owner, improving their earnings per share and balance-sheet ratios and thereby enhancing their ability to raise funds.

— Lenders required professional hotel management, creating opportunities for chain and independent operating companies to obtain contracts.

— The dearth of experienced hotel-management personnel contributed to the varying degrees of management expertise offered by chain and independent companies but also increased owners' reliance on these companies to operate the expanded number of properties.

— The recession of the mid-1970s strained the owner-operator relationships under existing contracts, increased the number of contracts between operators and owners-in-foreclosure, and led to greater owner-operator flexibility in the negotiation of contracts.

— The Economic Recovery Tax Act of 1981 and the Tax Equity and Fiscal Responsibility Act of 1982 created major tax incentives for real-estate developers to build hotels; since most developers had no hotel operating experience, they increased the demand for hotel-management expertise.

— Efforts by chain operators to expand their lodging product lines to target specific market segments in an effort to gain market share; developers of these properties were non-operators and relied on hotel operating companies for management.

B. Provisions of Concern During Negotiations

During contract negotiations, the operator attempts to gain maximum control over the property's operation for an uninterrupted and extended period. The owner, on the other hand, attempts to gain the authority to influence the operator's performance during the term of the contract.

In the course of negotiations, both parties identify contract provisions likely to affect their control over the property and its performance. These provisions of concern relate to eleven areas: **(1)** the nature of the contractual arrangement; **(2)** operator loan and equity contributions; **(3)** the term of the contract and its renewal options; **(4)** management fees and the services rendered for the fees; **(5)** operator system-reimbursable expenses; **(6)** conditions for contract termination, including operator-performance provisions; **(7)** personnel; **(8)** budgeting and spending limitations; **(9)** banking, accounting, and financial reporting; **(10)** dispute-settlement procedures; and **(11)** restrictive covenants.

The owner's and the operator's relative bargaining strengths influence the outcome of the negotiations. The eight factors with an impact on the operator's bargaining power are as follows: **(1)** the operator's reputation; **(2)** the number of properties managed by the operator; **(3)** the operator's growth record; **(4)** the extent and quality of the operator's management services; **(5)** the operator's willingness to make loan and equity contributions; **(6)** the experience of the operator's staff; **(7)** the operator's flexibility during negotiations; and **(8)** the operator's responsiveness to the owner's goals.

The seven factors relating to the owner's bargaining power are: **(1)** the owner's intent to maintain ownership; **(2)** the owner's experience and management capability; **(3)** the owner's financial commitment and financial background; **(4)** the type of owner (institutional or entrepreneurial); **(5)** the property's potential for achieving the operator's financial goals; **(6)** the operator's ability to enchance the owner's competitive position in the industry; and **(7)** substantial competition among operators for the property. The interplay of factors creates a continuum of relative bargaining strength ranging from strongly owner-favored to strongly operator-favored positions.

A shift is occuring in the relative strengths of owners and operators. With regard to the continuum, power is now shifting from the operator-dominated end toward the owner-dominated end. As they become more aware of the ownership risks in management contracts, owners are beginning to take advantage of the increased competition among operators, shifting risks formerly assumed by the owner to the operator.

As *owner bargaining strength increases,* the provisions of concern tend to be negotiated with the following outcomes:

— Nature of contractual arrangement: Concept of independent operator replaces the concept of agency. Indemnification of owner by operator is included. Operator's sole and exclusive right to manage remains unchanged, but owner gains additional options and approval rights in other contract provisions.

— Operator loan and equity contribution: The operator offers a nominal loan contribution that is increased in amount if necessary. An operator equity contribution may be substituted depending upon mutually agreeable objectives of both parties. The amount may first cover working capital, but may be expanded to include inventories, furniture, fixtures, and equipment, or a specified amount to be applied to operating deficits.

— Term of contract: Initial term length, number of renewal terms, and length of renewal terms tend to decrease. Options to renew sometimes shift to the owner or are tied to the operator's achieving specified performance objectives.

— Management fees: Technical-assistance and pre-opening management fees become negotiable. Incentive management fees play a greater role in the basic-incentive fee mix. Incentive fees are subordinated to a predetermined cash flow or are tiered with debt-service obligations and, sometimes, with a return on equity.

— Operator system-reimbursable expenses: Systematic monitoring of expenses increases. Dollar-amount limitations may be placed upon specific items.

— Contract termination by owner: Operator performance provisions are often included. Owner occasionally obtains right to terminate without cause for a termination fee. Right of first offer is substituted for right of first refusal in event of a sale.

— Personnel: Property employees may become employees of the operator. Owner may obtain the right to review and approve selection of general manager.

— Budgeting and spending limitations: Owner's approval rights for operating, reserve for replacement, and capital improvements/additions budgets increase. Replacement funds are on-call rather than in escrow accounts.

— Banking, accounting, and financial reporting: Cash-balance amounts required by operators become negotiable. Requirements for financial reporting become more specific to include submission of market plan, management analysis of operations, cash-flow projections, and audited reconciliation of operator system-reimbursable expenses.

— Dispute settlement: Dispute settlement or arbitration provisions are added and provisions subject to arbitration increase.

— Restrictive covenants: Geographical area in which operator is restricted from operating may be enlarged. Exclusions may decrease.

The effects of the four relative bargaining-strength positions on the provisions of concern negotiated are illustrated in Exhibits III-15 through III-18 for each of four operator-owner relationships (domestic contracts between chain operators and developer-owners, domestic contracts between independent operators and developer-owners, domestic contracts between operators and owners-in-foreclosure, and international contracts between operators and developer-owners).

C. Provisions of Concern During the Term of the Contract

Concerns left unresolved during the contract negotiations tend to escalate during the term of the contract but can be reduced if certain operating results or owner-operator compromises are reached. When property performance meets both owner and operator expectations, the contract relationship generally follows the functional lines outlined in the contract. When financial expectations are not met, concerns expand into the operational area as one party attempts to resolve the financial concerns by altering the contractual relationships involving the owner, the operator's corporate staff, and the property's general manager. If these operational concerns remain unresolved, the aggrieved party attempts to take legal action against the other party to the contract. If the concern is not resolved at this juncture, the contract is unilaterally terminated. When concerns at each level are satisfactorily addressed and the conditions ameliorated, concerns return to the next lower level. The expansion of concern from one level to the next can be initiated by either the owner or the operator, but is usually initiated by the owner because he generally bears a greater financial risk than does the operator.

Three underlying factors were identified as contributing to owner and operator concerns during the term of the contract. The first factor is the failure of the owner and the operator to evaluate the proposed project critically—to establish the compatibility of owner and operator objectives and to determine the proposed project's ability to achieve these objectives.

The second factor is the nature of the triangular relationship of the owner, the operator's corporate staff, and the general manager, and the division of legal and operating responsibilities as outlined in the management contract. The contractual relationship and division of responsibilities dictate that the owner must accept the financial results of the property but may lack the authority to influence those financial results. If the owner is dissatisfied with the financial results, he attempts to skew the relationship and division of responsibilities by actively participating in the operation of the property.

The third factor is the failure of the operator to establish and coordinate an effective communications network within the triangular relationship. An owner experiences concern when he concludes the operator is failing to provide accurate information for the education of the owner in the hotel business; supply the owner with realistic projections and advise him of strategies designed to achieve those projections; or communicate to the owner the property's operating problems and the cause of variances from budgeted figures.

Operators' past attempts to establish effective communication networks have seldom been successful, resulting in owner and operator misperceptions of the other party's intentions.

D. Preparing for Negotiations

To prepare for negotiations, each party should:

Assess his position, establishing his objectives for the hotel project, evaluating his bargaining strength, and identifying his concerns regarding the management contract.

Assess the other party, analyzing his past performance, present level of expertise, and short- and long-term plans and strategies.

Conduct a thorough analysis of the proposed project's likely financial performance, including **(1)** a market profile; **(2)** a long-term capital-investment analysis to determine the returns available to the owner and to the operator; and **(3)** a short-term cash-flow projection covering the critical pre-opening and start-up period. Computer-analysis techniques can be extremely helpful in assessing various financing and management-fee structures as well as conducting sensitivity analyses on key variables in the projections.

Develop going-in and fall-back positions to be used during the actual negotiating process.

This procedure, as outlined in Chapter V, does not guarantee the elimination of unrealistic expectations or of misunderstandings, but it does permit ample opportunity for potential problems to surface and be addressed. The mutual trust essential to successful negotiations develops from the candor and cooperation of the parties during the steps listed above.

E. Management Contracts for Commercial Restaurants

Management contracts for commercial restaurant operators tend to exist in two specific types of situations: when an owner develops a free-standing commercial restaurant, wishes to lease it, and the operator is not willing to assume the downside risk associated with a lease; or when an owner operates a hospitality or other multi-purpose facility but wishes to employ an operator to manage the restaurant operations within the facility.

Operator and owner rights and responsibilities in restaurant contracts parallel closely those in hotel contracts but center on more explicit agreements involving operating policies such as the establishment of hours, days, and seasons of operation, type and extent of services to be offered, and pricing decisions especially when prices are coordinated with non-restaurant services.

Operators seldom make loan or equity contributions in restaurant contracts. The initial length of the contract term ranges from three to ten years. Management fees are usually based upon a basic-incentive fee mix with basic fees being a fixed amount or a percentage or revenues and the incentive fee being a percentage of a negotiated profit level. Conditions for contract termination are similar in nature to those found in hotel contracts.

In most contracts, the owner has the right to approve the budget, but his approval cannot be unreasonably withheld. Seldom is a reserve-for-replacement fund established. Provisions providing for dispute settlement are absent in more than half of the contracts reviewed; those contracts that contain dispute settlements provisions utilize procedures similar to those contained in hotel contracts. Restrictive covenants are of major concern to restaurant owners; they are willing to grant exceptions within the restricted area only if the operator's other facilities differ significantly in theme, concept, and type of service offerred.

F. Conclusions

On the basis of the author's research, the following conclusions are advanced:

— Despite controversy concerning its fairness to the parties, the management contract has become a firmly established operating-agreement form in the United States lodging industry.

— The rapid and widespread adoption of management contracts prevented an orderly evolution of the management-contract concept. The rush by lenders to lend, owners to build, and operators to expand the number of properties they managed created a preoccupation with growth and left too little time for an adequate evaluation of the concept.

— The unexpected recession of the mid-1970s dramatically revealed to owners the significant downside risk that accompanies the potential for high returns from hotel investments and the restrictions placed upon owners under the management-contract form of operating agreement.

— The nature of the contractual arrangement creates an unhappy situation for the owner: he is responsible for the property's financial results but does not have the authority to influence them. The investor's limited control over the productivity of his assets leads to ownership concerns both expressed during negotiations and during the term of the contract.

— Owners are not willing to assume full financial risk without maintaining some degree of influence or control over operations.

— Operators are unwilling to enter into contracts that do not assure them adequate compensation for their commitment of effort and funds during the early years of a contract's life.

— The recent shift toward a more equitable balance between owner and operator bargaining strengths is a favorable trend for the hotel industry and for the future employment of management contracts. The contract provisions currently being negotiated transfer some of the owner's financial risk to the operator, provide for increased owner influence in operational matters, and create greater incentives for operators.

— When the economy is healthy, fewer concerns are expressed during the term of the contract; in times of an economic downturn or of overbuilding, concerns increase.

— The compatibility of the owner's and the operator's short-, intermediate-, and long-term objectives is essential to the success of a management contract. A critical evaluation of these objectives, as outlined in Chapter V, should be performed jointly by the owner and the operator before they enter into a contract.

— An effective communications network linking the owner, the operator's corporate office, and the general manager is essential to the success of a management contract.

— Operators and owners must share their management-contract experiences so that both groups may benefit. The formation of the American Hotel & Motel Association's International Council of Hotel-Motel Management Companies was the first major effort in this direction.

G. Implications for the Future

Having surveyed the available information, the author concludes that the following trends are probable:

— The number of management contracts will continue to increase. Chain operators will expand contract management with large (300 or more rooms), full-service properties, while independent operators will expand by managing smaller, market-segmented properties. The number of contracts between owners-in-foreclosure and operators will also increase during the next several years as the number of distressed properties increases.

— As competition among operators for additional properties heightens, the bargaining power of owners will continue to increase.

— Owners will bargain for and receive concessions from operators, resulting in greater sharing of operating and financial responsibilities. Operator loan and equity contributions will more likely be the rule rather than the exception, especially in large hotel ventures. Operator performance provisions will become more numerous as long as performance criteria are viewed by both parties to be reasonable and flexible. Owner initiated termination-without-cause provisions incorporating penalty fees to protect the time and effort invested by the operator will become more prevalent. Management fee structures will place greater emphasis on the incentive fee, reducing the portion of the management company's revenues derived from the basic fee. The tiering of management fees with ownership returns will become common in most contracts.

— Operators dissatisfied with the increase in owner influence will be forced to return to traditional ownership, lease, or franchise arrangements as vehicles for further growth.

— As hotel companies gain more experience operating under management contracts, more effective communication procedures will develop to facilitate information exchange in the relationship of owner, operator, and general manager.

— Greater emphasis will be placed on cooperative owner-operator analysis and planning of new projects to determine the feasibility of satisfying both parties' objectives. Increased use of computer-aided analysis techniques will assist in the decision-making process.

— Competition for properties among chain operating companies will continue to increase. The ability of chain operating companies to provide loans and/or equity contributions, to be flexible in negotiating contract provisions, and to service contracts adequately will determine their success in maintaining present contracts and obtaining new ones.

— As a group, independent operating companies should maintain their competitive niche, serving properties of fewer than 300 rooms without significant competition from chain operators.

— As competition for the number of foreclosed and new properties intensifies, there will be a continued reduction in the number of independent operating companies. Some independent operating companies will merge to maintain their competitive status; others will simply go out of business. Independent operating companies that maintain or improve their competitive strength will have above-average managerial talent, sophisticated management information and analysis systems, and adequate funds to make loan and equity contributions.

— One to two dozen strong, regional independent operating companies will probably surface, with each controlling 10 to 20 properties. Those attempting to expand to a national base will probably lose their control and effectiveness, as has been the experience of independent operating companies striving for similar widespread growth in the past.

— Both chain and independent operating companies will gain reputations for strengths in different areas of expertise—financial, marketing, controls, food and beverage, etc.—and owners wishing emphasis in a particular area will seek out operators who best fulfill their needs.

— The restaurant-contract concept has, as has the hotel-contract concept, matured in recent years and can offer, if negotiated astutely, an equitable business agreement between owner and operator.

— Significant future growth in the growth of management contracts for commercial restaurants is uncertain due to more profitable options and opportunites that may exist for operators to own or to lease restaurants that offer good value and are well-targeted to existing, adequate markets.

Appendix A:

Description of Management-Contract Provisions

This appendix provides an overview of the management-contract agreement. It enumerates the provisions contained in contracts, indicates how frequently each occurs and what the common variations of each provision are, and assesses the relative degree to which each provision is of concern to the owner and to the operator during contract negotiations and during the term of the contract. The provisions of concern to owners and operators are discussed in Chapter III.

Typical management-contract agreements vary in length from a three-page letter briefly outlining contract provisions to an 85-page legal document detailing each contract provision and the specific steps each party is permitted to take in response to a variety of contingencies.

The order of the contract provisions presented below is that of the most widely used contract format. The first ten sections are contained in contracts for a property in which the operator assumes no supervisory or managerial responsibilities during the property's pre-opening phases. Sections XI through XIII are part of contracts in which the operator assumes an active role in the management of the property's pre-opening phase.

The wording of the following provisions and their variations in this Appendix have been adapted from actual contracts to represent the typical language of hotel-management contracts. The frequency of occurrence of specific contract provisions has been indicated separately for chain-operator contracts and independent-operator contracts. Common variations on standard provisions are discussed in Chapter III. The reader should refer to Chapter III when attempting to structure provisions for a specific property, since a more detailed analysis is presented there. The contract provisions the author found to be of concern to the owner or the operator are so indicated through notations in the two right-hand columns. The word "Owner" or "Operator" appears in **boldface** when the provision is of major concern to the party indicated; it appears in regular type when the provision is of moderate concern.

Format of a Typical Management Contract

Section Heading	Section Title
I.	General Provisions
II.	Operator's duties
III.	Management fees
IV.	General covenants of owner and operator
V.	Trade name
VI.	Notices
VII.	Successors and assigns
VIII.	Condemnation of, damage to, or destruction of property
IX.	Termination rights
X.	Miscellaneous provisions
XI.	Construction of property
XII.	Opening date
XIII.	Pre-opening management services

EXHIBIT A-1

Description of Management-Contract Provisions

Provisions	Frequency of Occurrence: Chain	Frequency of Occurrence: Independent	Comments on Variations of Provisions	Concern* during: Negotiations	Concern* during: Term
Section I—General provisions			**I.**		
A. Introduction (paragraphs beginning with "whereas")			A.		
1. Owner owns hotel (motor inn) completely constructed, furnished, and equipped.	100%	100%	1. "Owner proposes to construct, has leased, or expects to become lessee of . . ."	—	—
2. Operator is qualified in supervision, operation, and management of hotels (motor inns).	100%	59%	**2.** —	—	Owner
3. Owner turns over to operator all control and discretion in the operation, direction, management, and supervision of the property.	100%	100%	**3.** —	**Owner Operator**	**Owner**
4. Operator desires to assume all such control and discretion upon terms set forth in this agreement.	100%	100%	**4.** —	—	—
B. Definitions [includes terms of basic fee, budget (annual plan), building, fiscal year, franchise, furnishings, operating equipment, incentive fee, operator, operating supplies, operating year, owner, property, replacement reserve, term, renewal term, working capital, debt service, gross revenues, gross operating profit, net profit, executive staff, operating expenses, annual house profit, accounting period, opening date, premises, capital improvements, technical-assistance services, and group services].	100%	100%	**B.** All chain contracts and 34% of independent contracts list definitions here; 66% of independent contracts list definitions throughout contract.	—	—
C. Owner's Title			**C.**		
1. Owner is owner or lessee of the property and has full power and authority to enter into agreement.	100%	100%	**1.** —	—	—
2. Property is zoned for use as a hotel (motor inn).	60%	31%	**2.** —	—	—
3. Owner owns all necessary food and liquor licenses authorizing sale and consumption upon the premises.	10%	45%	**3.** Operator occasionally owns licenses.	Owner Operator	—
4. Owner will keep in full force and effect the franchise, if any, and will comply with all terms and conditions of such franchise required to be performed by the owner.	10%	21%	**4.** Operator occasionally holds the franchise; 30% of chain contracts state that if management contract terminates prior to termination of the franchise license agreement, the franchise shall remain in effect until its termination.	—	—

5. Owner convenants that operator shall and may peacefully and quietly possess, manage, and operate the property during the operating term, and owner will, at its expense, undertake to assume such peaceful and quiet possession by the operator.	40%	3%	**5.** —	—	—
D. Term			**D.**		
1. This agreement shall remain in effect for an initial period of ________ years, commencing ______________ , 19______ .	100%	100%	**1.** Length of initial term for chain operators ranges from 10 to 30 years, the median being 20 years; length of initial term for independent operators ranges from 6 months to 25 years, the median being 5 years.	Owner **Operator**	—
2. This agreement shall be automatically renewed for ________ successive ________-year terms unless terminated upon ______ days' written notice by operator.	100%	93%	**2.** Number of renewal terms for chain operators ranges from 2 to 3 terms, with the length of a renewal term ranging from 5 to 20 years; number of renewal terms for independent operators ranges from 1 to 5 terms with the length of a renewal term ranging from 1 to 10 years; several independent operator contracts can be canceled by owner at any time after initial term if owner pays a predetermined cancellation penality fee.	Owner **Operator**	—
E. Sole and exclusive right. Owner grants sole and exclusive right to supervise and direct the management and operation of the property.	100%	100%	**E.** The phrase "without interference from owner" is occasionally added.	Owner **Operator**	Owner **Operator**
F. Operator as agent			**F.**		
1. Operator shall act solely in behalf of and as agent for owner and not in its own behalf.	100%	100%	**1.** —	**Owner Operator**	—
2. All debts, obligations, and other liabilities incurred by the operator in performance of its duties shall be incurred in behalf of the owner, and the operator shall not be liable for the payment of any such debts, obligations, and other liabilities.	100%	90%	**2.** —	**Owner Operator**	**Owner**
3. If any such debts or obligations are paid by the operator, it shall be entitled to reimbursement by owner.	100%	90%	**3.** Operator can withdraw reimbursable funds from operating cash flow.	—	—

***Boldface** type indicates major concern; regular type indicates moderate concern.

Appendix A, Description of Management-Contract Provisions (continued)

Provisions	Frequency of Occurrence: Chain	Independent	Comments on Variations of Provisions	Concern* during: Negotiations	Term
Section II—Operator's duties			**II.**		
A. Operating policies			**A.**		
1. To provide such services as are customarily provided by operators of hotels, motor hotels, or resorts of comparable class and standing, consistent with the property's facilities.	100%	90%	**1.** Chain operators add "in accordance with standards and policies established by [chain name] for the operation of all other [chain name] properties."	—	Owner
2. To keep owner advised as to all major policy matters affecting the property.	100%	100%	**2.** —	—	Owner
3. Operator will make no major policy change not reflected in the budget without prior approval of owner.	40%	72%	**3.** —	—	Owner
4. Operator shall have all reasonable discretion in the operation, direction, management, and supervision of the property.	100%	93%	**4.** Operator shall use "best efforts," "due diligence," "professional expertise."	—	—
5. Operator shall use its best efforts to operate and manage the property in compliance with the rules or requirements of any frachisor with whom the owner may have a franchise agreement.	0%	28%	**5.** —	—	—
B. Establishment of prices. To establish prices and rate schedules for guest rooms, meeting rooms, commercial space, food, beverage, and other salable or rentable items making up the property or its business.	100%	100%	**B.** Operator occasionally required to obtain owner's approval of specific price and rate schedules.	Owner Operator	Owner
C. Submission of budget			**C.**		
1. Operator shall submit to owner for its approval an annual budget of operations ________ days before the beginning of each fiscal year.	100%	97%	**1.** Usually includes schedules of room rentals, expected special repairs and maintenance terms, and capital-replacement items; submission date varies between 30 and 90 days prior to the beginning of each fiscal year.	—	—
2. If the budget is disapproved by owner, operator and owner shall enter into negotiations in an effort to determine a mutually satisfactory budget.	20%	48%	**2.** —	—	—
3. Operator may deviate from such budget if in operator's reasonable judgment a deviation is necessary or desirable for the efficient operation of the property.	100%	83%	**3.** Written approval of owner often necessary.	Owner	**Owner** Operator

4. Operator makes no guarantee, warranty, or representation whatsoever in connection with the budget, such being intended as reasonable estimates only.	70%	63%	**4.** —	—	—
5. Minimum and maximum amounts for certain expenditures established in budget.	80%	55%	**5.** Usually includes minimum and maximum amounts for advertising, repairs and maintenance, and replacement of furnishings and equipment based upon a percentage of gross revenues, a specified dollar amount per room, or a specified dollar amount; operator required to receive owner's written approval for excess expenditures.	Owner	—
D. Personnel			**D.**		
1. To hire, promote, discharge, and supervise the work of the executive staff (i.e., general manager, assistant managers, and department heads) of the property and supervise through said executive staff the hiring, promotion, discharge, and work of all other operating and service employees performing services in or about the property, all in the name of the owner.	100%	100%	**1.** Occasionally employees are employed in the name of operator; operator is then reimbursed by owner for all employee compensation payroll taxes, and fringe benefits.	**Owner Operator**	—
2. All employees shall be on owner's payroll and operator shall not be liable to such employees for their wages or compensation.	100%	100%	**2.** Same as (1) above.	**Owner Operator**	—
3. Operator will negotiate, on owner's behalf, with any labor union lawfully entitled to represent such employees, but any collective-bargaining agreements or labor contracts resulting therefrom shall be first approved by owner who shall be the only authorized person to execute the same.	80%	69%	**3.** —	—	—
4. Operator will not enter into any agreement with an employee for an annual basic salary in excess of $______ without the consent in writing of owner.	70%	86%	**4.** Amount ranges from $12,000 to $20,000.	—	—
5. Since the general manager may need to reside at the property and be available full-time to perform properly the duties of his employment, he may receive, free of charge and in addition to his salary, free room and board and reimbursement for any expenses which he may reasonably incur in performance of his duties.	100%	93%	**5.** —	—	—

*__Boldface__ type indicates major concern; regular type indicates moderate concern.

Appendix A, Description of Management-Contract Provisions (continued)

Provisions	Frequency of Occurrence: Chain	Independent	Comments on Variations of Provisions	Concern* during: Negotiations	Term
6. The general manager shall be an employee of operator, and owner shall reimburse operator monthly for the manager's salary and fringe benefits.	100%	100%	**6.** The general manager is often an employee of the owner.	**Operator**	**Operator**
7. Operator may assign other employees of operator as members of the property's executive staff and have such employees treated as employees of owner, and owner shall reimburse operator monthly for their salaries and fringe benefits.	100%	90%	**7.** Same as (1) above.	—	Owner
8. Operator may, with owner's approval, find it desirable to assign one or more of its supervisory employees to the property on a temporary basis. Owner agrees to reimburse operator for all actual expenses to and from the property and for all room and board while at the property for such employees.	100%	90%	**8.** —	—	—
9. Owner shall not interfere or give orders or instructions to personnel employed at the property.	100%	76%	**9.** —	**Owner** **Operator**	**Owner** **Operator**
10. Operator may change or replace the general manager of the property at any time. The decision in regard to any change or replacement shall be at the sole discretion of the operator.	100%	83%	**10.** —	Operator	Owner
11. Owner agrees that if the general manager of the property leaves the employ of operator for any reason owner shall not hire the general manager in any capacity for at least one year following such termination.	10%	72%	**11.** Time period ranges from 1 to 3 years.	**Operator**	Owner
E. Arrangements with concessionaires. To consummate, in the name and for the benefit of the owner, arrangements with concessionaires, licensees, and tenants, or other intended users of the facilities of the property.	100%	93%	**E.** Consummation is often subject to owner's approval, which owner agrees not to withhold unreasonably; in some instances, operator "shall advise owner as to the advisability of maintaining the franchise license, obtaining another franchise, or operating without any franchise affiliation. Operator will negotiate any new franchise."	—	—

F. Service contracts			**F.**		
1. Operator shall negotiate and enter into service contracts required in the ordinary course of business in operating the property, including, without limitation, contracts for electricity, gas, telephone, cleaning, vermin extermination, elevator and boiler maintenance, and other services which operator deems advisable.	100%	97%	**1.** —	—	—
2. No contract for more than ________ year(s) or involving an expenditure of more than $________ in the aggregate shall be entered into without owner's consent.	60%	24%	**2.** Term varies from 1 to 5 years; amount of expenditure ranges from $1,000 to $25,000, depending upon the size of the property; in emergency situations, operator can enter into contracts in excess of the agreed-upon sum.	—	—
G. Purchase of operating supplies			**G.**		
1. Operator shall purchase or arrange for the purchase of all inventories, provisions, supplies, and operating equipment which in the normal course of business are necessary to maintain and operate the property properly.	100%	100%	**1.** —	Owner	—
2. At operator's discretion, all or any part of such purchases may be made in operator's or owner's name.	70%	72%	**2.** —	—	—
3. Owner shall be credited with the full amount of any discounts or commissions obtained by operator on any of such purchases.	50%	79%	**3.** —	Owner	—
H. Repairs, replacements, and improvements			**H.**		
1. Operator shall make or install, or cause to be made or installed, at owner's expense and in the name of owner, all necessary or desirable repairs, decorations, renewals, revisions, alterations, rebuildings, replacements, additions, and improvements in and to the site, building, furnishings, and equipment; provided, however, that such are included in the budget or do not exceed $________ per item.	100%	100%	**1.** Approximately 20% of the contracts contain no dollar limitations. Dollar limitations range from $500 to $100,000, depending upon the size of the property.	Owner	—
2. Operator shall be required to obtain the written consent of owner before entering into any contract, agreement, or purchase if the amount payable exceeds the amount specified in (1) above.	100%	66%	**2.** In emergency situations, operator can enter into contracts in excess of the agreed-upon sum without prior approval of owner.	—	—
I. Licenses and permits			**I.**		
1. Operator shall apply for and obtain and maintain in the name and at the expense of owner all licenses and permits required of the owner or operator in connection with the management and operation of the property.	100%	100%	**1.** Occasionally, the owner or operator is entitled to terminate the agreement upon 10 days' notice to the other party in the event such licenses or permits cannot be obtained or retained.	—	—

*__Boldface__ type indicates major concern; regular type indicates moderate concern.

Appendix A, Description of Management-Contract Provisions (continued)

Provisions	Frequency of Occurrence: Chain	Independent	Comments on Variations of Provisions	Concern* during: Negotiations	Term
2. Owner agrees to execute and deliver any and all applications and other documents and to otherwise cooperate to the fullest extent with operator in applying for, obtaining, and maintaining such licenses and permits.	80%	86%	**2.** —	—	—
J. Laws and ordinances			**J.**		
1. Operator shall make all reasonable effort at owner's expense to comply with all applicable laws, rules, regulations, requirements, and ordinances of any federal, state, or municipal authority, including any alcoholic beverage control board or board of fire underwriters, and the requirements of any insurance companies covering any of the risks against which the property is insured.	60%	55%	**1.** —	—	—
2. Owner shall have the right at owner's expense to contest or to have operator contest by proper legal proceedings the validity or application of the above.	60%	48%	**2.** —	—	—
3. If owner's failure to comply with the above would result in the suspension of operations of the property or would expose owner or operator to danger of criminal liability, then operator may, but shall not be obligated to, cause the same to be complied with at owner's expense.	50%	21%	**3.** —	—	—
K. Banking			**K.**		
1. Operator shall deposit in a banking institution in accounts in operator's name all monies furnished by owner as working capital and all monies received by operator for or on behalf of owner and to disburse and pay the same as required in connection with the ownership, maintenance, and operation of the property, to include: taxes; all costs and expenses of maintaining, operating, and supervising the operation of the property, including compensation for operator; and reserves for replacement.	100%	100%	**1.** Often, monies are deposited in owner's name, with operator the only party authorized to withdraw funds; operator may be authorized to pay mortgage payment and land rent; operator's representatives signing checks or withdrawing funds must usually be bonded.	Owner	—
2. Subject to maintaining reasonable reserves for replacements and working-capital requirements, operator, at owner's request, shall transfer such funds as owner shall request to a bank account opened and maintained solely by owner.	100%	100%	**2.** Transfer can also be made monthly or quarterly on an automatic basis.	—	—

3. Monies received by operator in the operation of the property shall not be mingled with operator's own funds.	50%	24%	**3.** —	Owner	—
L. Insurance			**L.**		
1. Owner shall provide or operator shall purchase, at owner's expense, public and employer's liability, workmen's compensation, fire and extended coverage, and other such customary insurance deemed necessary for the protection of the interests of owner or operator, and shall name both owner and operator as insured parties.	100%	100%	1. A specific dollar amount of coverage is usually listed for each type of insurance.	Operator	—
2. Operator may make available to owner the opportunity to reduce insurance costs by participating with other properties operated by operator in blanket insurance policies.	60%	31%	**2.** —	—	—
3. Owner assumes all risks in connection with the adequacy of any insurance program.	100%	97%	**3.** —	—	—
4. Owner releases operator from any liability for any damage or destruction to the property caused by any act or omission on part of operator.	100%	86%	**4.** —	Owner	—
M. Accounting and financial statements			**M.**		
1. On or before the end of each calendar month, operator shall deliver to owner a profit-and-loss statement showing results of property's operation for the preceding calendar month and fiscal year to date and to include a computation of the management fee.	100%	100%	1. The monthly statements can often be prepared by the independent public accountants who prepare the annual statements. Owner often requires monthly statement of changes in financial position.	Owner	—
2. Within ninety days after the end of each fiscal year, operator will deliver to owner a balance sheet and profit-and-loss statement, including supporting schedules prepared by independent public accountants approved by both operator and owner.	100%	100%	**2.** —	Owner	—
3. All costs and expenses incurred in connection with the preparation of statements, budgets, and computations shall be borne by owner.	100%	86%	**3.** —	—	—
N. Legal actions for tenant or guest default			**N.**		
1. Operator shall institute, in its own name or in name of owner, but at expense of owner, legal actions or proceedings to collect charges or rent, to oust guests or tenants, or to cancel or terminate leases for breach or default.	60%	55%	1. —	—	—

*__Boldface__ type indicates major concern; regular type indicates moderate concern.

Appendix A, Description of Management-Contract Provisions (continued)

Provisions	Frequency of Occurrence: Chain	Independent	Comments on Variations of Provisions	Concern* during: Negotiations	Term
2. Operator must receive owner's prior consent before instituting legal actions or proceedings to oust tenants having an unexpired term of one year or more.	60%	49%	**2.** —	—	—
O. Legal actions to protest court decision against property			**O.**		
1. Unless otherwise directed by owner, operator may (but shall not be obligated to) take at owner's expense appropriate steps to protest or litigate final court decisions for any violation, order, rule, or regulation affecting the property.	40%	38%	**1.** —	—	—
2. Any counsel to be engaged shall be mutually approved by owner and operator.	40%	38%	**2.** —	—	—
P. Advertising and promotion			**P.**		
1. Operator shall arrange and contract for, at owner's expense, all advertising and promotion which operator may deem necessary for the operation of the property.	100%	100%	**1.** —	Owner	—
2. The property generally shall be advertised by operator as part of the [operator's name] system.	100%	21%	**2.** —	—	—
3. If advertising is supplied in conjunction with advertising for other of operator's owned, operated, or affiliated properties, cost of such advertising shall be prorated to properties benefited.	80%	21%	**3.** Based on a dollar amount per room or on a percentage of gross rooms revenue.	Owner	Owner
4. No expense for advertising and promotion in excess of the budget for any fiscal year shall be incurred or contracted for by operator without owner's approval.	80%	72%	**4.** Budgeted amount normally 3 to 4% of gross revenues.	—	—
5. Owner authorizes operator to accept operator-sponsored credit card and all other credit cards designated by operator for charges authorized in accordance with operator's credit-card billing system.	60%	0%	**5.** —	—	—
6. Owner shall be charged for costs of reservations equipment directly allocable to the property and for each reservation originating through operator's reservation system.	90%	0%	**6.** —	—	—

Q. Group services			**Q.**		
1. Operator shall provide those group benefits, services, and facilities generally made available by operator of other operator-owned or operator-managed properties, to include: convention, business, and sales-promotion services; advertising and public-relation services; food and beverage, personnel, and other operational departmental supervision and control services; centralized reservations services; computerized management-information service; accounting services for payroll accounts payable; accounts receivable and financial-statements preparation; educational and training programs and facilities; and central purchasing and procuring services.	100%	62%	**1.** Extent of group services varies, depending upon ability of operator to offer them; owner is usually required to receive all group services except the accounting and purchasing services, which he may elect to receive.	**Owner**	Owner
2. Owner shall not charge any profit for these services but shall be entitled to reimbursement for the cost of those specific services elected by owner to be performed centrally and for the property's pro-rata share of all costs and expenses incurred in connection with the rendition of group advertising, business promotion, and reservations services, allocated on the same basis as allocated to other properties owned or operated by the operator.	100%	55%	**2.** Pro-rata allocation usually based on the number of guest rooms; separate charges are made for services owner elects to receive.	Owner	Owner
3. Operator shall provide a statement to owner supporting group-service charges.	70%	52%	**3.** In addition, owner usually has right to have operator's books audited to substantiate charges.	—	Owner
Section III—Management fees			**III.**		
A. As compensation for the services to be rendered by operator, owner shall pay to operator a management fee. On the first day of each month, owner shall be sent a statement and shall pay the basic fee derived from the property from the preceding month; the incentive fee, if any, shall be paid by owner upon delivery to owner of the profit-and-loss statement and fee computation.	100%	100%	**A.** The management fee may be: (1) a basic fee only; (2) a basic fee plus an incentive fee; or (3) a basic fee or an incentive fee, whichever is greater. The basic fee may be: (1) a flat dollar amount; (2) a stipulated percentage of gross revenues; or (3) a flat dollar amount *or* a stipulated percentage of gross revenues, whichever is greater. The incentive fee may be: (1) a percentage of the gross operating profit, which is sometimes subordinated to the adequacy of operating cash flow for debt-service payments; (2) a percentage of operating cash flow after debt service; or (3) a percentage of the increase in gross revenues achieved. Specific fee structures are discussed in Chapter II.	**Owner** **Operator**	Owner

*__Boldface__ type indicates major concern; regular type indicates moderate concern.

Appendix A, Description of Management-Contract Provisions (continued)

Provisions	Frequency of Occurrence: Chain	Independent	Comments on Variations of Provisions	Concern* during: Negotiations	Term
B. Gross revenues and gross operating profits shall be determined in accordance with the Uniform System of Accounts for Hotels.	100%	79%	**B.** —	—	—
Section IV—General convenants of owner and operator			**IV.**		
A. Books and records			**A.**		
1. Operator shall keep on behalf of owner full and adequate books of accounts reflecting the results of the operation of the property.	100%	86%	**1.** Books are usually kept in accordance with the Uniform System of Accounts for Hotels.	—	—
2. Books and records shall be kept at the property or other such place as the parties agree.	100%	76%	**2.** Books and records are often kept at operator's central office if operator performs centralized accounting services for owner.	—	—
3. Proper identification must be given to operator before inspection or review is granted.	40%	66%	**3.** —	—	—
B. Opening inventories and working capital			**B.**		
1. Owner agrees to provide at its expense sufficient initial inventories of operating supplies and to provide and maintain all working capital required for the uninterrupted and efficient operation and maintenance of the property.	100%	97%	**1.** Operator occasionally provides initial working capital.	**Owner** **Operator**	Owner
2. Operator shall in no event be required to advance any of its own funds for the operation of the property.	60%	83%	**2.** —	—	Owner
C. Operating expenses. Owner shall be solely liable for the costs and expenses of maintaining and operating the property and shall pay all costs and expenses of maintaining, operating, and supervising the operation of the property, including without limitation the salaries of all of its personnel.	100%	100%	**C.** —	—	—
D. Owner's right of inspection and review. Operator shall accord to owner and its duly authorized agents the right to enter upon any part of the property at all reasonable times for the purpose of examining or inspecting the property, its records, or operation or any other purpose which owner, in its discretion, shall deem advisable.	90%	93%	**D.** It is often stipulated that operator must be given proper identification by inspecting party before operator will grant right to inspect and review.	—	Owner

E. Replacement reserve			**E.**		
1. Replacement reserve shall be created by owner in accordance with the annual budget for the purpose of making capital replacements, substitutions, and additions to the furnishing and equipment of the property.	100%	72%	**1.** Amount placed in reserve each year is based upon either a specified dollar amount per room, which increases annually from the first year through the sixth year of operation, or upon a predetermined percentage of gross revenue (1–4%) up to a maximum dollar amount per room; the dollar amount per room is often adjusted upward in accordance with the Cost of Living Index.	Owner Operator	**Owner**
2. Such funds will be deposited in an account in operator's name.	100%	72%	**2.** Usually deposited by operator in trust for owner.	Owner	—
3. Any expenditure for replacement, substitution, and additions during each fiscal year may be made by operator without owner's consent up to the then-remaining balance in such reserve fund.	60%	58%	**3.** Occasionally, operator must obtain written approval of owner to spend amounts over a stipulated amount, even though balance of the reserve exceeds the desired expenditure.	Owner	—
4. Any expenditure in excess of the reserve fund shall be subject to owner's approval, which approval shall not be unreasonably withheld.	80%	52%	**4.** The phrase "which approval shall not be unreasonably withheld" is often not in the provision.	Owner	—
5. Upon termination of the agreement, any remaining balance of the reserve fund shall be paid to owner.	100%	72%	**5.** —	—	—
F. Right of set-off. Operator shall have the right to set-off against any payments to be made to owner by operator hereunder and against all funds from time to time in the bank accounts provided for herein.	50%	28%	**F.** —	—	—
G. Indemnification of operator			**G.**		
1. Operator shall not be liable to owner or to any other person for any act or omission, negligent, tortious, or otherwise, of any agent or employee of owner or operator in the performance of this agreement, except only the fraud or gross negligence of operator.	90%	97%	**1.** —	**Owner Operator**	**Owner Operator**
2. Owner hereby agrees to indemnify and hold harmless operator from and against any liability, loss, damage, cost, or expense (including attorneys' fees) by reason of such act or omission.	80%	52%	**2.** —	**Owner Operator**	**Owner Operator**

*__Boldface__ type indicates major concern; regular type indicates moderate concern.

Appendix A, Description of Management-Contract Provisions (continued)

Provisions	Frequency of Occurrence: Chain	Independent	Comments on Variations of Provisions	Concern* during: Negotiations	Term
H. Restrictive covenant (noncompetition). As long as this agreement is in full force and effect, owner or operator will not, directly or indirectly, own, operate, manage, or otherwise have an interest in any other similar establishment within a radius of ________ miles of the property.	30%	7%	**H.** Occasionally restricted only to operator or to owner; occasionally restricted to a particular franchise; geographical area may be expressed in miles (2 to 10) or by a listing of specific counties.	Owner Operator	—
I. Arbitration and litigation			**I.**		
1. Any and all disputes and controversies arising out of or in any manner relating to the performance of this agreement which cannot be settled by agreement between operator and owner shall be settled by arbitration in accordance with the rules, then obtaining, of the American Arbitration Association.	80%	41%	**1.** —	Owner	Owner Operator
2. This agreement shall be enforceable, and judgment upon any award rendered by all or a majority of the arbitrators may be entered in any court having jurisdiction.	60%	38%	**2.** —	—	—
3. The arbitrator or arbitrators shall have the right only to interpret and apply the terms of this agreement, and may not change any such terms or deprive any party to this agreement of any right or remedy expressly or implicitly provided in this agreement.	20%	10%	**3.** —	—	—
4. The expenses of arbitration shall be borne equally by operator and owner.	60%	17%	**4.** —	—	—
5. In the event a dispute arises under this agreement which results in litigation, such litigation shall be filed only in a court of competent jurisdiction in ________ .	20%	14%	**5.** Location is usually the county in which operator's corporate office is located, but occasionally is the county where property is located.	—	—
J. Operator not to pledge owner's credit			**J.**		
1. Operator shall not pledge owner's credit without owner's prior consent except for purchases made in the ordinary course of business in the operation of the property and within the scope of this agreement.	20%	17%	**1.** —	—	—
2. Operator shall not, in the name of owner, borrow any money or execute any promissory note or other encumbrance without prior consent of owner.	10%	7%	**2.** —	—	—

Clause*			Variation		
K. Reimbursement of expenses. In the event that owner shall have advanced any funds in payment of expenses in the maintenance or operation of the property, or in performance of this agreement, owner agrees to reinburse operator for all such reasonable expenses incurred by operator.	70%	55%	**K.** —	—	—
Section V—Trade name			**V.**		
A. Trademarks and service marks of both owner and operator may be used in connection with the property, and neither party will acquire any right to any trademark or service mark of the other party.	100%	63%	**A.** —	—	—
B. Upon termination of this agreement, owner shall discontinue using trademarks and service marks in the conduct of its business and will not intentionally engage in a business or advertising practice which will lead the public to believe there is any relationship, affiliation, or identity with operator.	100%	51%	**B.** Usually, owner shall have the right to use all operating equipment and operating supplies then on hand bearing the trademarks or service marks but shall not reorder such items; operator, however, may replace such items at its own expense.	—	—
Section VI—Notices			**VI.**		
A. All notices, demands, and requests which may be or must be given by either party to the other shall be in writing.	100%	97%	**A.** Often, owner is required to designate one specific person within its firm to act as "coordinator" to whom all notices from operator will be directed.	—	—
B. Notices shall be personally delivered or sent by United States certified mail to the address set forth on the signature page hereto.	100%	93%	**B.** Either party may at any time change the address for notices to such party by delivery or mailing of a notice stating the change and setting forth the changed address.	—	—
Section VII—Successors and assigns			**VII.**		
A. Assignment by operator			**A.**		
1. Operator, without consent of owner, shall have the right to assign this agreement to any successor or assignee of operator which may result from any merger, consolidation, or reorganization, or to any corporation or firm, 50% or more of whose voting stock or control is owned directly or indirectly by operator, or to another corporation which shall acquire all or substantially all of the business and assets of operator.	100%	59%	**1.** In 41% of the independent contracts, operator must obtain owner's written consent to make the specific assignments enumerated.	—	—
2. Except as herein above provided, operator shall not assign this agreement without the prior written consent of owner.	100%	100%	**2.** See (1) above.	Owner	—

*__Boldface__ type indicates major concern; regular type indicates moderate concern.

Appendix A, Successors and Assigns, Condemnation of, Damage to, or Destruction of Property (continued)

Provisions	Frequency of Occurrence: Chain	Independent	Comments on Variations of Provisions	Concern* during: Negotiations	Term
3. Any consent granted by owner to any such assignment shall not be deemed a waiver against assignment in any subsequent case.	100%	28%	**3.** —	—	—
B. Sale, lease, or assignment by owner			**B.**		
1. Owner can sell or lease the property provided that purchaser expressly assures in writing all of the owner's obligations of this agreement.	100%	55%	**1.** Owners-in-foreclosure demand that this provision be eliminated. Operators who have right of first refusal (see (2) below) will modify this provision to read, "Owner shall not sell or lease the property or any part thereof or assign this agreement without the prior written consent of operator."	**Owner Operator**	—
2. If owner shall have received a bona fide written offer to purchase or lease the property and owner desires to sell or lease the property, owner shall give written notice to operator stating the name of the prospective purchaser or lessee and the conditions of such proposed sale or lease. Within sixty days after operator's receipt of such notice, operator shall elect, by written notice to owner, one of the following alternatives:	80%	34%	**2.** Part (a) of this provision known as operator's right of first refusal.	**Owner Operator**	—
a. To purchase or lease the property at the same price or rental and upon the same terms and conditions as those set forth in the written notice from owner to operator;			**a.** —	—	—
b. To consent to such sale or lease and to the assignment of this agreement to such purchaser or lessee, if such sale or lease is in fact consummated;			**b.** —	—	—
c. To terminate this agreement [if and only if operator shall not have exercised its rights under (a) and (b) above] at a date of termination between sixty and ninety days after the date of receipt by operator of owner's original sixty-day notice. If operator shall elect to terminate this agreement as provided in this clause, owner shall, and as a condition to such sale or lease, in the sales agreement or lease, require the prospective			**c.** —	—	—

purchaser or lessee to indemnify and save the operator harmless against any and all losses, costs, liabilities, and claims arising or resulting from the failure of owner or prospective purchaser or lessee to provide any services contracted for in connection with business booked for the property.					
3. Any consent granted by operator to any such sale, lease, or assignment shall not be deemed a waiver against sale, lease, or assignment in any subsequent case.	90%	97%	**3.** —	—	—
4. Nothing herein contained shall prevent owner from assigning this agreement to any bank, insurance company, or other financial institution as collateral security to any first mortgage on the property.	40%	21%	**4.** —	—	—
Section VIII—Condemnation of, damage to, or destruction of property			**VIII.**		
A. If all of the property shall be taken in condemnation proceedings, this agreement shall terminate as of the date of such taking.	100%	34%	**A.** —	—	—
B. If part of the property is taken or condemned by governmental action, and the operation of the remainder of the property becomes in the judgment of either owner or operator unreasonable or imprudent, either party may, upon _________ days' written notice, cancel this agreement at the expiration of such notice period.	100%	31%	**B.** Occasionally partial condemnation is defined as a specific percentage (usually 15–25%) of guest rooms condemned to total number of guest rooms; written notice time period varies from 30 to 90 days	—	—
C. If all or a material part of the property shall be damaged or destroyed by fire or other casualty or any other cause, either owner or operator may terminate this agreement by notice given not later than _________ days after the occurrence of the event, the date of termination to be not less than fifteen nor more than thirty days after giving such notice.	100%	62%	**C.** In some agreements, owner is required at operator's option to restore damaged or destroyed property for which insurance coverage was maintained by owner as long as cost of restoration does not exceed 30% of the replacement value for which the property was insured; a material part of the property is sometimes defined as 15 to 25% of the guest rooms or as a "significant portion" of the property's public space and food and beverage facilities.	—	—

*__Boldface__ type indicates major concern; regular type indicates moderate concern.

Appendix A, Description of Management-Contract Provisions (continued)

Provisions	Frequency of Occurrence: Chain	Independent	Comments on Variations of Provisions	Concern* during: Negotiations	Term
Section IX—Termination rights			**IX.**		
A. Termination by owner. Owner may terminate agreement if:			**A.**		
1. The operator shall fail to keep, observe, or perform any material covenant, agreement, term, or provision to be kept, observed, or performed by operator, and such default shall continue for a period of thirty days after notice thereof by owner to operator, or if such default cannot be cured within thirty days, then such additional period as shall be reasonable, provided that operator has proceeded to cure such default; or	100%	79%	**1.** —	—	**Owner**
2. The operator files a petition for adjudication as a bankrupt, for reorganization, or for an arrangement under any bankruptcy or insolvency law, or if any involuntary petition under any such law is filed against operator and not dismissed within sixty days; or	100%	79%	**2.** —	—	—
3. The operator shall make any assignment of its property for the benefit of creditors; or	100%	76%	**3.** —	—	—
4. The property's licenses or permits, including but not limited to occupancy, food, and alcoholic beverage service, are revoked because of the wrongful acts of the operator; or	40%	41%	**4.** It is often specified that the provision may not be invoked if revocation shall become stayed because of hearings, administrative proceedings, or litigation to contest the validity of such revocation.	—	—
5. The operator or operator's company is sold to another hotel (motor inn) chain or to a conglomerate which itself owns a hotel chain; or	0%	7%	**5.** —	—	—
6. Certain principal officers of the operator shall not be actively engaged in the management of the property; or	0%	7%	**6.** —	—	—
7. The owner shall not have received distributions at least equal to a predetermined dollar amount for each of a predetermined number of consecutive operating years occurring after a predetermined number of operating years; or	30%	14%	**7.** Distribution is usually defined as cash flow from operations and must be at least the amount to cover owner's debt-service payments (interest and principal); range of consecutive years varies from 2 to 4 years; range of the predetermined number of years varies from 3 to 8 years.	**Owner Operator**	**Owner Operator**

8. After a predetermined period of the term, owner, at its complete discretion, wishes to terminate the agreement by giving operator a predetermined number of days' written notice and a termination payment of a predetermined amount of money.	0%	28%	**8.** Often referred to as "cancellation clause"; owners-in-foreclosure usually demand that this provision be included to increase their ability to sell the property; developer-owners with substantial bargaining leverage can sometimes demand that this provision be included; length of notice ranges between 60 and 120 days; termination payment generally ranges from 3 months' basic management fee to 1 year's basic management fee.	**Owner Operator**	—
9. The owner must obtain any required consent from the holder of any mortgage prior to terminating this agreement.	90%	31%	**9.** —	Operator	—
B. Termination by operator. Operator may terminate agreement if:			**B.**		
1. The owner shall fail to keep, observe, or perform any material covenant, agreement, term, or provision to be kept, observed, or performed by owner, and such default shall continue for a period of thirty days after notice thereof by operator to owner, or if such default cannot be cured within thirty days, then such additional period as shall be reasonable, provided that owner has proceeded to cure such default; or	100%	97%	**1.** Often the operator shall have no right to terminate this agreement so long as any mortgagee shall cure such default respecting the payment of money or, for any other default, shall, within such 30-day period, proceed with diligence and good faith to cure such other defaults.	Operator	—
2. The owner files a petition for adjudication as a bankrupt, for reorganization, or for an arrangement under any bankruptcy or insolvency law, or if any involuntary petition under any such law is filed against owner and not dismissed within sixty days; or	100%	79%	**2.** Often mortgage holder can assume owner's role, which will prevent operator from unilaterally terminating agreement.	Operator	—
3. The owner shall make any assignment of its property for the benefit of creditors; or	100%	79%	**3.** See (2) above.	Operator	—
4. The property or any portion thereof shall be damaged or destroyed by fire or other casualty and if owner fails to undertake to repair, restore, rebuild, or replace any such damage or destruction within ________ days after such fire or other casualty, or shall fail to complete such work diligently; or	100%	62%	**4.** Number of days ranges from 30 to 120 days.	—	—
5. Any of the property's licenses or permits, including but not limited to occupancy, food and alcoholic-beverage service, are revoked for any cause other than through the wrongful act or acts of operator; or	40%	31%	**5.** —	—	—

*__Boldface__ type indicates major concern; regular type indicates moderate concern.

Appendix A, Description of Management-Contract Provisions (continued)

Provisions	Frequency of Occurrence: Chain	Independent	Comments on Variations of Provisions	Concern* during: Negotiations	Term
6. The property is condemned in whole or in part if operator determines that the remaining facilities are insufficient for the efficient and profitable operation of the property; or	100%	31%	**6.** Partial condemnation is usually defined again here.	—	—
7. The owner repeatedly fails or refuses to observe operator's right of noninterference from owner after having received written notice from operator to cease and desist such action; or	0%	14%	**7.** —	—	Owner Operator
8. Sale and transfer by owner of its right, title, and interest in the property except the sale to or merger with a subsidiary corporation or a corporation controlled by one or more of the stockholders of owner; or	100%	59%	**8.** Subject to operator's right of first refusal.	—	—
9. Because of a default by owner under the ground lease (if any) or the mortgage, the landlord or mortgagee shall declare a default, or take any other action in pursuance of the remedies arising as result of such default; or	100%	41%	**9.** Subject to right by mortgage holder to assume ownership role in agreement.	—	—
10. Failure of owner to maintain agreed-upon minimum balance in the property's operating bank account; or	100%	72%	**10.** —	Owner	**Owner**
11. Compensation due operator from owner is not received by operator ________ days after operator has made a written demand therefor; or	80%	86%	**11.** Time period varies from 10 to 30 days.	—	Owner
12. Owner has not secured firm investment commitments and firm financing commitments in amounts and upon terms approved by operator in order to finance the construction, furnishing, equipping, and operation of the property; or	90%	7%	**12.** —	—	—
13. Opening date of the property has not occurred prior to [a specific agreed-upon date]; or	90%	10%	**13.** —	—	Owner
14. Owner constructs a property that departs from what operator approved; or	50%	3%	**14.** —	—	—
15. Operator with or without cause gives ________ days' notice in writing without payment of any bonus or damages.	0%	14%	**15.** Usually after first year or first term of contract.	Owner Operator	—

Provision					
C. General			**C.**		
1. Notwithstanding the foregoing, neither owner nor operator shall be deemed to be in default under this agreement if a bona fide dispute with respect to any of the foregoing events of default has arisen between owner and operator and such dispute has been submitted to arbitration.	80%	31%	**1.** —	—	—
2. Upon termination of this agreement, all amounts due and owing between the parties shall become immediately due and payable.	90%	76%	**2.** —	—	—
3. At the termination of this agreement, operator shall remove all its property from the hotel's premises.	10%	10%	**3.** —	—	—
4. Operator shall transfer to owner all owner's books and records respecting the property in the custody and control of operator.	50%	7%	**4.** —	—	—
5. Operator shall assign and transfer to owner operator's right, title, and interest in and to all liquor, restaurant, and other licenses and permits, if any, used by operator in the operation of the property.	40%	14%	**5.** Applies when operator owns licenses.	—	—
6. If any mortgagee or other person or legal entity shall become the owner of the property, or any part thereof, as a result of any foreclosure or a conveyance in lieu of foreclosure, operator shall have no right or power to terminate this agreement solely because of such change in ownership of the property, or any part thereof, and shall recognize the mortgagee or such other person or legal entity as owner hereunder to the same extent as though it or they had been owner hereunder as of the execution of this agreement, provided that such mortgagee or such other person or legal entity shall agree in writing with operator to be bound by the terms and conditions of this agreement to the same extent as if such mortgagee or such other person or legal entity had been an original party hereto.	90%	21%	**6.** —	**Operator**	—
Section X—Miscellaneous provisions			**X.**		
A. No partnership or joint venture. Nothing contained in this agreement shall constitute or be construed to be or create a partnership or joint venture between the owner, its successors or assignees, on the one part, and operator, its successors and assignees, on the other part.	90%	62%	**A.** —	Operator	—

*__Boldface__ type indicates major concern; regular type indicates moderate concern.

Appendix A, Description of Management-Contract Provisions (continued)

Provisions	Frequency of Occurrence: Chain	Independent	Comments on Variations of Provisions	Concern* during: Negotiations	Term
B. Modification and changes. This agreement cannot be changed or modified except by another agreement in writing signed by the party sought to be charged therewith or by its duly authorized agent.	90%	59%	**B.** —	—	—
C. Understandings and agreements (entire agreement)			**C.**		
1. This agreement constitutes all of the understandings and agreements of whatsoever nature or kind existing between the parties with respect to operator's managership of the property.	90%	52%	**1.** —	—	—
2. Operator makes no guarantee, warranty, or representation that there will be profits or that there will not be losses from the operation of the property.	80%	48%	**2.** —	**Operator**	Owner
D. Headings. The article and paragraph headings contained herein are for convenience of reference only and are not intended to define, limit, or describe the scope or intent of any provision of this agreement.	90%	34%	**D.** —	—	—
E. Approval or consent. Whenever under any provision of this agreement the approval or consent of either party is required, said approval and consent shall be given or denied in a prompt manner.	60%	34%	**E.** Owner and operator are often each required to have a designated coordinator, so that whenever consent or approval is required or requested, the communication shall be directed to these coordinators.	—	—
F. Governing law. This agreement shall be deemed to have been made and shall be construed and interpreted in accordance with the laws of the state of ________ .	100%	69%	**F.** Usually the state where operator's corporate office is located.	Operator	—
G. Partial invalidity (enforceability). If any provisions of this agreement or the application of any provision to any person or circumstance is held invalid or unenforceable the remainder hereof and the application of such provision to other persons or circumstances shall remain valid and enforceable.	60%	35%	**G.** —	—	—
H. Binding effect (successors and assigns). This agreement shall be binding upon and insured to the benefit of the parties hereto and their respective heirs, personal representatives, successors, and permitted assigns.	100%	73%	**H.** —	—	—

I. Waiver of provisions			**I.**		
1. The failure of either party to insist upon a strict performance of any of the terms or provisions of this agreement or to exercise any option, right, or remedy herein contained, shall not be construed as a waiver or as a relinquishment for the future of such term, provision, option, right, or remedy, but the same shall continue and remain in full force and effect.	40%	28%	**1.** —	—	—
2. No waiver by either party or any term or provision hereof shall be deemed to have been made unless expressed in writing and signed by such party.	40%	24%	**2.** —	—	—
J. Third parties. Any provision herein to the contrary notwithstanding, it is agreed that none of the obligations hereunder of either party shall run to, or be enforceable by, any party other than the other party to this agreement.	90%	17%	**J.** Amended to include mortgage lender when lender may take action to correct a default of a contract provision caused by owner.	Operator	—
K. Estoppel certificates. At the request of either party, the parties hereto will execute an appropriate memorandum constituting notice of the existence of this agreement, in recordable form, and cause the same to be put of record in the jurisdiction where the property is located.	40%	3%	**K.** —	—	—
L. Counterparts. This agreement may be executed in several counterparts, each of which shall be an original, but all of which shall constitute but one and the same instrument.	20%	10%	**L.** —	—	—
M.Further Instruments. The parties shall execute and deliver all other appropriate supplemental agreements and other instruments, and take any other action necessary to make this agreement fully and legally effective, binding, and enforceable, as between the parties, and as against third parties.	20%	0%	**M.**—	—	—
N. Construction of additional facilities. In the event a casino, restaurant, or cocktail lounge should be operated at the property, operator shall have the exclusive right to operate same and to include gross revenues in the total revenues of the property and gross revenues less operating expenses in the gross operating profit of the property.	20%	7%	**N.** —	—	—

*Boldface type indicates major concern; regular type indicates moderate concern.

Appendix A, Description of Management-Contract Provisions (continued)

Provisions	Frequency of Occurrence: Chain	Independent	Comments on Variations of Provisions	Concern* during: Negotiations	Term
O. Owner not to use operator's name in obtaining financing			**O.**		
1. Owner shall not represent in any proposed financing arrangement or to any proposed lender or participant in a private or public investment that operator shall be in any way responsible for owner's obligation in financing arrangement other than to state that the property will bear the name of operator, will be managed by operator, and will be a part of the operator's hotel (motor inn) system.	20%	3%	**1.** —	—	—
2. In order to insure owner's full and faithful compliance with the above and to prevent any misunderstanding on the part of a proposed lender or participant in any such investment offering, owner shall, prior to the closing of any such proposed financing arrangement, inform and furnish operator with the identity of the proposed lender and copies of the proposed closing documents and owner shall, prior to the printing of any prospectus concerning said private or public investment offering, furnish operator with a copy of said prospectus, and said prospectus shall not be published or distributed without the prior written consent of operator.	20%	3%	**2.** —	—	—
P. Signatures. In witness whereof, the parties hereto have executed, or caused to be executed, this agreement all as of the day and year first above written. [Owner signature, operator signature, and two attestor signatures.]	100%	100%	**P.** —	—	—
Note: *Sections XI, XII, and XIII are included only where operator assumes responsibilities during a property's pre-opening phase.*					
Section XI—Construction of property			**XI.**		
A. Owner shall construct and equip the property to include purchase of all furniture, fixtures, and operating supplies reasonably deemed by operator and owner to be necessary for the operation of a first-class facility as per agreed-upon plans and specifications.	100%	100%	**A.** —	—	—

B. If owner does not commence construction within ________ months after the date of this agreement, operator may terminate this agreement by giving notice to owner.	100%	63%	**B.** Time period generally ranges from 3 to 18 months.	—	—
C. Owner shall afford operator's personnel reasonable access to the construction site in order that operator may perform its duties and obligations under this agreement.	40%	13%	**C.** —	—	—
D. Owner shall furnish operator with a time schedule of the design and construction stage in respect of the property and shall revise and update such schedule from time to time as appropriate.	60%	25%	**D.** —	—	—
Section XII—Opening date			**XII.**		
A. The specific opening date is defined by operator and is considered to be reached after: (1) architects have issued a certificate of completion; (2) certificates and approvals for the legal use and occupancy of the property have been obtained; (3) furniture, fixtures, equipment, and operating supplies have been installed, and (4) owner has established an adequate financing plan and has provided sufficient working capital.	100%	88%	**A.** —	—	—
B. If the conditions referred to above have not been met by [a specified date], operator may either terminate this agreement by giving notice to owner or may continue this agreement in full force.	70%	31%	**B.** —	Owner Operator	—
Section XIII—Pre-opening management services			**XIII.**		
A. Pre-opening plan			**A.**		
1. Operator shall prepare and deliver to owner a detailed plan and budget in respect of the various services to be performed by operator to include: (a) an estimated time schedule for the performance of such services; (b) a schedule of the personnel of operator assigned to the property on a full-time basis; (c) a budget showing the proposed expenditures during the pre-opening period; (d) a description of the sales, marketing, and promotional programs for the property during the pre-opening period; and (e) a description of the plan for the architectural design and construction consulting services to be provided by operator.	100%	100%	**1.** Plan occasionally excludes some items listed.	**Owner Operator**	—

*__Boldface__ type indicates major concern; regular type indicates moderate concern.

Appendix A, Description of Management-Contract Provisions (continued)

Provisions	Frequency of Occurrence: Chain	Independent	Comments on Variations of Provisions	Concern* during: Negotiations	Term
2. Owner has ________ days to approve the plan. In the event owner's comments and objections are such that operator believes they will not be able adequately to perform the obligations required by this agreement and they are unable to resolve such differences, operator shall have the right to terminate this agreement. Within thirty days after termination, owner shall pay operator all fees and other payments earned or due.	100%	100%	**2.** Inability to agree is usually not subject to arbitration; number of days for approval varies from 30 to 90 days.	—	—
B. Payment of pre-opening expenses. At least once each calendar month, operator shall furnish owner a statement itemizing costs and expenses incurred on owner's behalf pursuant to the pre-opening plan, and owner shall insure that sufficient funds are available to pay the costs and expenses.	100%	100%	**B.** —	—	—
C. Operating plan and budget. Operator shall furnish to owner a proposed operating plan and budget for the first operating year and shall update and revise such as appropriate during the pre-opening period.	80%	75%	**C.** —	—	—
D. Personnel services			**D.**		
1. Operator shall develop and furnish to owner copies of operational organization charts, staffing tables, schedules of employment, and beginning ranges of compensation for persons to be employed by owner.	40%	19%	**1.** —	—	—
2. Operator shall select a general manager and such other personnel as are necessary for proper implementation of the pre-opening plan and for the proper staffing on and after the opening date and shall indoctrinate and train all such personnel.	100%	100%	**2.** Some contracts specify when (prior to opening) operator may place management personnel on owner's payroll (e.g., general manager, 6 months to 1 year; department heads, 3 to 6 months; other personnel, 30 to 45 days).	Owner Operator	—
E. Sales and advertising			**E.**		
1. Operator shall plan and implement a marketing program consisting of advertising, public relations, and related activities for the purpose of promoting vigorously the name and business of the property.	100%	100%	**1.** —	Owner **Operator**	—

2. Operator shall arrange programs to secure bookings and business, such as conventions and catered events, for periods from and after opening date.	100%	44%	**2.** —	—	—
3. Owner agrees to pay operator a fee, payable monthly, for the services described in (1) and (2) above.	100%	100%	**3.** Operator often charges fee for pre-opening sales and advertising in addition to the normal pre-opening management fee; fee usually based upon (a) number of guest rooms and period of time over which sales and advertising are conducted (e.g., $2 to $4 per room per month, commencing with the date of the agreement and continuing until opening date, up to a maximum number of dollars); or (b) at cost or cost-plus.	Owner **Operator**	—
F. Rental space. Operator shall negotiate leases, licenses, and concession agreements covering the property's rental space. The general terms and provisions of such shall be subject to prior approval of owner.	80%	69%	**F.** —	—	—
G. Accounting services. During the pre-opening period, operator shall implement and provide to owner operator's standard pre-opening accounting services.	40%	13%	**G.** —	—	—
H. Purchasing services			**H.**		
1. Operator shall make available to owner operator's services in regard to procurement of all initial furniture, fixtures, equipment, and operating supplies required for the property.	100%	81%	**1.** Operator usually receives a procurement fee for purchasing services which is paid in addition to normal pre-opening management fee; procurement fee is based upon a percentage of items purchased or leased and ranges from 2% to 4% of invoice price of items purchased or leased.	—	—
2. Terms and conditions of all purchases made by operator for owner's account shall be approved by owner in writing.	100%	63%	**2.** —	—	—
I. Design and planning of facilities (consultation and technical-assistance services). Operator may make available to owner the expertise and experience of operator, its affiliates, and consultants in the design and planning of facilities.			**I.**		

*__Boldface__ type indicates major concern; regular type indicates moderate concern.

Appendix A, Description of Management-Contract Provisions (continued)

Provisions	Frequency of Occurrence: Chain	Independent	Comments on Variations of Provisions	Concern* during: Negotiations	Term
1. Architecture: assistance to owner's architects in developing schematic plans; consultation with owner's architects in preparation of detailed preliminary plans; review of preliminary and final architectural plans and specifications; and on-site inspections during and at the completion of construction.	100%	75%	**1.** Degree and value of assistance are dependent upon operator's ability to perform services.	Owner **Operator**	—
2. Interior design and lighting: assistance to owner's interior designers with suggestions on theme treatment, functional layout, and lighting requirements; review of preliminary plans for interiors, including layout plans, elevations, and color schemes; advice on specifications for carpeting, furniture, draperies, and fabrics; review of working drawings for interiors; and on-site inspections of the work in progress and after completion.	100%	56%	**2.** Some chain operators require owner to contract with operator's own interior designers to perform interior design and lighting planning; cost of these services is in addition to normal pre-opening management fee; degree and value of assistance are dependent upon operator's ability to perform services.	**Owner** **Operator**	—
3. Mechanical installations: consultation with owner's mechanical consultants during the plan development; review and recommendation concerning preliminary and final system plans and specifications prepared by owner's mechanical consultants; on-site inspection during the construction period; and submission of names of acceptable manufacturers and suppliers of equipment.	50%	25%	**3.** Degree and value of assistance are dependent upon operator's ability to perform services.	Owner	—
4. Food-facilities layout and equipment: consultation regarding layouts for equipment; recommendations of experienced suppliers; analysis of bids; and on-site inspections and recommendations of acceptance of installation.	100%	75%	**4.** Some operators require that owner contract with operator's own food-facilities consultants to perform layout and design work; cost of those services is in addition to normal pre-opening management fee; degree and value of assistance are dependent upon operator's ability to perform services.	**Owner** **Operator**	—
5. Graphic work: consultation regarding graphic designs and mechanical artwork for folders, brochures, and food and beverage menus, and development of uniform designs.	60%	38%	**5.** Degree and value of assistance are dependent upon operator's ability to perform services.	—	—

J. Compensation			**J.**		
1. In consideration of the performance by operator of the services specified above, owner agrees to pay operator $________ , to be paid in monthly installments of $________ each, commencing ______________ , 19_____ .	100%	100%	**1.** Usually does not include services performed by operator for interior design planning, food-facilities planning, or purchasing if operator assumes more than a consulting role in these areas; pre-opening management-fee structures are usually based upon number of guest rooms.	Owner	—
2. Owner agrees to pay all travel and out-of-pocket expenses reasonably incurred by operator for those personnel not assigned to the property on a full-time basis but performing services of this agreement.	100%	100%	**2.** —	—	—
3. Owner agrees to reimburse operator for salaries, wages, travel, and out-of-pocket expenses for those personnel assigned to the property on a full-time basis.	100%	88%	**3.** Except salaries and wages paid to those personnel performing interior design, food facilities, purchasing, and sales and advertising services, for which owner is being charged over and above the normal pre-opening management fee.	—	—

*__Boldface__ type indicates major concern; regular type indicates moderate concern.

Appendix B:

Factors Influencing the Adoption of Management Contracts

The nine market, economic, and business-policy factors influencing the rapid acceptance of management contracts are described below in the chronological order of their impact. Although no factor should be considered to have caused another, individually and in combination these factors have influenced the nature of contract use today.

The material used in this analysis was derived from three sources: a review of real-estate and hospitality literature; the author's interviews with lodging operators, owners, lenders, and consultants; and the author's independent observations.

A. Factor 1: Chain Operating Companies' Market Concentration and Competition

The growth of chain operating companies in the lodging field since 1950 and their related increase in market power at the expense of independent properties parallels the growth toward concentration in market power in most retail and service sectors. The benefits of cultivating brand identification and a national network of properties or outlets—assuming that the firm's growth and administration are characterized by an effective degree of control and flexibility-are the same whether the firm operates a chain of supermarkets, department stores, discount houses, or hotels and motor inns.

The benefits include economies of scale in advertising, central purchasing, and other centralized services—including marketing, financing, accounting, research and development, and real-estate investment, access to capital markets,

EXHIBIT B-1
Chain Operating Companies' Market Penetration (1963 to 1975)

Year	Rooms	Revenues
1963	19.1%	25.4%
1967	25.4%	33.6%
1970	33.2%	41.5%
1973	40.6%	60.7%
1975	47.5%	68.0%

Source: Carl F. DeBiase, *A Critical Analysis of the Domestic Hotel-Motel Industry* (New York: Moore and Schley, Cameron and Company, 1971), p. 42.

and established career ladders designed to attract and hold highly qualified managerial talent.[1]

Growth becomes the primary goal of firms seeking rapid market penetration—especially when entry into the market by new firms is unrestricted. In 1950, the three major national hotel chains—Sheraton, Statler, and Hilton—operated properties with a total of approximately 38,600 rooms, which accounted for only two percent of the total number of rooms available in the United States.[2]

Between 1950 and 1960, entry into the market was relatively unrestricted for new individual properties and chain firms. Hilton, which acquired the Statler chain in 1954, and Sheraton were soon joined by Holiday Inns, Howard Johnson's, TraveLodge, Western International, Marriott, Ramada Inns, and Downtowner—all of them emerging as domestic chain operating companies with similar objectives: to increase their nationwide market penetration through the cultivation of brand identification and national reservations systems, and to rapidly increase their earnings bases (number of rooms).

Despite some variations from the norm, most chain operating companies supplemented owned properties with leased properties during the 1950s and expanded by franchise in the 1960s. The franchising trend, which permitted chain operating companies to expand rapidly with little or no capital outlay of their own, was the major impetus for the accelerated market penetration of chain operating companies during the 1960s and early 1970s (Exhibits B-1 and B-2). The trade-off for this penetration was a significant loss of control in regulating quality and service standards.

1. F. M. Scherer, *Industrial Market Structure and Economic Performance* (Chicago: Rand McNally, 1970), pp. 72-130; and Arthur H. Martel, "An Economic Analysis of the Market Structure of the Hotel-Motel Industry" (doctoral dissertation, University of Massachusetts, 1974), pp. 79-87.
2. Compiled from telephone interview with William Morton and Vernon Herndon during 1975-1976; and from John D. Glover, Edmund P. Learned, and Arthur B. Moss, *Hilton Hotels Corporation: Cases on Business Policy and Administration* (Cambridge: Harvard University Graduate School of Business Administration, 1956).

EXHIBIT B-2
Estimated Penetration of Top 90 Percent of Industry Volume by Chain-Type Organizations (1963 to 1975)

Year	Rooms	Revenues
1963	25.9%	38.1%
1967	37.2%	51.3%
1970	48.8%	63.9%
1973	59.8%	72.1%
1975	66.4%	76.7%

Source: Carl F. DeBiase, *A Critical Analysis of the Domestic Hotel-Motel Industry* (New York: Moore and Schley, Cameron and Company, 1971), p. 42.

The market penetration resulted from chain identification for the majority of new rooms available and from increased competition between chain-affiliated properties and independent properties, and among chain organizations, for the changing—but not increasing—demand for rooms. Exhibit B-3 compares the occupancy of chain-affliliated and independent properties since 1969 and illustrates the decrease in the independent properties' ability to compete with chain-affiliated properties.

Many developer-owners currently employing management contracts expressed bitterness about the chain operating companies' push for growth with what the owners perceive to be little regard for the risk involved in overbuilding. "I bear all the risk," one developer-owner stated, "while the chain bears none." Chain operators feel differently. One chain operating company replied:

> We haven't pushed anyone into building a hotel. Developers come to us and want to employ us in order to maximize their returns or because their lenders insist on professional management. It's their [owners'] decision that they're in the hotel business, not ours. We feel we can maximize their returns given the existing competitive factors and economic conditions.

This difference of opinion is one reason management contracts are continually a subject of controversy.

B. Factor 2: More Money for Real-Estate Ventures

The increased availability of money for real estate ventures in the late 1960s and early 1970s and again in the early and mid 1980s contributed to the growth in the number of available rooms. Since the value of real estate increased faster than the inflation rate after World War II, investors sought promising real-estate opportunities as a hedge against inflation. In addition to the traditional sources of investment capital for loans or equity (savings and loan associations, savings

EXHIBIT B-3
Occupancy Comparisons Between Chain-Affiliated and Independent Properties (1966–1985)

Year	Median Occupancies Chain-Affiliated	Independent	Independent Differs by
1969	72.0 %	75.0 %	4.0 %
1971	64.8	65.4	0.9
1973	67.3	66.6	(1.0)
1975	63.5	64.3	1.3
1977	68.5	69.5	1.5
1979	72.1	72.5	0.6
1981	71.3	63.3	(11.2)
1983	66.6	60.8	(8.7)
1985	65.8	60.0	(8.8)

Source: Compiled from Laventhol and Horwath *Lodging Industry* studies, 1969–1986 editions (Philadelphia: Laventhol and Horwath).

banks, pension funds, and life-insurance companies), two new investment-fund vehicles emerged—the real-estate investment trust (REIT) and the limited partnership—offering greater opportunities for individuals to participate in the benefits of real-estate investment. Combined with traditional investment sources, REITs and limited partnerships accentuated the real-estate boom—in an inherently "boom-or-bust" business—by providing increased capital for real-estate investments.

1. Real-Estate Investment Trust (REIT)

Introduced in the early 1960s by the federal government to spur real-estate development, REITs were permitted to operate tax-free, provided they returned at least 90 percent of their profits to their shareholders. The REIT did not create any new funds *per se*, but it did represent a conduit for the shifting of capital into the construction and real-estate industries.[3]

> Just as the mutual fund industry grew because it enabled the investor to share professionally managed securities portfolios, the REIT industry has grown primarily by being able to channel funds from institutional and public investors into the real estate, mortgage, and construction sectors. Both entities also enable the small investor to share in a diversified portfolio, and both [by law] release earnings to investors immediately upon receipt of income.[4]

Investment policies of the various REITs are "generally broad and flexible,

3. Securities and Exchange Commission, Office of Economic Research, "Real Estate Investment Trusts: A Background Analysis and Recent Industry Developments—1961—1974," *Economic Staff Paper*, 75, No. 1 (February 1975), pp. 4-5.
4. Ibid., p. 6.

leaving considerable discretion to the respective trust management and trustees."[5] The REIT can emphasize short-term construction and development loans, long-term mortgages, real properties, or a combination of these; however, REIT investments are concentrated in short-term development and construction loans, where attractive yields ranging from 13 to 16 percent can be earned due to the greater risk involved.[6] In addition to the loan's stated interest, the REIT typically charges the borrowers additional points as consideration for making the loan. To maximize its earnings, the REIT will try both to maximize the average spread between its cost of money and its rate of return from loans and to leverage its debt.

2. Limited Partnership

The limited partnership was the second major vehicle that has drawn capital funds into lodging construction since the early 1970s. Before 1970, the limited-partnership form of ownership was infrequently used and limited to "risky ventures that showed losses in the early years but held vague promise of a hefty capital gain in the future."[7] During the early 1970s, limited partnerships became popular; an estimated 1,600 were formed to finance new lodging projects. One 1972 financial publication promoted the limited partnership as offering "the advantages of owning major income property while eliminating the headaches that are so often part of being a landlord."[8] The advantages were said to include:

— **Tax Shelters:** Net rental income or gross operating income can be sheltered from income taxes if the property owned by the partnership is operating at a paper loss due to accelerated depreciation expenses; the limited partner can apply this loss against income from other business revenue, thus reducing his tax liability.

— **Cash-Flow Income:** Although the property is operating at a paper loss, a positive cash flow is usually generated if cash revenues exceed cash expenses.

— **Capital Gains:** When the real estate is ultimately sold, any profits realized due to an increase in the value of the real estate are taxed at the lower capital-gains tax rate.[9]

In a limited partnership, the general partner provides the professional expertise in developing and managing the real estate and accepts all responsibility for the partnership's obligations, management duties, and personal liability. The limited partners, who provide the majority of the equity capital, have no legal liabilities beyond their original investment, which can range from $5,000

---

5. Ibid.
6. Ibid.
7. "New Popularity for Limited Partnerships," *Business Week,* December 11, 1971, p. 88.
8. "Herbert Glasser, "Teaming Up to Tap the Real Estate Market," *Stock Market Magazine,* March 1972, p. 12.
9. Ibid., pp. 13-14.

per partner to a usual maximum of $150,000 per partner, depending upon state law. It is critical to the success of the limited partnership—but seldom pointed out in promotional material—that a property generate positive cash flows. If positive cash flows are not generated immediately, the general partner or the limited partners must make additional contributions to maintain the project's solvency. Sensitive to the normally risky nature of the limited partnership, some states restrict the sale of participations to a well-defined class of investors.

In the late 1970s and early 1980s, chain and independent operating companies began sponsoring limited partnership offerings for two purposes. The first purpose was as a means to develop new properties. In this situation, the operating company would serve as the general partner to exercise control over the development of the properties and the partnership and, through a management contract on the properties, exercise long-term control of the properties' operations. Marriott's Potomac Hotel Limited Partnership offering in 1982 was the first large public offering of this type by a chain operator. The second purpose was as a means to sell existing properties owned by a hotel operating company to provide capital for the chain's future developement and to retain operational control of the properties through a management contract negotiated with the limited partnership. Holiday Inns' sale of 24 properties in 1985 through the VMS National Hotel Portfolio I was the first large private offering of this type by a chain operator.

The future use of limited partnerships to finance hotel and motor-inn projects will be reduced due to the 1986 Tax Reform Act provisions that severely curtail the previous passive-income benefits of limited partnerships. Projects financed in the future by limited partnerships will have to attract investors based on project economic viability rather than on tax-shelter benefits.

The race to invest available capital during these real-estate booms resulted in a lack of conservatism in lending and a lack of sophistication in the analysis of proposed projects. These two criticisms are not restricted to the lodging industry but can also be applied to industrial-park, apartment, condominium, and office-building construction.

Lack of caution in lending was characteristic mainly of loan officers who were younger, more aggressive, and less conservative than traditional lenders. During these periods, reports Whitehead:

> ... the trusts introduced many types of financing [that] had not previously been used to any extent, such as three-to-five year standby mortgages and construction loans without take-outs [permanent mortgages]. The combination of new money sources and the availablility of larger loans attracted far greater development than in previous years. For the privilege of obtaining such lenient financing arrangements, developers had to pay substantially higher interest rates. Project costs began to rise

as construction costs increased; and when the developer commenced operation, he was faced with extremely high debt service.[10]

Robert Lee, of the national accounting firm of Peat, Marwick, Mitchell, made the following observation to the author:

> Most every hotel or motor-inn property the REITs loaned to had been "shopped" by the conservative lending institutions. Developers first went to the lenders who offered lower rates. Then when they [the developers] were turned down, they went to the REITs. As a result, the less competitive projects borrowed money from the REITs at higher interest rates, making an already shaky project even shakier.

Lack of sophistication in the analysis of proposed projects and of the markets to which these projects would cater resulted in the granting of mortgage money to basically unsound projects.

Insufficient hotel experience among REIT and mortgage officers or general and limited partners in many of the partnership arrangements is considered a major factor in the lack of adequate project analysis. "Most trusts did not have competent hotelmen on their staffs, nor did they hire consultants to provide them with the expertise they needed in the areas of hotel development, operation, real estate, and financing."[11] Hotelmen who have been hired by the REITs to supervise and monitor distressed or foreclosed REIT-financed lodging properties cite the following reasons to explain why the REITs are now owners-in-foreclosure of many properties:[12]

— The loans were based on feasibility studies describing future markets that never materialized, due to overbuilding and economic recessions.

— Developer-owners were unaware of the negative cash flow associated with lodging operations during the first years of operation.

— Lenders did not thoroughly investigate the financial background of the developer-owner to determine his financial depth and stability.

— Lenders did not properly monitor construction of the properties.

— Lenders felt that as long as a chain operating company was willing to put its name on the property and manage it, the project was a sound investment. As a result, independent operators manage several hundred foreclosed properties under management contracts.

---

10. Donald E. Whitehead, "An Analysis of Distressed Properties," *The Cornell Hotel and Restaurant Administration Quarterly*, 16, No. 4 (February 1976), p. 34.
11. Whitehead, op. cit.
12. "How REITs Are Reacting," *The Cornell Hotel and Restaurant Administration Quarterly*, 16, No. 4 (February 1976), p. 40.

C. Factor 3: Changes in Property Size and Ownership Risk

Changing markets, the industry's increasingly competitive nature, and inflation led to an increase in the size of projects, the amount of investment, and the risk of new lodging properties.

During the late 1960s, demand for rooms shifted from highway locations to center-city and suburban locations (with the exception of the demand in Orlando created by the opening of Walt Disney World). The new center-city hotels were often part of large, multipurpose complexes or redevelopment programs and were promoted by metropolitan business interests to attract and maintain business and convention activity. Clusters of large convention hotels were developed in several dozen American cities. In addition, new full-service, resort-type suburban properties were built to attract the potential business and convention activity that follows the dispersion of commercial, light manufacturing, and corporate-office activities into the cities' peripheries. Most new center-city and suburban properties stress extensive public-space areas, creative architectural design, and luxurious atmospheres. Many are based upon Portman's revolutionary atrium concept. These properties are expensive to build and to maintain. To pay for extensive public spaces producing no revenue, developers found it necessary to increase the number of guest rooms at an increasing cost per room.

In addition to the projected cost per room and the expected increased maintenance expenses, the risk of cost overruns has risen substantially due to the following factors: **(1)** the increased complexity of coordinating construction—the result of increased property size and, often, dependence upon non-hotel projects in a complex (e.g., office buildings, convention centers); **(2)** inflationary increases in materials over longer construction periods; **(3)** delays due to material shortages and labor stoppages; and **(4)** higher interest rates on construction loans. The owners and operators interviewed estimated that fewer than 20 percent of the lodging projects they had opened since 1968 were completed either on time or with negligible cost overruns.

The overall financial risk for owners of these larger properties has also increased because of the larger debt-service charges attributable to greater financial leverage, higher interest rates, and the increase in undistributed operating expenses, especially in utility costs. Most of the above expenses are fixed costs. In areas where competitive pricing drives down room rates or where customers resist paying increased room rates, ownership risk is substantially increased. Chain and independent operating companies usually do not share in the financial risk of achieving adequate cash flow for debt service, unless their incentive management fees are subordinated to debt service, in which case the fees are usually deferred and not waived.

D. Factor 4: Chain Operating Companies' Decision to Change from Being Real-Estate Companies to Operating Companies

The policy decision to change from being a real-estate company to an operating company relates primarily to a chain operating company's ability to raise and manage funds for rapid growth. A chain operating company may expand rapidly in one or more of the following ways: **(1)** merge with another hotel chain; **(2)** merge with a non-hotel company that has a broader financial base; or **(3)** improve its own growth record by concentrating on the Wall Street criterion of maximizing earnings per share, which in turn would open up funding from the Wall Street capital market.

The first alternative has not been viable in recent years, with the exception of the Dunfey-Omni merger, due to the extensive duplication of properties that would result if two nation-wide chains merged. Sheraton, Westin, and Dunfey chose the second alternative by merging with ITT, Allegis, and Aer Lingus, respectively, to achieve a broader financial base to support expansion. Most chain operating companies, including the three companies listed above, employed the third method. One vice president of development remarked, "Since we [major hotel companies] did not put up a united front to Wall Street's preoccupation with earnings per share as the only measure for growth, we had no chance of convincing the investing public that the value of a company can also increase through appreciation of its real-estate assets." As a result, hotel chains are minimizing ownership in additional real-estate ventures and divesting themselves of full or partial ownership of existing real-estate holdings in order, as another director of development reports, to make "lethal use of our cash." These actions minimize the company's investment, assets, and liabilities while maintaining or increasing its earnings base.

Operating-company executives interviewed cited the following reasons that their companies prefer to increase the number of properties managed while making little or no equity investment of their own:

— Marginal revenue significantly exceeds marginal costs for each additional property once the basic contract staff is established at the corporate office.

— The negative cash flow of the pre-opening period and the first years of operation—which requires substantial cash reserves—must be funded by the owner.

— The depreciation expenses resulting from ownership of assets are minimized for the operator, thus improving the operating company's earnings per share of common stock and maximized for the owner, who can use the depreciation expenses to shelter his taxable income and improve his cash flow.

— An investment of 50 percent or less in a property allows the operating company to report the investment under the equity method of accounting so that a company's liability regarding the investment will not be recorded on the company's balance sheet; and maintain a degree of influence in ownership decision-making.

— The operator's hazard from cost overruns, changing markets, overbuilding, and recession is reduced.

— The ability to obtain a property with potential for long-term capital appreciation is desirable for an owner with cash he can afford to commit for extended periods of time.

The sale of existing properties and the assumption of management contracts on them create the following additional benefits for the operating company:[13] immediate cash flow, which can be used to expand services and to fund efforts to generate additional contracts, and an immediate increase in earnings for the year in which the sale is made, assuming—in most cases—that the property's book value is below its market value.

Although an operator generally does not want to provide equity investment, he is often forced to at the owner's or lender's insistence, if he wants the project offered. Voluntary operator investment has increased as the competition among operators for property locations has increased. Institutional owners, such as life-insurance companies and REITs, confirm they are now better able to bargain during negotiations with both chain and independent operating companies because of the increasing competition among operating companies for the fewer good projects now available.

---

13. The sale of a 50-percent interest in six Hilton-owned hotels to the Prudential Insurance Company of America in March 1975 illustrates the benefits accruing to each party. The aggregate sale price was approxiatmely $83,350,000, consisting of $65,950,000 in cash and approximately $17,400,000 in existing mortgage indebtedness. The transaction resulted in a gain (after applicable income taxes) of approximately $27,300,000. Hilton used about $20,700,000 of this cash to retire outstanding debt and used the remaining amount to repurchase one million of 7.5 million shares of stock outstanding on the open market. As a result, Hilton achieved: **(1)** cash; **(2)** increased earnings per share, which resulted from the gain on sale of assets combined with the reduction of outstanding shares; **(3)** reclassification of the hotels' remaining asset value from the asset-and-liability accounts to the investment account, thus decreasing the company's leverage; and **(4)** reduction in ownership risk while maintaining adequate ownership control in the properties to protect its interests in the property and its management contract. Prudential achieved 50-percent interest in six properties with potential for long-term capital appreciation; a long-term management contract with an established hotel operator with adequate equity in the property to have the incentive to perform well; and depreciation expense, which shelters taxable income and maximizes cash flow. (From Hilton Hotels Corporation 1974 Annual Report, p. 33, and from "Hilton Hotels Slates Cash Tender Offer for 1 Million Shares," *The Wall Street Journal,* March 10, 1975, p. 10.)

E. Factor 5: Lenders' Insistence on Professional Management

Beginning in the late 1960s, lenders increasingly demanded that hotel developers obtain a national chain franchise as a condition to obtaining financing. Hospitality consulting firms were generally willing to point out in feasibility studies the potential increase in occupancy a proposed property would have if it could draw on an established national reservations system and receive regular inspections by national chain operating company supervisors. As the average dollar investment of lodging projects increased and the realization grew that chain operating companies were losing supervisory control over many of their franchise operations, lenders began to insist that developer-owners without established lodging management experience employ the management of a chain operating company or an established regional independent operating company with a chain franchise to increase the probability of the property's success. The result of linking a national chain name and professional management to a property gave the developer increased borrowing power and was often the deciding factor in his ability to obtain funding.

F. Factor 6: Supply of Professional Management Personnel

During the expansionary period of the late 1960s and early 1970s, the pool of trained management and supervisory personnel was increasing at a slower rate than the increase in the number of existing properties,[14] and the industry ran "the risk of giving up expertise in an effort to show expansion."[15] Franchised and independent properties were at a competitive disadvantage in bidding for current managerial and supervisory talent in comparison to the larger chain organizations or established franchise groups, which could offer well-defined career ladders. With their difficulties intensified by the recession, many over-extended developers faced foreclosure, and the lenders who were not in the business of operating lodging properties began to search for management expertise.

In response to this need, independent operating companies were formed and established a competitive niche alongside the chain operating companies. The independent operating companies, with their lower overhead, could charge lesser fees that small properties could afford to pay. As a result, competition for these smaller properties was not between chain operating companies and

14. Booz, Allen, and Hamilton, and Cornell School of Hotel Adminstration, *Operation Breakthrough: An Approach to Hotel-Motel Operations in 1978* (New York: American Hotel and Motel Association, 1969), p. 64.
15. Michael A. Leven, "The Management Contract," *Hospitality,* 14 (January 1974), p. 10.

independent operating companies, but among independent operating companies.

The ease of entry into the independent operating-company field and the need for professional services created a proliferation of new companies with varying levels of competence and offering a range of professional services. The writer's survey of independent operating companies indicated the following reasons for the formation of these companies:

— Hotel managers with all degrees of operating experience found the management-contract company a vehicle for self-employment and an opportunity to purchase—with minimal equity—distressed properties.

— Owners who were already operating lodging properties added management-contract properties to employ more fully their existing corporate staffs, which were underutilized when construction was curtailed during the recession.

— Operators leasing lodging properties found they could rapidly expand their earnings bases with little or no additional financial commitment.

— Lodging consulting firms offered to manage foreclosed properties, improve the properties' profitability, and sell them for the owner-in-foreclosure to collect the brokerage fees.

— A partner in a joint venture that had built and owned lodging properties often employed a management contract to maintain complete operating control; this partner became the operator, and the joint-venture partner became the owner.

— Food-service companies diversified into the lodging industry with minimal equity participation.

— Several REITs converted from their trust status to operating-company status to manage and improve the operational efficiencies of their foreclosed properties.

Due to the ease of entering the hotel business, independent operating companies' qualifications, abilities, and depth vary significantly. The writer categorizes these firms into the following three groups:

— **Firms with national coverage**: Several of the earliest independent operating companies attempted to expand too rapidly on a national basis and extended their management expertise too thinly. As a result, their market penetration seriously deteriorated to the benefit of newer, more slowly growing national independent operating companies and strong regional independent operating companies. These earlier companies are in the process of consolidating. Firms with national coverage generally manage between 15 and 45 properties.

— **Firms with regional coverage**: A number of operating companies have purposely restricted themselves to regional operations, maintained strong support staffs, and exerted progressive and effective marketing control over their properties. Many regional operating companies exist with marginal support staffs and rely heavily upon the management of foreclosed properties for their fees, and as a result, their futures are relatively uncertain. Operating companies with regional coverage generally manage between five and 15 properties.

— **Firms with state, local, and sometimes regional coverage**: The majority of independent operating companies are in this category. These companies consist of one person who, with minimal office assistance, supervises one to three properties. The experience and competence among these persons are extremely varied, and their companies' mortality rates are high.

G. Factor 7: The Recession of the Mid-1970s

The recession of the mid-1970s, coupled with the overbuilt state of the lodging industry and rapidly rising utility, food, beverage, and payroll costs, affected the evolution of management contracts in two ways. First, it strained operator-owner relationships in existing contracts. Second, it led to an increase in management contracts between operators and owners-in-foreclosure. During the recession, many marginal properties operated by developer-owners fell behind in their mortgage payments and were foreclosed by mortgage holders. The owners-in-foreclosure, in an attempt to salvage their inherited properties, mostly hired independent operating companies to improve the properties' operating results so the properties could be sold with minimal losses.

With the existing contracts, developer-owners were forced to resupply their operations with unanticipated cash infusions, since cash flows from operations were often inadequate to cover the increased operating expenses and high debt-service payments. It was during this time that many developer-owners, frustrated by disappointing financial results, became critical of the quality of management offered by the operating companies they employed. Developer-owners often advised their operators how to manage their properties and subsequently began to search for alternatives to their existing contract arrangements.

The writer found numerous and often conflicting claims by owners and operators interviewed concerning who was to blame for the insufficient returns of the properties. Claims frequently made by developer-owners included the following:

— The operator continually presented overly optimistic projections to keep his contract. One developer-owner stated his operator "kept surprising us with the poor operating results of each operating period after it was too late for us to do anything about it. What we didn't need was surprises. We wanted to have a clear picture so that we could make better financial decisions."

— The operator was unable to see obvious things in the operation—poor food, low housekeeping standards, impolite employees—that were causing customer dissatisfaction, and he failed to correct them.

— The operator's corporate staff received inadequate supervision and support. Owners often claimed that operators placed more experienced general managers in operator-owned properties and that corporate sales staffs favored operator-owned properties when booking business—at the expense of the management-contract properties—since financial returns in properties owned by operating companies were higher than in management-contract properties.

Operators interviewed by the researcher defended their management practices, saying:

— Operators were doing the best they could, given the economic conditions of the recession.

— Operators were treating management-contract properties in the same way as operator-owned properties, since this policy was advantageous in the long run to their management-contract business.

— Developer-owners were often too highly leveraged and had high fixed expenses, so that they could not afford declines in business volume.

One operating company's executive commented, "Operators are being blamed by owners for the owners' indiscretions in sound investment decision-making. We're the scapegoats."

Whether the developer-owner criticisms of operating companies' management reflected real or imagined conditions, operator-owner relationships became strained and owners became actively aware of the adverse effect of the high-risk, high-return nature of the management contract during economic downturns.

The second outgrowth of the recession, the increase in the number of management contracts between owners-in-foreclosure and operating companies, liberalized the traditional contract, creating more flexibility in the contract's provisions regarding term of contract, fee structure, and rights of owner termination. The majority of contracts signed by owners-in-foreclosure were with independent operating companies, but some chain operating companies were willing to sign management contracts on foreclosed franchised properties carrying their names to assist owners-in-foreclosure in selling the property. This assistance was offered primarily as a goodwill gesture to maintain a strong business relationship with lenders for future business opportunities.

H. Factor 8: Tax-Incentive Legislation of 1981 and 1982

The Economic Recovery Tax Act of 1981 and the Tax Equity and Fiscal Responsibility Act of 1982 created a significant impetus for the development of commercial real estate by offering wide ranging tax incentives in the form of investment tax credits for furniture, fixtures, and equipment; expanded accelerated depreciation allowances; shorter useful lives for buildings, equipment,

EXHIBIT B-4

Hotel Market and Product Segmentation

Aircoa (2)
- Wynfield Inns (moderate priced)
- Clarion Hotels (highly diversified)

Doubletree (2)
- Doubletree (upscale)
- Compri (midpriced)

Holiday Corporation (5)
- Holiday Inn Hotels (midscale)
- H.I. Crowne Plaza (upper midscale)
- Hampton Inns (economy)
- Embassy Suites/Granada Royale (low end of upscale)

Marriott (4)
- Marriott Hotels and Resorts (diversified)
- Courtyard by Marriott (midpriced)
- Marriott Marquis (luxury)
- Marriott Suites (suites)

Quality Inns (5)
- Quality Inns (midprice)
- Comfort Inns (budget)
- Comfort Inn Suites (suites)
- Quality Inn Suites (suites)
- McSleep (budget)
- Clarion (upper end)

Radisson (5)
- Radisson Hotels (upper middle)
- Radisson Inns (midrange)
- Radisson Resorts (middle to upper)
- Radisson Plaza Hotels (upper end)
- Radisson Suite Hotels (suites)

Ramada (3)
- Ramada Inns (midprice)
- Ramada Hotels (midprice)
- Ramada Renaissance (upper midprice)

Royce Hotels (3)
- Royce Inns (midrange)
- Royce Hotels (upscale)
- Royce Resorts (luxury suites)

Trusthouse Forte (2)
- Travelodge (economy)
- Viscount (upscale)

Wyndham (2)
- Wyndham Hotels and Resorts (upscale)
- Wyndham Garden Hotels (upper midscale)

Source: "A Burst of Tiers," *The Cornell Hotel and Restaurant Administration Quarterly,* November 1985, pp. 36–38.

---

and furniture; and tax credits for improvements in the rehabilitation of historic buildings. The combination of the above significantly improved ownership returns of proposed projects. The basis of this improvement, however, was in tax shelter benefits, not in the property's economic returns.

Hotel developers were able to take significant advantage of these incentives in two ways. First, since the furniture, fixtures, and equipment component of total project cost is larger than that for other types of real-estate projects, investment tax credits, and the shorter useful-life schedules for this component provided greater tax shelters. Second, the tax credits on improvements for the renovation of historic buildings created incentives for hotel conversions in urban market areas where new hotel sites were nonexistent or were severely limited in number.

The tax incentives, coupled with the optimistic economic outlook and inflation-fueled economy, created unusually high rates of return on investment for hotel projects. These returns attracted significant equity and debt capital to fund hotel projects. As in the past, most of this capital was provided by investors and lenders with little or no hotel expertise who had to rely on hotel operating companies to promote and manage their properties. It was during this expansionary period that such internationally based hotel companies as Inter-Continental Hotels, Hilton International (Vista), Meridien, and Trusthouse Forte entered the U.S. market, further increasing competition among chain operators.

I. Factor 9: Market and Product Segmentation

During the early and mid 1980s, operating companies began expanding their lodging product lines to target a range of specific market segments in an effort to gain market share. Chain operators who catered primarily to the mid-market developed products for up-scale markets, while operators who catered to up-scale markets entered the mid-market business. Many entered the all-suite market. Exhibit B-4 summarizes the product-differentiation efforts of ten chain operators.

The segmentation efforts by hotel operators increased the perceived need for additional lodging development, in which the product is generated to cater to the specific needs of defined market segments. Much of this product is being built by developers and investors with no hotel experience. This development has created opportunities for chain operators to manage additional larger upscale properties and for independent operators to manage additional mid-size and smaller properties.

Appendix C

Present-Value Tables

This appendix presents the present value of one dollar tables for use in the capital budgeting decision analysis in Chapter III.

EXHIBIT C-1

Present Value of One Dollar

N	1.0%	2.0%	3.0%	4.0%	5.0%	6.0%	7.0%	8.0%	9.0%	10.0%
1	0.9901	0.9804	0.9709	0.9615	0.9524	0.9434	0.9346	0.9259	0.9174	0.9091
2	0.9803	0.9612	0.9426	0.9246	0.9070	0.8900	0.8734	0.8573	0.8417	0.8264
3	0.9706	0.9423	0.9151	0.8890	0.8638	0.8396	0.8163	0.7938	0.7722	0.7513
4	0.9610	0.9238	0.8885	0.8548	0.8227	0.7921	0.7629	0.7350	0.7084	0.6830
5	0.9515	0.9057	0.8626	0.8219	0.7835	0.7473	0.7130	0.6806	0.6499	0.6209
6	0.9420	0.8880	0.8375	0.7903	0.7462	0.7050	0.6663	0.6302	0.5963	0.5645
7	0.9327	0.8706	0.8131	0.7599	0.7107	0.6651	0.6228	0.5835	0.5470	0.5132
8	0.9235	0.8535	0.7894	0.7307	0.6768	0.6274	0.5820	0.5403	0.5019	0.4665
9	0.9143	0.8368	0.7664	0.7026	0.6446	0.5919	0.5439	0.5002	0.4604	0.4241
10	0.9053	0.8204	0.7441	0.6756	0.6139	0.5584	0.5084	0.4632	0.4224	0.3855
11	0.8963	0.8043	0.7224	0.6496	0.5847	0.5268	0.4751	0.4289	0.3875	0.3505
12	0.8875	0.7885	0.7014	0.6246	0.5568	0.4970	0.4440	0.3971	0.3555	0.3186
13	0.8787	0.7730	0.6810	0.6006	0.5303	0.4688	0.4150	0.3677	0.3262	0.2897
14	0.8700	0.7579	0.6611	0.5775	0.5051	0.4423	0.3878	0.3405	0.2992	0.2633
15	0.8614	0.7430	0.6419	0.5553	0.4810	0.4173	0.3624	0.3152	0.2745	0.2394
16	0.8528	0.7285	0.6232	0.5339	0.4581	0.3936	0.3387	0.2919	0.2519	0.2176
17	0.8444	0.7142	0.6050	0.5134	0.4363	0.3714	0.3166	0.2703	0.2311	0.1978
18	0.8360	0.7002	0.5874	0.4936	0.4155	0.3503	0.2959	0.2502	0.2120	0.1799
19	0.8278	0.6864	0.5703	0.4746	0.3957	0.3305	0.2765	0.2317	0.1945	0.1635
20	0.8196	0.6730	0.5537	0.4564	0.3769	0.3118	0.2584	0.2145	0.1784	0.1486
21	0.8114	0.6598	0.5376	0.4388	0.3589	0.2942	0.2415	0.1987	0.1637	0.1351
22	0.8034	0.6468	0.5219	0.4220	0.3419	0.2775	0.2257	0.1839	0.1502	0.1228
23	0.7955	0.6342	0.5067	0.4057	0.3256	0.2618	0.2109	0.1703	0.1378	0.1117
24	0.7876	0.6217	0.4919	0.3901	0.3101	0.2470	0.1971	0.1577	0.1264	0.1015
25	0.7798	0.6095	0.4776	0.3751	0.2953	0.2330	0.1843	0.1460	0.1160	0.0923
26	0.7721	0.5976	0.4637	0.3607	0.2812	0.2198	0.1722	0.1352	0.1064	0.0839
27	0.7644	0.5859	0.4502	0.3468	0.2679	0.2074	0.1609	0.1252	0.0976	0.0763
28	0.7569	0.5744	0.4371	0.3335	0.2551	0.1956	0.1504	0.1159	0.0896	0.0693
29	0.7494	0.5631	0.4243	0.3207	0.2430	0.1846	0.1406	0.1073	0.0822	0.0630
30	0.7419	0.5521	0.4120	0.3083	0.2314	0.1741	0.1314	0.0994	0.0754	0.0573

N	10.5%	11.0%	11.5%	12.0%	12.5%	13.0%	13.5%	14.0%	14.5%	15.0%
1	0.9050	0.9009	0.8969	0.8929	0.8889	0.8850	0.8811	0.8772	0.8734	0.8696
2	0.8190	0.8116	0.8044	0.7972	0.7901	0.7831	0.7763	0.7695	0.7628	0.7561
3	0.7412	0.7312	0.7214	0.7118	0.7023	0.6931	0.6839	0.6750	0.6662	0.6575
4	0.6707	0.6587	0.6470	0.6355	0.6243	0.6133	0.6026	0.5921	0.5818	0.5718
5	0.6070	0.5935	0.5803	0.5674	0.5549	0.5428	0.5309	0.5194	0.5081	0.4972
6	0.5493	0.5346	0.5204	0.5066	0.4933	0.4803	0.4678	0.4556	0.4438	0.4323
7	0.4971	0.4817	0.4667	0.4523	0.4385	0.4251	0.4121	0.3996	0.3876	0.3759
8	0.4499	0.4339	0.4186	0.4039	0.3897	0.3762	0.3631	0.3506	0.3385	0.3269
9	0.4071	0.3909	0.3754	0.3606	0.3464	0.3329	0.3199	0.3075	0.2956	0.2843
10	0.3685	0.3522	0.3367	0.3220	0.3079	0.2946	0.2819	0.2697	0.2582	0.2472
11	0.3334	0.3173	0.3020	0.2875	0.2737	0.2607	0.2483	0.2366	0.2255	0.2149
12	0.3018	0.2858	0.2708	0.2567	0.2433	0.2307	0.2188	0.2076	0.1969	0.1869
13	0.2731	0.2575	0.2429	0.2292	0.2163	0.2042	0.1928	0.1821	0.1720	0.1625
14	0.2471	0.2320	0.2178	0.2046	0.1922	0.1807	0.1698	0.1597	0.1502	0.1413
15	0.2236	0.2090	0.1954	0.1827	0.1709	0.1599	0.1496	0.1401	0.1312	0.1229
16	0.2024	0.1883	0.1752	0.1631	0.1519	0.1415	0.1318	0.1229	0.1146	0.1069
17	0.1832	0.1696	0.1572	0.1456	0.1350	0.1252	0.1162	0.1078	0.1001	0.0929
18	0.1658	0.1528	0.1409	0.1300	0.1200	0.1108	0.1023	0.0946	0.0874	0.0808
19	0.1500	0.1377	0.1264	0.1161	0.1067	0.0981	0.0902	0.0829	0.0763	0.0703
20	0.1358	0.1240	0.1134	0.1037	0.0948	0.0868	0.0794	0.0728	0.0667	0.0611
21	0.1229	0.1117	0.1017	0.0926	0.0843	0.0768	0.0700	0.0638	0.0582	0.0531
22	0.1112	0.1007	0.0912	0.0826	0.0749	0.0680	0.0617	0.0560	0.0508	0.0462
23	0.1006	0.0907	0.0818	0.0738	0.0666	0.0601	0.0543	0.0491	0.0444	0.0402
24	0.0911	0.0817	0.0734	0.0659	0.0592	0.0532	0.0479	0.0431	0.0388	0.0349
25	0.0824	0.0736	0.0658	0.0588	0.0526	0.0471	0.0422	0.0378	0.0339	0.0304
26	0.0746	0.0663	0.0590	0.0525	0.0468	0.0417	0.0372	0.0331	0.0296	0.0264
27	0.0675	0.0597	0.0529	0.0469	0.0416	0.0369	0.0327	0.0291	0.0258	0.0230
28	0.0611	0.0538	0.0475	0.0419	0.0370	0.0326	0.0288	0.0255	0.0226	0.0200
29	0.0553	0.0485	0.0426	0.0374	0.0329	0.0289	0.0254	0.0224	0.0197	0.0174
30	0.0500	0.0437	0.0382	0.0334	0.0292	0.0256	0.0224	0.0196	0.0172	0.0151

EXHIBIT C-1, Present Value of One Dollar (continued)

N	15.5%	16.0%	16.5%	17.0%	17.5%	18.0%	18.5%	19.0%	19.5%	20.0%
1	0.8658	0.8621	0.8584	0.8547	0.8511	0.8475	0.8439	0.8403	0.8368	0.8333
2	0.7496	0.7432	0.7368	0.7305	0.7243	0.7182	0.7121	0.7062	0.7003	0.6944
3	0.6490	0.6407	0.6324	0.6244	0.6164	0.6086	0.6010	0.5934	0.5860	0.5787
4	0.5619	0.5523	0.5429	0.5337	0.5246	0.5158	0.5071	0.4987	0.4904	0.4823
5	0.4865	0.4761	0.4660	0.4561	0.4465	0.4371	0.4280	0.4191	0.4104	0.4019
6	0.4212	0.4104	0.4000	0.3898	0.3800	0.3704	0.3612	0.3521	0.3434	0.3349
7	0.3647	0.3538	0.3433	0.3332	0.3234	0.3139	0.3048	0.2959	0.2874	0.2791
8	0.3158	0.3050	0.2947	0.2848	0.2752	0.2660	0.2572	0.2487	0.2405	0.2326
9	0.2734	0.2630	0.2530	0.2434	0.2342	0.2255	0.2170	0.2090	0.2012	0.1938
10	0.2367	0.2267	0.2171	0.2080	0.1994	0.1911	0.1832	0.1756	0.1684	0.1615
11	0.2049	0.1954	0.1864	0.1778	0.1697	0.1619	0.1546	0.1476	0.1409	0.1346
12	0.1774	0.1685	0.1600	0.1520	0.1444	0.1372	0.1304	0.1240	0.1179	0.1122
13	0.1536	0.1452	0.1373	0.1299	0.1229	0.1163	0.1101	0.1042	0.0987	0.0935
14	0.1330	0.1252	0.1179	0.1110	0.1046	0.0985	0.0929	0.0876	0.0826	0.0779
15	0.1152	0.1079	0.1012	0.0949	0.0890	0.0835	0.0784	0.0736	0.0691	0.0649
16	0.0997	0.0930	0.0869	0.0811	0.0758	0.0708	0.0661	0.0618	0.0578	0.0541
17	0.0863	0.0802	0.0746	0.0693	0.0645	0.0600	0.0558	0.0520	0.0484	0.0451
18	0.0747	0.0691	0.0640	0.0592	0.0549	0.0508	0.0471	0.0437	0.0405	0.0376
19	0.0647	0.0596	0.0549	0.0506	0.0467	0.0431	0.0398	0.0367	0.0339	0.0313
20	0.0560	0.0514	0.0472	0.0433	0.0397	0.0365	0.0335	0.0308	0.0284	0.0261
21	0.0485	0.0443	0.0405	0.0370	0.0338	0.0309	0.0283	0.0259	0.0237	0.0217
22	0.0420	0.0382	0.0347	0.0316	0.0289	0.0262	0.0239	0.0218	0.0199	0.0181
23	0.0364	0.0329	0.0298	0.0270	0.0245	0.0222	0.0202	0.0183	0.0166	0.0151
24	0.0315	0.0284	0.0256	0.0231	0.0208	0.0188	0.0170	0.0154	0.0139	0.0126
25	0.0273	0.0245	0.0220	0.0197	0.0177	0.0160	0.0144	0.0129	0.0116	0.0105
26	0.0236	0.0211	0.0189	0.0169	0.0151	0.0135	0.0121	0.0109	0.0097	0.0087
27	0.0204	0.0182	0.0162	0.0144	0.0129	0.0115	0.0102	0.0091	0.0081	0.0073
28	0.0177	0.0157	0.0139	0.0123	0.0109	0.0097	0.0086	0.0077	0.0068	0.0061
29	0.0153	0.0135	0.0119	0.0105	0.0093	0.0082	0.0073	0.0064	0.0057	0.0051
30	0.0133	0.0116	0.0102	0.0090	0.0079	0.0070	0.0061	0.0054	0.0048	0.0042

N	20.5%	21.0%	21.5%	22.0%	22.5%	23.0%	23.5%	24.0%	25.0%	26.0%
1	0.8299	0.8264	0.8230	0.8197	0.8163	0.8130	0.8097	0.8065	0.8000	0.7937
2	0.6887	0.6830	0.6774	0.6719	0.6664	0.6610	0.6556	0.6504	0.6400	0.6299
3	0.5715	0.5645	0.5575	0.5507	0.5440	0.5374	0.5309	0.5245	0.5120	0.4999
4	0.4743	0.4665	0.4589	0.4514	0.4441	0.4369	0.4299	0.4230	0.4096	0.3968
5	0.3936	0.3855	0.3777	0.3700	0.3625	0.3552	0.3481	0.3411	0.3277	0.3149
6	0.3266	0.3186	0.3108	0.3033	0.2959	0.2888	0.2818	0.2751	0.2621	0.2499
7	0.2711	0.2633	0.2558	0.2486	0.2416	0.2348	0.2282	0.2218	0.2097	0.1983
8	0.2250	0.2176	0.2106	0.2038	0.1972	0.1909	0.1848	0.1789	0.1678	0.1574
9	0.1867	0.1799	0.1733	0.1670	0.1610	0.1552	0.1496	0.1443	0.1342	0.1249
10	0.1549	0.1486	0.1426	0.1369	0.1314	0.1262	0.1212	0.1164	0.1074	0.0992
11	0.1286	0.1228	0.1174	0.1122	0.1073	0.1026	0.0981	0.0938	0.0859	0.0787
12	0.1067	0.1015	0.0966	0.0920	0.0876	0.0834	0.0794	0.0757	0.0687	0.0625
13	0.0885	0.0839	0.0795	0.0754	0.0715	0.0678	0.0643	0.0610	0.0550	0.0496
14	0.0735	0.0693	0.0655	0.0618	0.0584	0.0551	0.0521	0.0492	0.0440	0.0393
15	0.0610	0.0573	0.0539	0.0507	0.0476	0.0448	0.0422	0.0397	0.0352	0.0312
16	0.0506	0.0474	0.0443	0.0415	0.0389	0.0364	0.0341	0.0320	0.0281	0.0248
17	0.0420	0.0391	0.0365	0.0340	0.0317	0.0296	0.0276	0.0258	0.0225	0.0197
18	0.0349	0.0323	0.0300	0.0279	0.0259	0.0241	0.0224	0.0208	0.0180	0.0156
19	0.0289	0.0267	0.0247	0.0229	0.0212	0.0196	0.0181	0.0168	0.0144	0.0124
20	0.0240	0.0221	0.0203	0.0187	0.0173	0.0159	0.0147	0.0135	0.0115	0.0098
21	0.0199	0.0183	0.0167	0.0154	0.0141	0.0129	0.0119	0.0109	0.0092	0.0078
22	0.0165	0.0151	0.0138	0.0126	0.0115	0.0105	0.0096	0.0088	0.0074	0.0062
23	0.0137	0.0125	0.0113	0.0103	0.0094	0.0086	0.0078	0.0071	0.0059	0.0049
24	0.0114	0.0103	0.0093	0.0085	0.0077	0.0070	0.0063	0.0057	0.0047	0.0039
25	0.0094	0.0085	0.0077	0.0069	0.0063	0.0057	0.0051	0.0046	0.0038	0.0031
26	0.0078	0.0070	0.0063	0.0057	0.0051	0.0046	0.0041	0.0037	0.0030	0.0025
27	0.0065	0.0058	0.0052	0.0047	0.0042	0.0037	0.0033	0.0030	0.0024	0.0019
28	0.0054	0.0048	0.0043	0.0038	0.0034	0.0030	0.0027	0.0024	0.0019	0.0015
29	0.0045	0.0040	0.0035	0.0031	0.0028	0.0025	0.0022	0.0020	0.0015	0.0012
30	0.0037	0.0033	0.0029	0.0026	0.0023	0.0020	0.0018	0.0016	0.0012	0.0010

Appendix D

Quantitative Model for Project and Management-Contract Analyses

The model used for the quantitative analysis of the various management-contract fee structures was developed with Microsoft's Excel on an Apple MacIntosh Plus computer. The model contains the following major components: **(a)** development of operating proforma statements on a constant and inflated dollar basis; **(b)** development of the project's financing structure; **(c)** development of the depreciation and amortization schedules; **(d)** calculation of a simulated sale at the end of the ten-year operating period; and **(e)** development of cash flow schedules representing returns to the equity and to the operator for the various management-contract fee structures.

A major objective of the program design is to preserve maximum flexibility, so that the model can be used for various projects with different property characteristics and financing structures. Moreover, if the reader wishes to develop a comparable model, he should attempt to make the program as user-friendly as possible through extensive use of macro commands. In the present model, macro commands have been included that simply require the user to respond to numerous computer requests for information. Consequently, the user loads the program and then answers questions regarding the property's characteristics, expected business activity and operating costs, the financing arrangement, depreciation and taxation considerations, and the data about the fee structures under consideration. Finally the user can choose whether he wants a screen display of the present value returns to the operator and to the equity or an immediate print-out of the analysis. Each component of the model is discussed below.

A. Ten-Year Operating *Pro-Forma* Statements on a Constant and Inflated Dollar Basis

The *pro-forma* statement should be set up for eleven years so that the operating cashflows for the ten-year projection period and the sale price which is based upon the eleventh year's operating results can be calculated. In light of the importance of inflation on real estate investments, it is necessary to construct the *pro-forma* statement model so that the impact of inflation on the operating cash flows during the projection period can easily be calculated using various inflation rates. In addition, it is helpful to construct the proforma statement so that different inflation rates can be used for the various revenue and expense items in the operating statement. Consequently, different expectations about future revenue and expense increases can be considered in the *pro-forma* statement. Moreover, to assure a realistic reflection of the impact of different levels of activity on the operating cash flows, it is necessary to categorize the operating costs of each department in their fixed and variable components. Further, it is recommended to increase slightly certain operating costs (e.g., marketing, administrative and general, and payroll) as a percentage of gross revenues for the first two to three operating years until the hotel reaches its stabilized operating year. Sufficient time and effort should be invested in the proforma model since its efficient design and flexibility provide the basis for the later sensitivity analysis of owner and operator returns.

Major variables which can be changed in the program to determine their impact on the returns include: **(1)** average room rates; **(2)** occupancy percentages; **(3)** total number and amounts of the average food and beverage checks; **(4)** cost and profit percentages of all operating departments; **(5)** undistributed operating expenses and fixed charges adjusted to the property's characteristics, the local price level, and the operating policies of the management company; and **(6)** any expected inflation rate.

B. Analysis of the Project's Financing Structure

The model for the determination of the debt service should be designed so that various financing options can be analyzed. In the present model, it is possible to consider up to two amortized loans. These loans can be analyzed in any combination, and for any principal amount, interest rate, amortization period, and term period. Finally, it is possible to enter and analyse any roll-over loans that are planned during the operating period. Consequently, this analysis will calculate the returns to the owner and to the operator with various financing structures and will determine the financing arrangement that will maximize after-tax returns based on the revenue and cost assumptions in the proforma statement. In addition, it is possible to determine the returns to the lender based on the financing arrangement and the expected performance of the project.

C. Depreciation and Amortization Schedules

Development of the depreciation and amortization schedules requires a division of the total project cost into costs that can be amortized or depreciated over different periods. One should design the model to allow for various depreciation methods so that it is possible to determine the impact of various depreciation options on the returns.

D. Simulated Sale at the End of the Ten-Year Operating Period

To determine the after-tax proceeds from the stimulated sale at the end of the ten-year operating period under various fee structures, it is necessary to use as a basis for the sale price the income before fixed charges less replacement reserve, property taxes and insurance, and the total expected management fees due in the eleventh year for each management fee structure under consideration. When determining the sale price, it is important not to deduct any accrued fees from the income before fixed charges when determining the sale price, since deferred management fees do not represent normal annual fixed charges. However, these accrued fees must be deducted from the net sale proceeds of the present owner to arrive at the correct present value of the equity investment. To allow flexibility in the determination of the after-tax net sale proceeds, it is recommended to construct the sale model so that any capitalization rate, selling expense, and capital gain tax rate can be used.

E. Operator and Equity Cash Flow Returns and Present Value Analyses for the Various Management-Contract Fee Structures

The design of the management fee payout schedules should include the following components: **(1)** the base fee as a percentage of gross revenues; **(2)** the incentive fee as a percentage of income before fixed charges or other negotiated profit or cash flow level; **(3)** the option to subordinate the incentive fee to debt service, and/or a percentage of a preferred return on equity; **(4)** the percentage of the remaining cash flow that may be distributed to the operator; **(5)** the percentage of the appreciation of the project that may be distributed to the operator at the sale of the property; and **(6)** the interest rate paid on accrued incentive management fees. If the fee structure is constructed in this manner, it will allow for any combination of base and incentive fee percentages and subordination to debt service and/or to a preferred cumulative return on equity. Moreover, any participation of the operator in the returns traditionally accruing to the equity, (e.g., a percentage of appreciation and/or of the remaining cash flows) can also be considered. In respect to the annual cash flow and present value analysis, it is recommended that this analysis be performed for both parties, since it is important in the contract analysis and negotiations to be aware of the returns to the other party and of the impact of various fee alternatives on the returns to the other party.

The cash flow and present value analysis for the operator and the equity should include: **(1)** the annual base and incentive fees paid and accruing to the operator; **(2)** the annual operating cash flows and the net sale proceeds to the equity; **(3)** any discount rate percentages for the different cash flows to the operator and to the equity position; and **(4)** the present value of the annual cashflows.

The model used for the present value analysis should permit the discounting of cash flows at different discount rates due to the varying degrees of risk inherent in the different portions of the cash flows, particularly in very complex fee structures. For instance, in the case of a management fee payout schedule that subordinates a portion of the operator's incentive fees to a preferred return on equity, it is recommended that different discount rates be used for the different components of the total return to the owner and the operator. In the present value analysis presented in Exhibit IV-12, a general discount rate of 10 percent was used for the sake of clarity and comparability.

For the analysis of the annual operating cash flows, it is necessary to incorporate in the model the current provisions about tax loss carry forwards due to the importance of the tax losses in the earlier years of operation. These earlier tax losses offer a considerable shelter from taxation in the later years of the project, and therefore substantially increase the returns to the equity position.

F. Illustration of the Sensitivity Analysis

The graphs on the following pages illustrate the variations of the returns to the equity position and to the operator caused by changes in average room rate, occupancy level, mortgage interest rate, and inflation rate for each of four different management-fee structures. These fee structures are shown in the table on the following page.

All graphs are based on the initial projections for the Century 21 Hotel project (Exhibit V-7). It must be noted that on each graph the displayed variations of the returns are only caused by the variation of the variable under consideration, since all other variables were held constant at the level projected in the initial Century 21 Hotel projections.

Exhibit D-1 illustrates the present values of owner and operator returns when variations in the average room rate occur. Exhibit D-2 illustrates the present values of owner and operator returns when variations in the occupancy percentage occur. Exhibits D-3 illustrates the present values of owner and

Fee I:	Base fee: 3% of gross revenue Incentive fee: 10% of income before fixed charges, unsubordinated to debt service and reserve for replacement
Fee II:	Basic fee: 3% of gross revenues 1st incentive fee portion: 5% of income before fixed charges subordinated to debt service and reserve for replacement 2nd incentive fee portion: 5% of income before fixed charges subordinated to 10% cumulative return on equity 3rd incentive fee portion: 10% of remaining cashflow 4th incentive fee portion: 10% of property appreciation
Fee III:	Base fee: 3% of gross revenues Incentive fee: 15% of available cashflow
Fee IV:	Base fee: 3% of gross revenues Incentive fee: 10% of income before fixed charges subordinated to debt service and reserve for replacement

operator returns when variations in the inflation rate occur. Exhibit D-4 illustrates the present values of owner and operator returns when variations in the mortgage interest rate occur. In the present value analysis of the various fee structures, a general discount rate of 10 percent was used for the sake of clarity and comparability. However, it must be noted that using the same rate tends to reduce the apparent advantage to the equity position in tiered management fee structures. Therefore, the following graphs slightly understate the returns to the equity position and overstate the returns to the operator in the case of tiered fee structures.

EXHIBIT D-1

Owner and operator returns for four different management-fee structures: Variations of average room rate

Owner returns

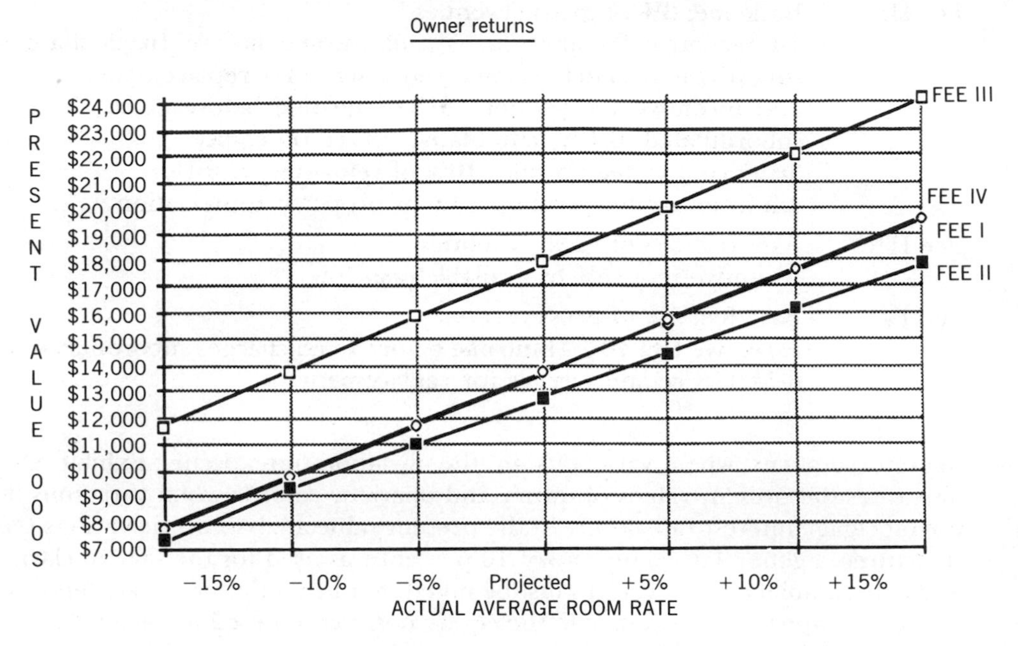

Note: Fee I is hidden under Fee IV; Fee IV offers slightly higher returns to the owner

Operator returns

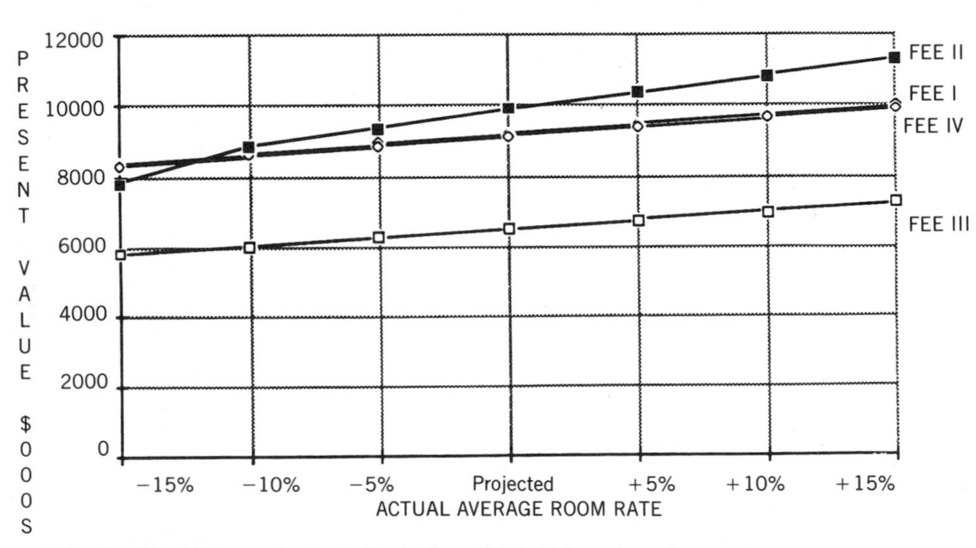

Note: Fee IV is hidden under Fee I; Fee I offers slightly higher returns to operator.

Note: All other variables held constant; a 10% discount rate is used to calculate present values

EXHIBIT D-2

Owner and operator returns for four different management-fee structures: Variations of occupancy level

Owner returns

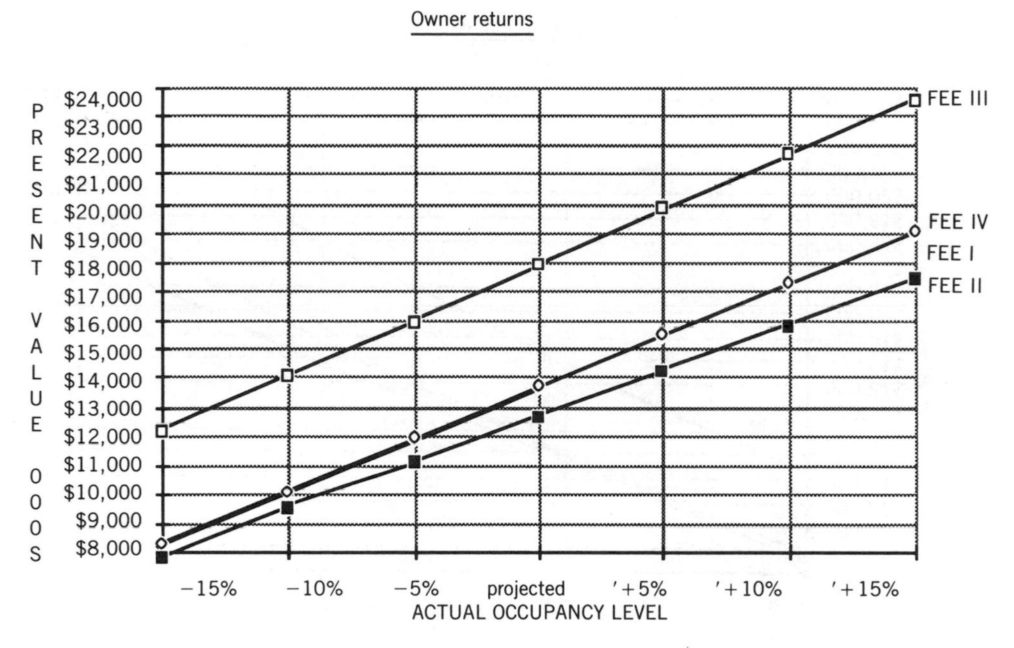

Note: Fee I is hidden under Fee IV; Fee IV offers slightly higher returns to the owner.

Operator returns

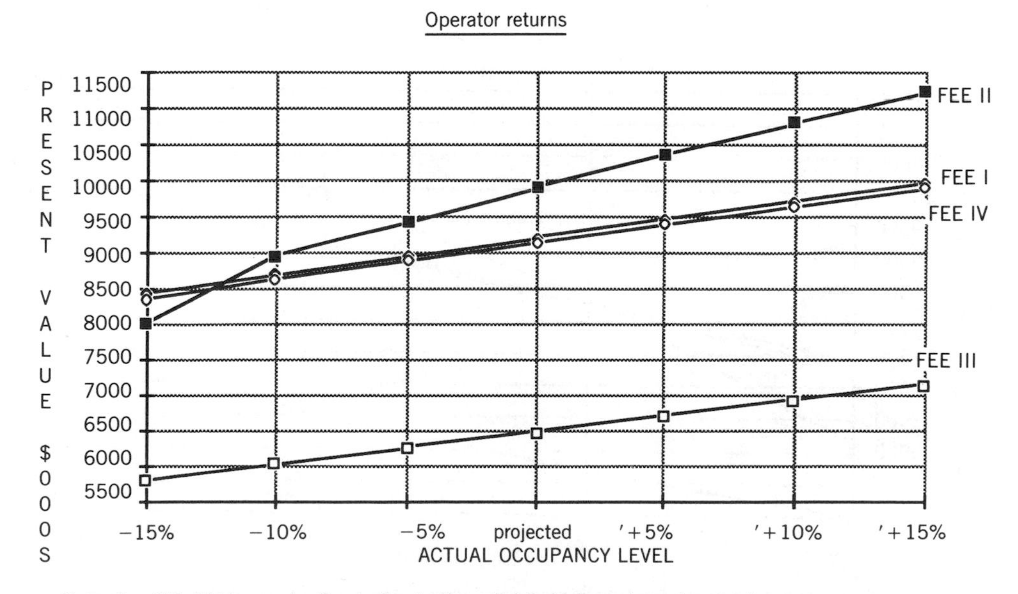

Note: Fee IV is hidden under Fee I; Fee I offers slightly higher returns to operator.

Note: All other variables held constant; a 10% discount rate is used to calculate present values

EXHIBIT D-3

Owner and operator returns for four different management-fee structures: Variations of inflation rate

Owner returns

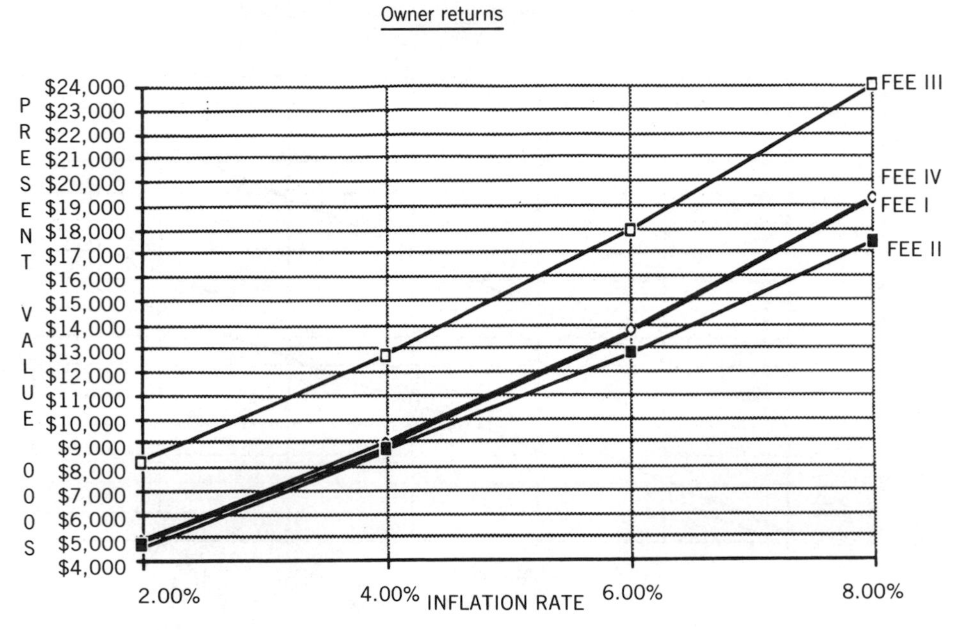

Note: Fee I is hidden under Fee IV; Fee IV offers slightly higher returns to the owner

Operator returns

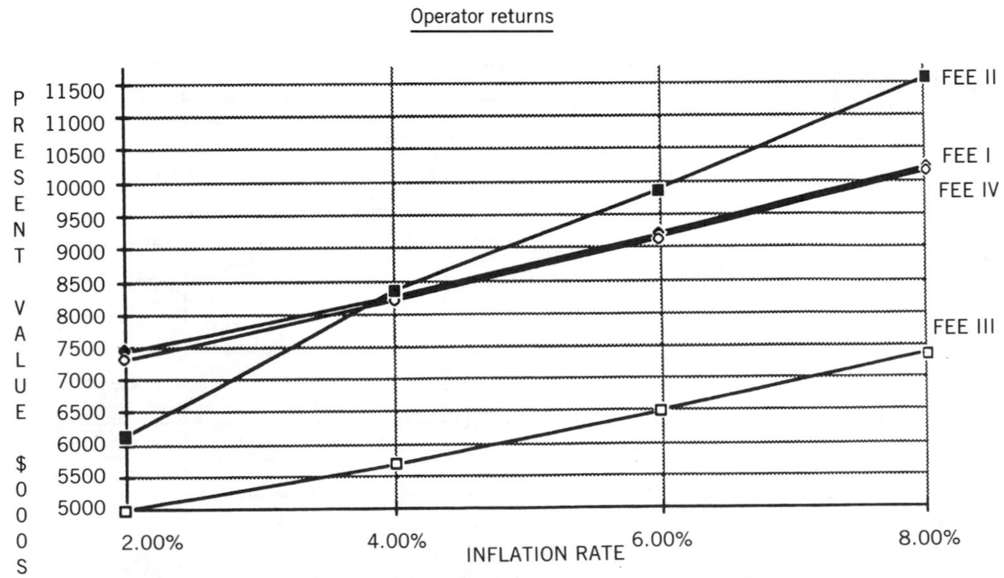

Note: Fee IV is hidden under Fee I; Fee I offers slightly higher returns to operator.

Note: All other variables held constant; a 10% discount rate is used to calculate present values

EXHIBIT D-4

Owner and operator returns for four different management-fee structures: Variations of interest rate

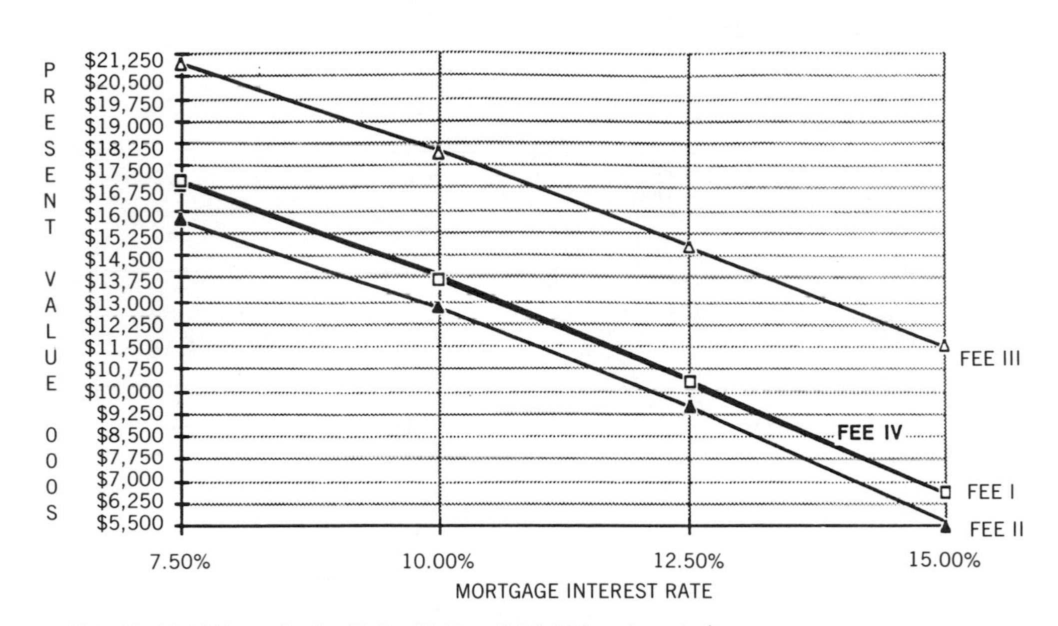

Note: Fee I is hidden under Fee IV; Fee IV offers slightly higher returns to the owner.

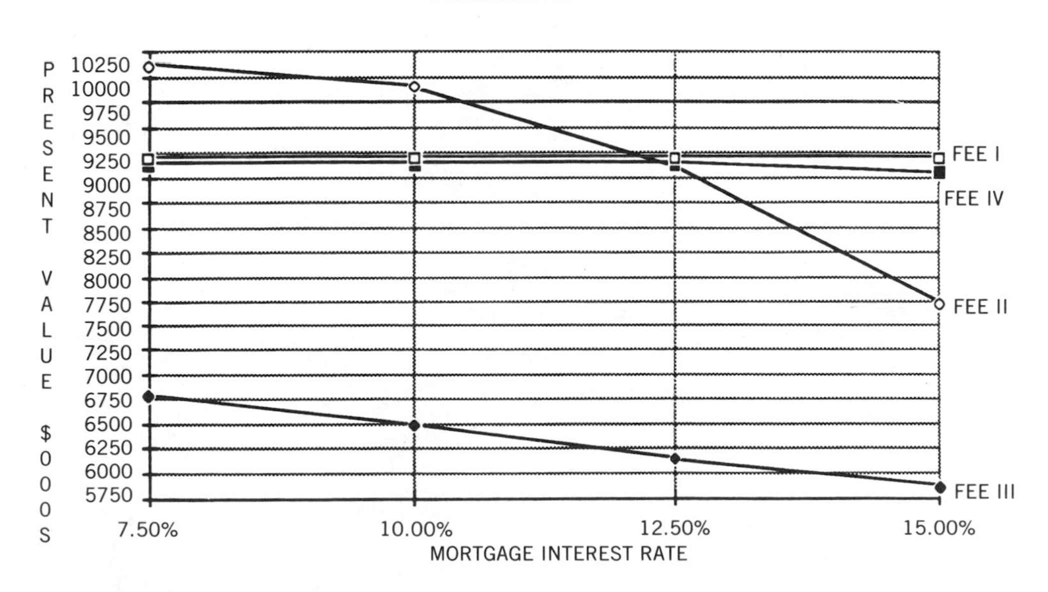

Note: All other variables held constant; a 10% discount rate is used to calculate present values